MW00736675

ISBN: 9781313710879

Published by:
HardPress Publishing
8345 NW 66TH ST #2561
MIAMI FL 33166-2626

Email: info@hardpress.net
Web: http://www.hardpress.net

GONE TO EARTH

BY

MARY WEBB

AUTHOR OF "THE GOLDEN ARROW"

"Take us the foxes, the little foxes that spoil the vines."
—Song of Solomon.

NEW YORK

E. P. DUTTON & CO.

681 FIFTH AVENUE

Printed in the United States of America

GONE TO EARTH

GONE TO EARTH

CHAPTER I

SMALL feckless clouds were hurried across the vast untroubled sky—shepherdless, futile, imponderable—and were torn to fragments on the fangs of the mountains, so ending their ephemeral adventures with nothing of their fugitive existence left but a few tears.

It was cold in the Callow—a spinney of silver birches and larches that topped a round hill. A purple mist hinted of buds in the tree-tops, and a fainter purple haunted the vistas between the silver and brown boles.

Only the crudeness of youth was here as yet, and not its triumph—only the sharp calyx-point, the pricking tip of the bud, like spears, and not the paten of the leaf, the chalice of the flower.

For as yet spring had no flight, no song, but went like a half-fledged bird, hopping tentatively through the undergrowth. The bright springing mercury that carpeted the open spaces had only just hung out its pale flowers, and honeysuckle leaves were still tongues of green fire. Between the larch boles and under the thickets of honeysuckle and blackberry came a tawny silent form, wearing with the calm dignity of woodland creatures a beauty of eye and limb, a brilliance of tint, that few women could have worn without self-consciousness. Clear-eyed, lithe, it stood for a moment in the full sunlight—a year-old fox, round-headed and velvet-footed. Then it slid into the shadows. A shrill whistle came from the interior of the wood, and the fox bounded towards it.

"Where you bin? You'm stray and lose yourself, certain sure!" said a girl's voice, chidingly motherly. "And if you'm alost, I'm alost; so come you whome. The sun's undering, and there's bones for supper!"

With that she took to her heels, the little fox after her, racing down the Callow in the cold level light till they came to the Woodus's cottage.

Hazel Woodus, to whom the fox belonged, had always lived at the Callow. There her mother, a Welsh gipsy, had born her in bitter rebellion, hating marriage and a settled life and Abel Woodus as a wild cat hates a cage. She was a rover, born for the artist's joy and sorrow, and her spirit found no relief for its emotions; for it was dumb. To the linnet its flight, to the thrush its song; but she had neither flight nor song. Yet the tongueless thrush is a thrush still, and has golden music in its heart. The caged linnet may sit moping, but her soul knows the dip and rise of flight on an everlasting May morning.

All the things she felt and could not say, all the stored honey, the black hatred, the wistful home-sickness for the unfenced wild—all that other women would have put into their prayers, she gave to Hazel. The whole force of her wayward heart flowed into the softly beating heart of her baby. It was as if she passionately flung the life she did not value into the arms of her child.

When Hazel was fourteen she died, leaving her

treasure—an old, dirty, partially illegible manuscript-book of spells and charms and other gipsy lore—to her daughter.

Her one request was that she might be buried in the Callow under the yellow larch needles, and not in a churchyard. Abel Woodus did as she asked, and was regarded askance by most of the community for not burying her in Chrissen-ground. But this did not trouble him. He had his harp still, and while he had that he needed no other friend. It had been his absorption in his music that had prevented him understanding his wife, and in the early days of their marriage she had been wildly jealous of the tall gilt harp with its faded felt cover that stood in the corner of the living-room. Then her jealousy changed to love of it, and her one desire was to be able to draw music from its plaintive strings. She could never master even the rudiments of music, but she would sit on rainy evenings when Abel was away and run her thin hands over the strings with a despairing passion of grieving love. Yet she could not bear to hear Abel play. Just as some childless women with all their accumulated stores of love cannot bear to see a mother with her child, so Maray Woodus, with her sealed genius, her incapacity for expression, could not bear to hear the easy self-expression of another. For Abel was in his way a master of his art; he had dark places in his soul, and that is the very core of art and its substance. He had the lissom hands and cheerful self-absorption that bring success.

He had met Maray at an Eisteddfodd that had been held in days gone by on a hill five miles from the Callow, called God's Little Mountain, and crowned by a chapel. She had listened, swaying and weeping, to the surge and lament of his harp, and when he won the harper's prize and laid it in her lap she had consented to be married in the chapel at the end of the Eisteddfodd week. That was nineteen years ago, and she was fled like the leaves and the birds of departed summers; but God's Little Mountain still towered as darkly to the eastward; the wind still leapt sheer from the chapel to the young larches of the Callow; nothing had changed at all; only one more young, anxious, eager creature had come into the towering, subluminous scheme of things.

Hazel had her mother's eyes, strange, fawn-coloured eyes like water, and in the large clear irises were tawny flecks. In their shy honesty they were akin to the little fox's. Her hair, too, of a richer colour than her father's, was tawny and foxlike, and her ways were graceful and covert as a wild creature's.

She stood in the lane above the cottage, which nestled below with its roof on a level with the hedge-roots, and watched the sun dip. The red light from the west stained her torn old dress, her thin face, her eyes, till she seemed to be dipped in blood. The fox, wistfulness in her expression and the consciousness of coming supper in her mind, gazed obediently where her mistress gazed, and was touched with the same fierce beauty. They stood there fronting the crimson pools over the far hills, two small sentient things facing destiny with pathetic courage; they had, in the chill evening on the lonely hill, a look as of those predestined to grief, almost an air of martyrdom.

The small clouds that went westward took each in its turn the prevailing colour, and vanished, each dipped in blood.

From the cottage, as Hazel went down the path,

came the faint thrumming of the harp, changing as she reached the door, to the air of "The Ash Grove." The cottage was very low, one-storied, and roofed with red corrugated iron. The three small windows had frames coloured with washing-blue and frills of crimson cotton within. There seemed scarcely room for even Hazel's small figure. The house was little larger than a good pigstye, and only the trail of smoke from its squat chimney showed that humanity dwelt there.

Hazel gave Foxy her supper and put her to bed in the old washtub where she slept. Then she went into the cottage with an armful of logs from the wood heap. She threw them on the open fire.

"I'm a-cold," she said; "the rain's cleared, and there'll be a duck's frost to-night."

Abel looked up absently, humming the air he intended to play next.

"I bin in the Callow, and I've gotten a primmyrose," continued Hazel, accustomed to his ways, and not discouraged. "And I got a bit of blackthorn, white as a lady."

Abel was well on in "Ap Jenkyn" by now.

Hazel moved about seeing to supper, for she was as hungry as Foxy, talking all the time in her rather shrilly sweet voice, while she dumped the cracked cups and the loaf and margarine on the bare table. The kettle was not boiling, so she threw some bacon-grease on the fire, and a great tongue of flame sprang out and licked at Abel's beard. He raised a hand to it, continuing to play with the other.

Hazel laughed.

"You be fair comic-struck," she said.

She always spoke in this tone of easy comradeship; they got on very well; they were so entirely indifferent to each other. There was nothing filial about her or parental about him. Neither did they ever evince the least affection for each other.

He struck up "It's a fine hunting day."

"Oh! shut thy row with that drodsome thing!" said Hazel with sudden passion. "Look'ee! I unna bide in if you go on."

"Ur?" queried Abel dreamily.

"Play summat else!" said Hazel, "not that; I dunna like it."

"You be a queer girl, 'Azel," said Abel, coming out of his abstraction. "But I dunna mind playing 'Why do the People?' instead; it's just as heartening."

"Canna you stop meddling wi' the music and come to supper?" asked Hazel. The harp was always called "the music," just as Abel's mouth-organ was "the little music."

She reached down the flitch to cut some bacon off, and her dress, already torn, ripped from shoulder to waist.

"If you dunna take needle to that, you'll be mother-naked afore a week's out," said Abel indifferently.

"I mun get a new un," said Hazel. "It unna mend. I'll go to town to-morrow."

"Shall you bide with yer auntie the night over?"

"Ah."

"I shanna look for your face till I see your shadow, then. You can bring a tuthree wreath frames. There's old Samson at the Yeath unna last long; they'll want a wreath made."

Hazel sat and considered her new dress. She never had a new one till the old one fell off her back, and then she usually got a second-hand one, as a shilling or two would buy only material if new, but would stretch to a ready-made if second-hand.

"Foxy'd like me to get a green velvet," said Hazel. She always expressed her intense desires, which were few, in this formula. It was her unconscious protest against the lovelessness of her life. She put the blackthorn in water and contemplated its whiteness with delight; but it had not occurred to her that she might herself, with a little trouble, be as sweet and fresh as its blossom. The spiritualization of sex would be needed before such things would occur to her. At present she was sexless as a leaf. They sat by the fire till it went out; then they went to bed, not troubling to say good-night.

In the middle of the night Foxy woke. The moon filled her kennel-mouth like a door, and the light shone in her eyes. This frightened her—so large a lantern in an unseen hand, held so purposefully before the tiny home of one defenceless little creature. She barked sharply. Hazel awoke, promptly as a mother at her child's cry. She ran straight out with her bare feet into the fierce moonlight.

"What ails you?" she whispered. "What ails you, little un?"

The wind stalked through the Callow, and the Callow moaned. A moan came also from the plain, and black shapes moved there as the clouds drove onwards.

"Maybe they're out," muttered Hazel. "Maybe the Black Meet's set for to-night and she's scented the jeath pack." She looked about nervously. "I can see summat driving dark o'er the pastures yonder; they'm abroad, surely."

She hurried Foxy into the cottage and bolted the door.

"There!" she said. "Now you lie good and quiet in the corner, and the jeath pack shanna get you."

It was said that the death pack, phantom hounds of a bad squire, whose gross body had been long since put to sweeter uses than any he put it to in life—changed into the clear-eyed daisy and the ardent pimpernel—scoured the country on dark stormy nights. Harm was for the houses past which it streamed, death for those that heard it give tongue.

This was the legend, and Hazel believed it implicitly. When she had found Foxy half dead outside her deserted earth, she had been quite sure that it was the death pack that had made away with Foxy's mother. She connected it also with her own mother's death. Hounds symbolized everything she hated, everything that was not young, wild and happy. She identified herself with Foxy, and so with all things hunted and snared and destroyed.

Night, shadow, loud winds, winter—these were inimical; with these came the death pack, stealthy and untiring, following for ever the trail of the defenceless. Sunlight, soft airs, bright colours, kindness—these were beneficent, havens to flee into. Such was the essence of her creed, the only creed she held, and it lay darkly in her heart, never expressed even to herself. But when she ran into the night to comfort the little fox, she was living up to her faith as few do; when she gathered flowers and lay in the sun, she was dwelling in a mystical atmosphere as vivid as that of the Saints; when she recoiled from cruelty, she was trampling evil underfoot, perhaps more surely than those great divines who destroyed one another in their zeal for their Maker.

CHAPTER II

AT six the next morning they had breakfast. Abel was busy making a hive for a next summer's swarm. When he made a coffin, he always used up the bits thus. A large coffin did not leave very much; but sometimes there were small ones, and then he made splendid hives. The white township on the south side of the lilac hedge increased as slowly and unceasingly as the green township around the distant churchyard. In summer the garden was loud with bees, and the cottage was full of them at swarming-time. Later it was littered with honey-sections; honey dripped from the table, and pieces of broken comb lay on the floor and were contentedly eaten by Foxy.

Whenever an order for a coffin came, Hazel went to tell the bees who was dead. Her father thought this unnecessary. It was only for folks that died in the house, he said. But he had himself told the bees when his wife died. He had gone out on that vivid June morning to his hives, and had stood watching the lines of bees fetching water, their shadows going and coming on the clean white boards. Then he had stooped and said with a curious confidential indifference, "Maray's jead." He had put his ear to the hive and listened to the deep, solemn murmur within; but it was the murmur of the future, and not of the past, the preoccupation with life, not with death, that filled the pale galleries within. To-day the eighteen hives lay under their winter covering, and the eager creatures within slept. Only one or two strayed sometimes to the early arabis, desultory and sad, driven home again by the frosty air to await the purple times of honey. The happiest days of Abel's life were those when he sat like a bard before the seething hives and harped to the muffled roar of sound that came from within.

All his means of livelihood were joys to him. He had the art of perpetual happiness in this, that he could earn as much as he needed by doing the work he loved. He played at flower shows and country dances, revivals and weddings. He sold his honey, and sometimes his bees. He delighted in wreath-making, gardening, and carpentering, and always in the background was his music—some new air to try on the gilded harp, some new chord or turn to master. The garden was almost big enough, and quite beautiful enough, for that of a mansion. In the summer white lilies haunted it, standing out in the dusk with their demure cajolery, looking, as Hazel said, like ghosses. Goldenrod foamed round the cottage, deeply embowering it, and lavender made a grey mist beside the red quarries of the path. Then Hazel sat like a queen in a regalia of flowers, eating the piece of bread and honey that made her dinner, and covering her face with lily pollen.

Now, there were no flowers in the garden; only the yew-tree by the gate had hung her waxen blossom along the undersides of the branches. Hazel hated the look of the frozen garden; she had an almost unnaturally intense craving for everything rich, vivid, and vital. She was all these things herself, as she communed with Foxy before starting. She had wound her hair round her head in a large plait, and her old black hat made the colour richer.

"You'm nigh on thirty miles to go there and back, unless you get a lift," said Abel.

"A lift? I dunna want never no lifts!" said Hazel scornfully.

"You'm as good a walker as John of No Man's Parish," replied Abel "and he walks for ever, so they do say."

As Hazel set forth in the sharp, fresh morning, the Callow shone with radiant brown and silver, and no presage moved within it of the snow that would hurtle upon it from mountains of cloud all night.

When Hazel had chosen her dress—a peacock blue serge—and had put it on there and then in the back of the shop, curtained off for this purpose, she went to her aunt's.

Her cousin Albert regarded her with a startled look. He was in a margarine shop, and spent his days explaining that margarine was as good as butter. But, looking at Hazel, he felt that here *was* butter—something that needed no apology, and created its own demand. The bright blue made her so radiant that her aunt shook her head.

"You take after your ma, 'Azel," she said. Her tone was irritated.

"I be glad."

Her aunt sniffed.

"You ought to be as glad to take after one parent as another, if you were jutiful," she said.

"I dunna want to take after anybody but myself." Hazel flushed indignantly.

"Well! we *are* conceited!" exclaimed her aunt. "Albert, don't give 'Azel all the liver and bacon. I s'pose your mother can eat as well as schoolgirls?"

Albert was gazing at Hazel so animatedly, so obviously approving of all she said, that her aunt was very much ruffled.

"No wonder you only want to be like yourself," he said. "Jam! my word, Hazel, you're jam!"

"Albert!" cried his mother raspingly, with a pathetic note of pleading, "haven't I always taught you to say preserve?" She was not pleading against the inelegant word, but against Hazel.

When Albert went back to the shop, Hazel helped her aunt to wash up. All the time she was doing this, with unusual care, and cleaning the knives—a thing she hated—she was waiting anxiously for the expected invitation to stay the night. She longed for it as the righteous long for the damnation of their enemies. She never paid a visit except here, and to her it was a wild excitement. The gas-stove, the pretty china, the rose-patterned wall-paper, were all strange and marvellous as a fairy-tale. At home there was no paper, no lath and plaster, only the bare bricks, and the ceiling was of bulging sailcloth hung under the rafters.

Now to all these was added the new delight of Albert's admiring gaze—an alert, live gaze, a thing hitherto unknown to Albert. Perhaps, if she stayed, Albert would take her out for the evening. She would see the streets of the town in the magic of lights. She would walk out in her new dress with a real young man—a young man who possessed a gilt watch-chain. The suspense, as the wintry afternoon drew in, became almost intolerable. Still her aunt did not speak. The sitting-room looked so cosy when tea was laid; the firelight played over the cups; her aunt drew the curtains. On one side there was joy, warmth—all that she could desire; on the other, a forlorn walk in the dark. She had left it until so late that her heart shook at the idea of the many miles she must cover alone if her aunt did not ask her.

Her aunt knew what was going on in Hazel's mind, and smiled grimly at Hazel's unusual meekness. She took the opportunity of administering a few home-truths.

"You look like an actress," she said.

"Do I, auntie?"

"Yes. It's a disgrace, the way you look. You quite draw men's eyes."

"It's nice to draw men's eyes, inna it, auntie?"

"Nice! Hazel, I should like to box your ears! You naughty girl! You'll go wrong one of these days."

"What for will I, auntie?"

"Some day you'll get spoke to!" She said the last words in a hollow whisper. "And after that, as you won't say and do what a good girl would, you'll get picked up."

"I'd like to see anyone pick me up!" said Hazel indignantly. "I'd kick!"

"Oh! how unladylike! I didn't mean really picked up; I meant allegorically—like in the Bible."

"Oh! only like in the Bible," said Hazel disappointedly. "I thought you meant summat *real.*"

"Oh! You'll bring down my grey hairs," wailed Mrs. Prowde.

An actress was bad, but an infidel!

"That I should live to hear it—in my own villa, with my own soda cake on the cake-dish—and my own son," she added dramatically, as Albert entered, "coming in to have his God-fearing heart broken!"

This embarrassed Albert, for it was true, though the cause assigned was not.

"What's Hazel been up to?" he queried.

The affection beneath his heavy pleasantry strengthened his mother in her resolve that Hazel should not stay the night.

"There's a magic-lantern lecture on to-night, Hazel," he said. "Like to come?"

"Ah! I should that."

"You can't walk home at that time of night," said Mrs. Prowde. "In fact, you ought to start now."

"But Hazel's staying the night, mother, surely?"

"Hazel must get back to her father."

"But, mother, there's the spare-room."

"The spare-room's being spring-cleaned."

Albert plunged; he was desperate and forgetful of propriety.

"I can sleep on this sofa," he said. "She can have my room."

"Hazel can't have your room. It's not suitable."

"Well, let her share yours, then."

Mrs. Prowde played her trump-card. "Little I thought," she said, "when your dear father went, that before three years had passed you'd be so forgetful of my comfort (and his memory) as to suggest such a thing. As long as I live, my room's mine. When I'm gone," she concluded, knocking down her adversary with her superior weight of years—"when I'm gone (and the sooner the better for you, no doubt), you can put her in my room and yourself, too."

When she had said this she was horrified at herself. What an improper thing to say! Even anger and jealousy did not excuse impropriety, though they excused any amount of unkindness.

But at this Hazel cried out in her turn:

"That he never will!" The fierce egoism of the consciously weak flamed up in her. "I keep myself to myself," she finished.

"If such things come to pass, mother," Albert said, and his eyes looked suddenly vivid, so that Hazel clapped her hands and said, "Yer lamps are lit! Yer lamps are lit!" and broke into peals of laughter. "If such things come to pass," laboured Albert, "they'll come decent, that is, they won't be spoken of."

He voiced his own and his mother's creed.

At this point the argument ended, because Albert had to go back after tea to finish some work. As he stamped innumerable swans on the yielding material, he never doubted that his mother had also yielded. He forgot that life has to be shaped with an axe till the chips fly.

As soon as he had gone, Mrs. Prowde shut the door on Hazel hastily, for fear the weather might bring relenting. She had other views for Albert. In after-years, when the consequences of her action had become things of the past, she always spoke of how she had done her best with Hazel. She never dreamed that she, by her selfishness that night, had herself set Hazel's feet in the dark and winding path that she must tread from that night onward to its hidden, shadowy ending. Mrs. Prowde, through her many contented years, blamed in turn Hazel, Abel, Albert, the devil, and (only tacitly and, as it were, in secret from herself) God. If there is any purgatorial fire of remorse for the hard and selfish natures that crucify love, it must burn elsewhere. It does not touch them in this world. They go as the three children went, in their coats, their hosen, and their hats all complete, nor does the smell of fire pass over them.

Hazel felt that heaven was closed—locked and barred. She could see the golden light stream through its gates. She could hear the songs of joy—joy unattained and therefore immortal; she could see the bright figures of her dreams go to and fro. But heaven was shut.

The wind ran up and down the narrow streets like a lost dog, whimpering. Hazel hurried on, for it was already twilight, and though she was not afraid of the Callow and the fields at night, she was afraid of the highroads. For the Callow was home, but the roads were the wide world. On the fringe of the town she saw lights in the bedroom windows of prosperous houses.

"My! they go to their beds early," she thought, not having heard of dressing for dinner. It made her feel more lonely that people should be going to bed. From other houses music floated, or the savoury smell of dinner. As she passed the last lamp-post she began to cry, feeling like a lost and helpless little animal. Her new dress was forgotten; the wreath-frames would not fit under her arm, and caused a continual minor discomfort, and the Callow seemed to be half across the country. She heard a trapped rabbit screaming somewhere, a thin anguished cry that she could not ignore. This delayed her a good deal, and in letting it out she got a large bloodstain on her dress. She cried again at this. The pain of a blister, unnoticed in the morning journey, now made itself felt; she tried walking without her boots, but the ground was cold and hard.

The icy, driving wind leapt across the plain like a horseman with a long sword, and stealthily in its track came the melancholy whisper of snow.

When this began, Hazel was in the open, half-way to Wolfbatch. She sat down on the step of a stile, and sighed with relief at the ease it gave her foot. Then, far off, she heard the sharp miniature sound, very neat and staccato, of a horse galloping. She held her breath to hear if it would turn down a by-road, but it came on. It came on, and grew in volume and in meaning, became almost ominous in the frozen silence. Hazel rose and stood in the fitful moonlight. She felt that the approaching hoof-beats were for her. They were the one sound in a dead world, and she nearly cried out at the thought of their dying in the distance. They must not; they should not.

"Maybe it's a farmer and his missus as have drove a good bargain, and the girl told to get supper fire-hot agen they come. Maybe they'll give me a lift! Maybe they'll say 'Bide the night over?'"

She knew it was only a foolish dream; nevertheless, she stood well in the light, a slim, brow-beaten figure, the colour of her dress wan in the grey world.

A trap came swaying round the corner. Hazel cried out beseechingly, and the driver pulled the horse up short.

"I must be blind drunk," he soliloquized, "seeing ghosts!"

"Oh, please sir!" Hazel could say no more, for the tears that companionship unfroze.

The man peered at her.

"What in hell are you doing here?" he asked.

"Walking home-along. She wouldna let me bide

the night over. And my foot's blistered in a balloon and blood on my dress." She choked with sobs.

"What's your name?"

"Hazel."

"What else?"

With an instinct of self-protection she refused to tell her surname.

"Well, mine's Reddin," he said crossly; "and why you're so dark about yours I don't know, but up you get, anyway."

The sun came out in Hazel's face. He helped her up, she was so stiff with cold.

"Your arm," she said in a low tremulous voice, when he had put the rug round her—"your arm pulling me in be like the Sunday-school tale of Jesus Christ and Peter on the wild sea—me being Peter."

Reddin looked at her sideways to see if she was in earnest. Seeing that she was, he changed the subject.

"Far to go?" he asked.

"Ah! miles on miles."

"Like to stop the night over?"

At last, late certainly, but no matter, at last the invitation had come, not from her aunt, but from a stranger. That made it more exciting.

"I'm much obleeged," she said. "Where at?"

"D'you know Undern?"

"I've heard tell on it."

"Well, it's two miles from here. Like to come?"

"Ah! Will your mother be angry?"

"I haven't one."

"Father?"

"No."

"Who be there, then?"

"Only Vessons and me."

"Who's Vessons?"

"My servant."

"Be you a gentleman, then?"

Reddin hesitated slightly. She said it with such reverence and made it seem so great a thing.

"Yes," he said at last. "Yes, that's what I am—a gentleman." He was conscious of bravado.

"Will there be supper, fire-hot?"

"Yes, if Vessons is in a good temper."

"Where you bin?" she asked next.

"Market."

"You've had about as much as is good for you," she remarked, as if thinking aloud.

He certainly smelt strongly of whisky.

"You've got a cheek!" said he. "Let's look at you."

He stared into her tired but vivid eyes for a long time, and the trap careered from side to side.

"My word!" he said, "I'm in luck to-night!"

"What for be you?"

"Meeting a girl like you."

"Do I draw men's eyes?"

"Eh?" He was startled. Then he guffawed. "Yes," he replied.

"*She* said so," Hazel murmured. "And she said I'd get spoke to, and she said I'd get puck up. I'm main glad of it, too. She's a witch."

"She said you'd get picked up, did she?"

"Ah."

Reddin put his arm round her.

"You're so pretty! That's why."

"Dunna maul me!"

"You might be civil. I'm doing you a kindness." They went on in that fashion, his arm about her, each wondering what manner of companion the other was.

When they neared Undern there were gates to open, and he admired her litheness as she jumped in and out.

In his pastures, where the deeply rutted track was already white with snow, two foals stood sadly by their mothers, gazing at the cold world with their peculiarly disconsolate eyes.

"Eh! look's the abron un! Abron, like me!" cried Hazel.

Reddin suddenly gripped the long coils that were loose on her shoulders, twisted them in a rope round his neck, and kissed her. She was enmeshed, and could not avoid his kisses.

The cob took this opportunity—one long desired—to rear, and Reddin flogged him the rest of the way. So they arrived with a clatter, and were met at the door by Andrew Vessons—knowing of eye as a blackbird, straw in mouth, the poison of asps on his tongue.

CHAPTER III

UNDERN HALL, with its many small-paned windows, faced the north sullenly. It was a place of which the influence and magic were not good. Even in May, when the lilacs frothed into purple, paved the lawn with shadows, steeped the air with scent; when soft leaves lipped each other consolingly; when blackbirds sang, fell in their effortless way from the green height to the green depth, and sang again—still, something that haunted the place set the heart fluttering. No place is its own, and that which is most stained with old tumults has the strongest fascination.

So at Undern, whatever had happened there went on still; someone who had been there was there still. The lawns under the trees were mournful with old pain, or with vanished joys more pathetic than pain in their fleeting mimicry of immortality.

It was only at midsummer that the windows were coloured by dawn and sunset; then they had a sanguinary aspect, staring into the delicate skyey dramas like blind, bloodshot eyes. Secretly, under the heavy rhododendron leaves and in the furtive sunlight beneath the yew-trees, gnats danced. Their faint motions made the garden stiller; their smallness made it oppressive; their momentary life made it infinitely old. Then Undern Pool was full of leaf shadows like multitudinous lolling tongues, and the smell of the mud tainted the air—half sickly, half sweet. The clipped bushes and the twisted chimneys made inky shadows like steeples on the grass, and great trees of roses, beautiful in desolation, dripped with red and white and elbowed the guelder roses and the elders set with white patens. Cherries fell in the orchard with the same rich monotony, the same fatality, as drops of blood. They lay under the fungus-riven trees till the hens ate them, pecking gingerly and enjoyably at their lustrous beauty as the world does at a poet's heart. In the kitchen-garden also the hens took their ease, banqueting sparely beneath the straggling black boughs of a red-currant grove. In the sandstone walls of this garden hornets built undisturbed, and the thyme and lavender borders had grown into forests and obliterated the path. The cattle drowsed in the meadows, birds in the heavy trees; the golden day-lilies drooped like the daughters of pleasure; the very principle of life seemed to slumber. It was then, when the scent of elder blossom, decaying fruit, mud, and hot yew brooded there, that the place attained one of its most individual moods—narcotic, aphrodisiac.

In winter the yews and firs were like waving funeral plumes and mantled, headless goddesses; then the giant beeches would lash themselves to frenzy, and, stooping, would scourge the ice on Undern Pool and the cracked walls of the house, like beings drunken with the passion of cruelty. This was the second mood of Undern—brutality. Then those within were, it seemed, already in the grave, heavily covered with the prison of frost and snow, or shouted into silence by the wind. On a January night the house seemed to lie outside time and space; slow, ominous movement began beyond the blind windows, and the inflexible softness of snow, blurred on the vast background of night, buried summer ever deeper with invincible, caressing threats.

The front door was half glass, so that a wandering candle within could be seen from outside, and it looked inexpressibly forlorn, like a glow-worm seeking escape from a chloroform-box or mankind looking for the way to heaven. Only four windows were ever lit, and of these two at a time. They were Jack Reddin's parlour, Andrew Vessons's kitchen, and their respective bedrooms.

Reddin of Undern cared as little for the graciousness of life as he did for its pitiful rhapsodies, its purple-mantled tragedies. He had no time for such trivialities. Fox-hunting, horse-breeding, and kennel lore were his vocation. He rode straight, lived hard, exercised such creative faculties as he had on his work, and found it very good. Three times a year he stated in the Undern pew at Wolfbatch that he intended to continue leading a godly, righteous, and sober life. At these times, with amber lights from the windows playing over his well-shaped head, his rather heavy face looked, as the Miss Clombers from Wolfbatch Hall said, "so chivalrous, so uplifted." The Miss Clombers purred when they talked, like cats with a mouse. The younger still hunted, painfully compressing an overfed body into a riding-habit of some forgotten cut, and riding with so grim a mouth and such a bloodthirsty expression that she might have had a blood-feud with all foxes. Perhaps, when she rode down the anxious red-brown streak, she thought she was riding down a cruel fate that had somehow left her life vacant of joy; perhaps, when the little creature was torn piecemeal, she imagined herself tearing so the frail unconquerable powers of love and beauty. Anyway, she never missed a meet, and she and her sister never ceased their long silent battle for Reddin, who remained as unconscious of them as if they were his aunts. He was, of course, beneath them, very much beneath them—hardly more than a farmer, but still—a man.

Reddin went on his dubious and discreditable way, and the woman Sally Haggard, of the cottage in the hollow, gained by virtue of a certain harsh beauty what the ladies Clomber would have given all their wealth for.

The other inhabitant of Undern, Andrew, revolved in his own orbit, and was entirely unknown to his master. He cut the yews—the peacocks and the clipped round trees and the ones like tables—twice a year. He was creating a swan. He had spent twenty years at it, and hoped to complete it in a few more, when the twigs that were to be the beak had grown sufficiently. It never occurred to him that the place was not his, that he might have to leave it. He had his spring work and his autumn work; in the winter he ordained various small indoor jobs for himself; and in the summer, in common with the rest of the place, he grew somnolent. He sat by the hacked and stained kitchen-table (which he seldom scrubbed, and on which he tried his knife, sawed bones, and chopped meat) and slept the afternoons away in the ceaseless drone of flies.

When Reddin called him, he rarely answered, and only deigned to go to him when he felt sure that his order was going to be reasonable.

Everything he said was non-committal, every movement was expostulatory. Reddin never noticed. Vessons suited his needs, and he always had such meals as he liked. Vessons was a bachelor. Monasticism had found, in a countryside teeming with sex, one silent but rabid disciple. If Vessons ever felt the irony of his own presence in a breeding stable, he never said so. He went about his work with tight disapproving lips, as if he thought that Nature owed him a debt of gratitude for his tolerance of her ways. Ruminative and critical, he went to and fro in the darkly lovely domain, with pig buckets or ash buckets or barrows full of manure. The lines of his face were always etched in dirt, and he always had a bit of rag tied round some cut or blister. He was a lonely soul, as he once said himself when unusually mellow at the Hunter's Arms; he was "wi'out mother, wi'out father, wi'out descent." He preferred it to the ties of family. He liked living with Reddin because they never spoke except of necessity, and because he was quite indifferent to Reddin's welfare and Reddin to his.

But to Undern itself he was not indifferent. Ties deep as the tangled roots of the bindweed, strong as the great hawsers of the beeches that reached below the mud of Undern Pool, held him to it, the bondslave of a beauty he could not understand, a terror he could not express. When he trudged the muddy paths, "setting taters" or earthing up; when he scythed the lawn, looking, with a rose in his hat, weirder and more ridiculous than ever; and when he shook the apples down with a kind of sour humour, as if to say, "There! that's what you trees get by having apples!"—at all these times he seemed less an individual than a blind force. For though his personality was strong, that of the place was stronger. Half out of the soil, minded like the dormouse and the beetle, he was, by virtue of his unspoken passion, the protoplasm of a poet.

CHAPTER IV

VESSONS took up the pose of one seeing a new patent.

"This young lady's lost her way," Reddin remarked.

"She 'as, God's truth! But you'll find it forra I make no doubt, sir. 'There's a way'" (he looked ironically at the poultry-basket behind the trap, from which peered anxious, beaky faces)—"'a way as no fowl knoweth, the way of a man with a maid.'"

"Fetch the brood mares in from the lower pasture. They should have been in this hour."

"And late love's worse than lad's love, so they do say," concluded Vessons.

"There's nothing of love between us," Reddin snapped.

"I dunna wonder at it!" Andrew cast an appraising look at his master's flushed face and at Hazel's tousled hair, and withdrew.

Hazel went into the elaborately carved porch. She looked round the brown hall where deep shadows lurked. Oak chests and carved chairs, all more or less dusty, stood about, looking as if disorderly feasters had just left them. In one corner was an inlaid sideboard piano.

Hazel did not notice the grey dust and the hearth full of matches and cigarette ends. She only saw what seemed to her fabulous splendour. A foxhound rose from the moth-eaten leopard-skin by the hearth as they came in. Hazel stiffened.

"I canna-d-abear the hound-dogs," she said. "Nasty snabbing things."

"Best dogs going."

"No, they kills the poor foxes."

"Vermin."

Hazel's face became tense. She clenched her hands and advanced a determined chin.

"Keep yer tongue off our Foxy, or I unna stay!" she said.

"Who's Foxy?"

"My little small cub as I took and reared."

"Oh! you reared it, did you?"

"Ah. She didna like having no mam. I'm her mam now."

Reddin had been looking at her as thoughtfully as his rather maudlin state allowed.

He had decided that she should stay at Undern and be his mistress.

"You'll be wanting something better than foxes to be mothering one of these days," he remarked to the fire, with a half embarrassed, half jocose air, and a hand on the poker.

"Eh?" said Hazel, who was wondering how long it would take her to learn to play the music in the corner.

Reddin was annoyed. When one made these arch speeches at such cost of imagination, they should be received properly.

He got up and went across to Hazel, who had played three consecutive notes, and was gleeful. He put his hand on hers heavily, and a discord was wrung from the soft-toned notes that had perhaps known other such discords long ago.

"Laws! what a din!" said Hazel. "What for d'you do that, Mr. Reddin?"

Reddin found it harder than ever to repeat his remark, and dropped it.

"What's that brown on your dress?" he asked instead.

"That? Oh, that's from a rabbit as I loosed out'n a trap. It bled awful."

"Little sneak, to let it out."

"Sneak's trick to catchen un, so tiny and all," replied Hazel composedly.

"Well, you'd better change your dress; it's very wet, and there's plenty here," said he, going to a chest and pulling out an armful of old-fashioned gowns. "If you lived at Undern you could wear them every day."

"If ifs were beans and bacon, there's few'd go clemmed," said Hazel. "That green un's proper, like when the leaves come new, and little small roses and all."

"Put it on while I see what Vessons is doing."

"He's grumbling in the kitchen, seemingly," said Hazel.

Vessons always grumbled. His mood could be judged only by the *piano* or *forte* effects.

Hazel heard him reply to Reddin.

"No. Supper binna ready; I've only just put 'im on." He always spoke of all phases of his day's work in the masculine gender.

Hazel stopped buttoning her dress to hear what Reddin was saying.

"Have you some hot water for the lady?" ("The lady! That's me!" she thought.)

"No, sir, I anna. Nor yet I anna got no myrrh, aloes, nor cassher. There's nought in my kitchen but a wold useless cat and an o'erdruv man of six-and-sixty, a pot of victuals not yet simmering, and a gentleman as ought to know better than to bring a girl to Undern and ruin her—a poor innicent little creature."

"Me again," said Hazel. She pondered on the remark and flushed. "Maybe I'd best go," she thought. Yet only vague instincts stirred her to this, and all her soul was set on staying.

"Never shall it be said"—Andrew's voice rose like a preacher's—"never shall it be said as a young female found no friend in Andrew Vessons; never shall it be said"—his voice soared over various annoyed exclamations of Reddin's—"as a female went from this 'all different from what she came."

"Shut up, Vessons!"

But Vessons was, as he would have phrased it himself, "in full honey-flow," and not to be silenced.

"Single she be, and single she'd ought to stay. This 'ere rubbitch of kissing and clipping!"

"But, Vessons, if there were no children gotten, the world'd be empty."

"Let 'un be! 'Im above'll get a bit of rest, nights, from their sins."

"Eh, I like that old chap," thought Hazel.

The wrangle continued. It was the deathless quarrel of the world and the monastery—natural man and the hermit. Finally Vessons concluded on a top note.

"Well, if you take this girl's good name off'n her——"

Suddenly something happened in Hazel's brain. It was the realization of life in relation to self. It marks the end of childhood. She no more saw herself throned above life and fate, as a child does. She saw that she was a part of it all; she was mutable and mortal.

She had seen life go on, had heard of funerals, courtings, confinements and weddings in their conventional order—or reversed—and she had remained, as it were, intact. She had starved and slaved and woven superstitions, loved Foxy, and tolerated her father.

Girl friends had hinted of a wild revelry that went on somewhere—everywhere—calling like a hidden merry-go-round to any who cared to hear. But she had not heard. They had let fall such sentences as "He got the better of me," "I cried out, and he thought someone was coming, and he let me go." Later, she heard, "And I thought I'd ne'er get through it when baby came."

She felt vaguely sorry for these girls; but she realized nothing of their life. Nor did she associate funerals and illness with herself.

As the convolvulus stands in apparent changelessness in a silent rose and white eternity, so she seemed to herself a stationary being. But the convolvulus has budded and bloomed and closed again while you thought her still, and she dies—the rayed and rosy cup so full of airy sweetness—she dies in a day.

Hazel got up from her chair by the fire and went restlessly, with a rustle as of innumerable autumn leaves, to the hall door. She gazed through the glass, and saw the sad feather-flights of snow wandering and hesitating, and finally coming to earth. They held to their individuality as flakes as long as they could, it seemed; but the end came to all, and they were [illegible]n earth and their own multitudes.

Hazel opened the door and stood on the threshold, so that snow-flakes flattened themselves on the yellow roses of her dress. Outside there was no world, only a waste of grey and white. Like leaves on a dead bird, the wrappings of white grew deeper over Undern. Hazel shivered in the cold wind off the hill, and saw Undern Pool curdling and thickening in the frost. No sound came across the outspread country. There were no roads near Undern except its own cart-track; there were no railways within miles. Nothing moved except the snow-flakes, fulfilling their relentless destiny of negation. She saw them only, and heard only the raised voices in the house arguing about herself.

"I mun go," she said, strong in her spirit of freedom, remote and withdrawn.

"I mun stay," she amended, weak in her undefended smallness, and very tired. She turned back to the fire. But the instinct that had awakened as childhood died clamoured within her and would not let her rest.

She softly took off the silk dress, and put on her own.

She picked up the wreath-frames with a sigh and opened the door again. She would have a long, wild walk home, but she could creep in through her bedroom window, which would not latch, and she could make a great fire of dry broom and brew some tea.

"And I'll let Foxy in and eat a loaf, I will, for I'm clemmed!" she said.

She slipped out through the door that had seen so many human lives come and go. Even as she went, the door betrayed her, for Reddin, coming from the kitchen, saw her through the upper panes.

CHAPTER V

I BE going homealong," she said, but he pulled her in and shut the door.

"Why did you want to go?"

"I'm alost in this grand place."

"Your hair's grander than anything in the place. And your eyes are like sherry."

"Truth on your life?"

"Yes. Now you'd better change your dress again."

He reached down an old silver candlestick, very tarnished.

"You can go upstairs. There's a glass in the first room you come to. Then we'll have supper."

"Sitting at the supper in a grand shining gown wi' roses on it," said Hazel, ecstatically, her voice rising to a kind of chant, "with a white cloth on table like school-treat, and the old servant hopping to and agen like thrussels after worms."

"Thrussel yourself!" muttered Andrew, peering in at the door. He retired again, remarking to the cat in a sour lugubrious voice, as he always did when ruffled: "There's no cats i' the Bible." He began to sing "By the waters of Babylon."

Upstairs Hazel coiled her hair, running her fingers through its bright lengths, as she had no comb, and turning in her underbodice to make it suit the low dress. Outside, his rough hair wet with snow, stood

Reddin, watching her from the vantage-ground of the darkness. He saw her stand with head erect and bare white shoulders, smiling at herself in the glass. He saw her slip into the rich gown and pose delightedly, mincing to and fro like a wagtail. He noted her lissom figure and shining coils of hair.

"She'll do," he said, and did not wonder whether he would do himself. Then he gave a smothered exclamation. She had opened the window, pushing the snowy ivy aside, and she leant out, her breast under its folds of silk resting on the snow.

She looked over his head into the immensity of night.

"Dunna let 'un take my good name, for the old feller says I'd ought to keep it," she said. "And let me get back to Foxy quick in the morning light, and no harm come to us for ever and ever."

The night received her prayer in silence. Whether or not any heard but Reddin none could say.

Reddin tiptoed into the house, rather downcast. This was a strange creature that he had caught.

Vessons was still at the waters of Babylon when Hazel came down.

"Why canna he get beyond them five words?" asked Hazel. "He allus stops and goes back like a dog on a chain." She sang it through in her high clear voice. There was silence in the kitchen.

Reddin stared at Hazel.

"Who taught you to sing?" he asked.

"Father. He's wonderful with the music, is father." Hazel found that in the presence of strangers her feeling for her father was almost warm "Playing the harp nights, he makes your flesh creep; ah! and he makes the place all on a charm, like the spinneys in

Maymonth. And he says, 'Sing!' says he, and I ups and sings, and whiles I don't never know what I bin singing."

"That I can well believe," said Vessons.

Reddin swung round.

"What the devil are you doing here?" he asked.

"I've acome to say"—Vessons' tone was dry—"as supper's burnt."

"Burnt?"

"Ah, to a cinder."

"How did you do that, you fool?"

"Harkening at the lady teaching me to sing."

Reddin was furious. He knew why supper was burnt.

"Get out!" he said. "Get out into the stable and stay there. I'll get supper myself."

Vessons withdrew composedly.

Since Hazel had offended him, he had decided that she must take care of herself.

"Couldna he bide in the house?" asked Hazel uneasily.

"No."

They fetched in bread and beer and cold meat. Her host was jubilant and, during supper, quite deferential. He had been awed by Hazel's request to the night and by her beauty. But when his hunger was satisfied, his voice grew louder and his eyes sultry.

Restraint fell between them. Looking at his face, Hazel again had an impulse for flight. When he said, "I want to stroke that silk dress," and came towards her, knocking the candle over as if by accident, she edged away, saying sharply:

"Dunna maul me!"

He paid no attention.

"I'll do right by you," he said; "I swear I will. I'll—yes, I'll even marry you to-morrow. But to-night's mine."

It was not a question of marrying or not marrying in Hazel's eyes. It was a matter of primitive instinct. She would be her own.

He had pulled the low dress off one shoulder. She twitched it out of his hand and slipped from his grasp like a fish from a net. He was too surprised to follow at once.

"Old feller!" she called, running into the yard, "quick! quick!" A rough grey head appeared.

"What? after the old 'un?"

"I wunna stay along of him!"

Vessons looked at her interestedly. Apparently she also was a devotee of his religion—celibacy; one who dared to go against the explicit decrees of nature.

"I think the better of you," he said. "So he's had his trouble for nothing," he chuckled. "You can have my room. You shanna say Andrew Vessons inna a man of charitable nature. Never shall you! There's a key to it."

He led the way to his room through the back door and up the kitchen stairs.

Most people would have suffered anything rather than sleep in the room he revealed when he proudly flung the door open.

He had the hermit's love of little possessions and daily comforts.

On an upturned box by the bed were his clay pipe, matches, a treacle-tin containing whisky, and some chicken-bones. He usually kept a few bones to pick at his ease. A goldfinch with a harassed air occupied a wooden cage in the window, and the mantelpiece was fitted up with white mice in home-made cages. It seemed quite a pleasant room to Hazel.

"Mind as you're very careful of all my things," said Vessons wistfully. "I hanna slep away from this room for nigh twenty year. That bird's ne'er slep without me. He'll miss me. He unna sing for anybody else." He always asserted this, and the bird always belied it by singing to Reddin and any chance visitor. But Vessons continued to believe it. There are some things that it is necessary to believe; doubt of them means despair.

Vessons was conscious that he was being generous.

"You can drink a sup of whisky if you like," he said. "Now I'm going, afore that bird notices, or I shall never get away."

The bird sat in preoccupied silence. He was probably thinking of the woods and seeded dandelions. He was of the fellowship to which comfort means little and freedom much. So was Hazel.

"Lock the door!" Vessons said in a sepulchral whisper from the stairs.

Hazel did so, and curled up to sleep in the creaking house, thoughtless as the white mice, defenceless as they, as little grateful to Vessons for his protection, and in as deep an ignorance of what the world could do to her if it chose.

CHAPTER VI

EARLY next morning, while the finch still dreamed its heavy dream and the mice were still motionless balls, Hazel was awakened by a knock at the massive oak door. She ran across and opened it a crack, peering out from amid her hair like a squirrel from autumn leaves.

Vessons stood there with a pint mug of beer, which he proffered. But Hazel had a woman's craving for tea.

"If so be the kettle's boiling," she said apologetically.

"Tay!" said Vessons. "Laws! how furiously the women do rage after tay! I s'pose it's me as is to make it?"

"If kettle's boiling."

"Kettle! O' course kettle's boiling this hour past. Or how would the ca'ves get their meal?"

"Well, you needna shout. You'll waken 'im."

Fright was in her eyes, strong and inexplicable to herself.

"I mun go!" she whispered.

"Ah! You go," said Vessons, glad that for once duty and inclination went hand in hand.

"I'll send you," he added. "Where d'yer live?"

She hesitated.

"You needna be frit to tell *me*," said Vessons. "I'm

six-and-sixty, and you're no more to me"—he surveyed her flushed face contemplatively—"than the wold useless cat," he concluded.

Hazel frowned; but she wanted a promise from Vessons, so she made no retort.

"You wunna tell 'im?" she pleaded.

"'Im? Never will I! Wild 'orses shanna drag it from me, nor yet blood 'orses, nor 'unters, nor cart-'orses, nor Suffolk punches!" Vessons waxed eloquent, for again righteousness and desire coincided. He did not want a woman at Undern.

"Well," said Hazel, whispering through the crack, "I lives at the Callow."

"What! that lost and forgotten place t'other side the mountain?"

"Ah! But it inna lost and forgotten; it's better'n this. We've got bees."

"So've I got bees."

"And a music."

"Music? What's a music? You canna eat it."

"And my dad makes coffins."

"Does 'e, now?" said Vessons, interested at last. Then he bethought him of the credit of Undern. "But you anna got a mulberry-tree," he said triumphantly. "Now then! *I* 'ave!"

He creaked downstairs.

In a few moments Hazel also went down, and drank her tea by the red fire in the kitchen, watching the frost-flowers being softly effaced from the window as if someone rubbed them away with a sponge. Snow like sifted sugar was heaped on the sill, and the yard and outbuildings and fields, the pool and the ricks, all had the dim radiance of antimony.

"Where be the road?" asked Hazel, standing on

the doorstep and feeling rather lost. "How'll I find it?"

"You wunna find it."

"Oh, but I mun!"

"D'you think Andrew Vessons 'll let an 'ooman trapse in the snow when he's got good horses in stable?" queried Vessons grandly. "I'll drive yer."

"I'm much obleeged, I'm sure," said Hazel. "But wunna he know?"

"He'll sleep till noon if I let 'im," said Andrew.

They drove off in silence, the snow muffling the plunging hoofs. Hazel looked back as the sky crimsoned for dawn. The house fronted her with a look of power and patience. She felt that it had not yet done with her. She wondered how she would feel if Reddin suddenly appeared at his window. And a tiny traitorous wish slipped up from somewhere in her heart. She watched the windows till a turn hid the house, and then she sighed. Almost she wished that Reddin had awakened.

But soon she forgot everything in delight; for the snow shone, the long slots of the rabbits and hares, the birds' tracks in orderly rows, the deep footprints of sheep, all made her laugh by their vagaries, for they ran in loops and in circles, and appeared like the crazy steps of a sleep-walker to those who had not the key of their activity. Hazel's own doings were like that; everyone's doings are like it, if one sees the doings without the motive.

Plovers wheeled and cried desolately, seeing the soft relentless snow between themselves and their green meadows, sad as those that see fate drawing thick veils between themselves and the meadows of their hope and joy.

At the foot of the Callow Hazel got out.

"Never tell him," she said, looking up.

"Never in life," said Vessons.

Hazel hesitated.

"Never tell him," she added, "unless he asks a deal and canna rest."

"He may ask till Doomsday," said Vessons, "and he may be restless as the ten thousand ghosses that trapse round Undern when the moon's low, but I'll ne'er tell 'im."

Hazel sighed, and turned to climb the hill.

"A missus at Undern!" said Andrew to the cob's ears as they trotted home. "No, never will I!"

A magpie rose from a wood near the road, jibing at him. He looked round almost as if it had been someone laughing at his resolve, and repeated, "Never will I!"

"Where's Hazel?" asked Reddin.

"Neither wild 'orses, nor blood 'orses, nor race-'orses, nor cart-'orses, nor Suffolk punches——" began Vessons, whose style was cumulative, and who, when he had made a good phrase, was apt to work it to death like any other artist.

"Oh, you're drunk, Vessons!" said his master.

"Shall drag it from me," finished Vessons.

Reddin knew this was true, and felt rather hopeless. Still, he determined not to give up the search until he had found Hazel.

He inquired at the Hunter's Arms, but Vessons had been there before him, and he was met by pleasant stupidity.

Vessons was of the people, Reddin of the aristocracy, so the frequenters of the Hunter's Arms sided as one man against Reddin.

"You'll not get another bite of that apple," said Vessons with satisfaction, when his master returned with downcast face.

"I can't stand your manners much longer, Vessons," said he irritably.

"Gie me notice, then," said Vessons, falling back on the well-worn formula, and scoring his usual triumph.

Reddin had the faults of his class, but turning an old servant adrift was not one of them. Vessons traded on this, and invariably said and did exactly what he liked.

CHAPTER VII

WHEN Hazel got in, her father had finished his breakfast, and was busy at work.

"Brought the wreath-frames?" he asked, without looking up.

"Ah."

"He's jead at last. At the turn of the night. They came after the coffin but now. I'll be able to get them there new section crates I wanted. He's doing more for me, wanting a coffin, and him stiff and cold, than what he did in the heat of life."

"Many folks be like that," said Hazel out of her new wisdom. Neither of them reflected that Abel had always been like that towards Hazel, that she was becoming more like it to him every year.

Abel made no remark at all about Hazel's adventures, and she preserved a discreet silence.

"That little vixen's took a chicken," said Abel, after a time; "that's the second."

"She only does it when I'm away, being clemmed," said Hazel pleadingly.

"Well, if she does it again," Abel announced, "it's the water and a stone round her neck. So now you know."

"You durstn't."

"We'll see if I durst."

Hazel fled in tears to the unrepentant and dignified

Foxy. Some of us find it hard enough to be dignified when we have done right; but Foxy could be dignified when she had done wrong, and the more wrong, the more dignity.

She was very bland, and there was a look of deep content—digestive content, a state bordering on the mystic's trance—in her affectionate topaz eyes.

It had been a tender and nourishing chicken; the hours she had spent in gnawing through her rope had been well repaid.

"Oh! you darlin' wicked little thing!" wailed Hazel. "You munna do it, Foxy, or he'll drown you dead. What for did you do it, Foxy, my dear?"

Foxy's eyes became more eloquent and more liquid.

"You gallus little blessèd!" said Hazel again. "Eh! I wish you and me could live all alone by our lonesome where there was no men and women."

Foxy shut her eyes and yawned, evidently feeling doubtful if such a halcyon place existed in the world.

Hazel sat on her heels and thought. It was flight or Foxy. She knew that if she did not take Foxy away, her renewed naughtiness was as certain as sunset.

"You was made bad," she said sadly but sympathetically. "Leastways, you wasn't made like watchdogs and house-cats and cows. You was made a fox, and you be a fox, and its queer-like to me, Foxy, as folk canna see that. They expect you to be what you wanna made to be. You'm made to be a fox; and when you'm busy being a fox they say you'm a sinner!"

Having wrestled with philosophy until Foxy yawned again, Hazel went in to try her proposition on Abel. But Abel met it as the world in general usually meets a new truth.

"She took the chick," he said. "Now, would a tarrier do that—a well-trained tarrier? I says 'e would *not.*"

"But it inna fair to make the same law for foxes and terriers."

"I make what laws suit me," said Abel. "And what goes agen me—gets drownded."

"But it inna all for you!" cried Hazel.

"Eh?"

"The world wunna made in seven days, only for Abel Woodus," said Hazel daringly.

"You've come back very peart from Silverton," said Abel, reflectively—"very peart, you 'ave. How many young fellers told you your 'air was abron this time? That fool Albert said so last time, and you were neither to hold nor to bind. Abron! Carrots!"

But it was not, as he thought, this climax that silenced Hazel. It was the lucky hit about the young fellows and the reminiscence called up by the word "abron." He continued his advantage, mollified by victory.

"Tell you what it is, 'Azel; it's time you was married. You're too uppish."

"I shall ne'er get married."

"Words! words! You'll take the first as comes—if there's ever such a fool."

Hazel wished she could tell him that one had asked her, and that no labouring man. But discretion triumphed.

"Maybe," she said, tossing her head, "I *will* marry to get away from the Callow."

"Well, well, things couldna be dirtier; maybe they'll be cleaner when you'm gone. Look's the floor!"

Hazel fell into a rage. He was always saying things about the floor. She hated the floor.

"I swear I'll wed the first as comes!" she cried—"the very first!"

"And last," put in Abel. "What'll you swear by?"

"By God's Little Mountain."

"Well," said Abel contentedly, "now you've sworn *that* oath, you're bound to keep it, and so now I know that if ever an 'usband *does* come forrard you canna play the fool."

Hazel was too wrathful for consideration.

"You look right tidy in that gownd," Abel said. "I s'pose you'll be wearing it to the meeting up at the Mountain?"

"What meeting?"

"Didna I tell you I'd promised you for it—to sing? They'm after me to take the music and play."

Hazel forgot everything in delight.

"Be we going for certain sure?" she asked.

"Ah! Next Monday three weeks."

"We mun practise."

"They say that minister's a great one for the music. One of them sort as is that musical he canna play. There'll be a tea."

"Eh!" said Hazel, "it'll be grand to be in a gentleman's house agen!"

"When've you bin in a gentleman's house?"

Hazel was taken aback.

"Yesterday!" she flashed. "If Albert inna a gent I dunno who is, for he's got a watch-chain brass-mockin'-gold all across his wescoat."

Abel roared. Then he fell to in earnest on the coffin, whistling like a blackbird. Hazel sat down and watched him, resting her cheek on her hand. The cold snowlight struck on her face wanly.

"Dunna you ever think, making coffins for poor souls to rest in as inna tired, as there's a tree growing somewhere for yours?" she asked.

"Laws! What's took you? Measles? What for should I think of me coffin? That's about the only thing as I'll ne'er be bound to pay for." He laughed. "What ails you?"

"Nought. Only last night it came o'er me as I'll die as well as others."

"Well, have you only just found that out? Laws! what a queen of fools you be!"

Hazel looked at the narrow box, and thought of the active, angular old man for whom it was now considered an ample house.

"It seems like the world's a big spring-trap, and us in it," she said slowly. Then she jumped up feverishly. "Let's practise till we're as hoarse as a young rook!" she cried.

So amid the hammering their voices sprang up, like two keen flames. Then Abel threw away the hammer and began to harp madly, till the little shanty throbbed with the sound of the wires and the lament of the voices that rose and fell with artless cunning. The cottage was like a tree full of thrushes.

After their twelve o'clock dinner, Abel cut holly for the wreaths, and Hazel began to make them. For the first time home seemed dull. She thought wistfully of the green silk dress and the supper in the old, stately room. She thought of Vessons, and of Reddin's eyes as he pulled her back from the door. She thought of Undern as a refuge for Foxy.

"Maybe sometime I'll go and see 'em," she thought.

She went to the door and looked out. Frost tingled in the air; icicles had formed round the water-butt; the strange humming stillness of intense cold was about her. It froze her desire for adventure.

"I'll stay as I be," she thought. "I wunna be his'n."

To her, Reddin was a terror and a fascination. She returned to the prickly wreath, sewing on the variegated holly-leaves one by one, with clusters of berries at intervals.

"What good'll it do 'im?" she asked; "he canna see it."

"Who wants him to see it?" Abel was amused. "When his father died he 'ad his enjoyment—proud as proud was Samson, for there were seven wreaths, no less."

Hazel's thoughts returned to the coming festivity. Her hair and her peacock-blue dress would be admired. To be admired was a wonderful new sensation. She fetched a cloth and rubbed at the brown mark. It would not come out. As long as she wore the dress it would be there, like the stigma of pain that all creatures bear as long as they wear the garment of the flesh.

At last she burst into tears.

"I want another dress with no blood on it!" she wailed. And so wailing she voiced the deep lament, old as the moan of forests and falling water, that goes up through the centuries to the aloof and silent sky, and remains, as ever, unassuaged.

Hazel hated a burying, for then she had to go with Abel to help in carrying the coffin to the house of mourning. They set out on the second day after her return. The steep road down to the plain—called the Monkey's Ladder—was a river, for a thaw had set in. But Hazel did not mind that, though her boots let in the water, as she minded the atmosphere of gloom at old Samson's blind house. She would never, as Abel always did, "view the corpse," and this was always taken as an insult. So she waited in the road, half snow and half water, and thought with regret of Undern and its great fire of logs, and the green rich dress, and Reddin with his force and virility, loud voice, and strong teeth. He was so very much alive in a world where old men would keep dying.

Abel came out at last, very gay, for he had been given, over and above the usual payment, glove-money and a glass of beer.

"Us'll get a drop at the public," he said.

So they turned in there. Hazel thought the red-curtained, firelit room, with its crudely coloured jugs and mugs, a most wonderful place. She sat in a corner of the settle and watched her boots steam, growing very sleepy. But suddenly there was a great clatter outside, the sound of a horse, pulled up sharply, slipping on the cobbles, and a shout for the landlord.

"Oh, my mortal life!" said Hazel, "it met be the Black Huntsman himself."

"No, I won't come in," said the rider, "a glass out here."

Hazel knew who it was.

"Can you tell me," he went on, "if there's any young lady about here with auburn hair? Father plays the fiddle."

"He's got it wrong," thought Hazel.

"Young lady!" repeated the landlord. "Haw-burn? No, there's no lady that colour hereabouts. And what ladies there be are weathered and case-hardened."

"The one I'm looking for's young—young as a kitten, and as troublesome."

Hazel clapped her hands to her mouth.

"There's no fiddler chap hereabouts, then?"

Abel rose and went to the door.

"If it's music you want, I know better music than fiddles, and that's harps," he said. "Saw! saw! The only time as ever I liked a fiddle was when the fellow snabbed at the strings with his ten fingers—despert-like."

"Oh, damn you!" said Reddin. "I didn't come to hear about harps."

"If it's funerals or a forester's supper, a concert or a wedding," Abel went on, quite undaunted, "I'm your man."

Reddin laughed.

"It might be the last," he said.

"Wedding or bedding, either or both, I suppose," said the publican, who was counted a wit.

Reddin gave a great roar of laughter.

"Both!" he said.

"Neither!" whispered Hazel, who had been poised indecisively, as if half prepared to go to the door. She sat further into the shadow. In another moment he was gone.

"Whoever she be," said the publican, nodding his large head wisely, "have her he will, for certain sure!"

All through the night, murmurous with little rivulets of snow-water, the gurgling of full troughing, and the patter of rain on the iron roof of the house and the miniature roofs of the beehives, Hazel, waking from uneasy slumber, heard those words and muttered them.

In her frightened dreams she reached out to something that she felt must be beyond the pleasant sound of falling water, so small and transitory; beyond the drip and patter of human destinies—something vast, solitary, and silent. How should she find that which none have ever named or known? Men only stammer of it in such words as Eternity, Fate, God. All the outcries of all creatures, living and dying, sink in its depth as in an unsounded ocean. Whether this listening silence, incurious, yet hearing all, is benignant or malevolent, who can say? The wistful dreams of men haunt this theme for ever; the creeds of men are so many keys that do not fit the lock. We ponder it in our hearts, and some find peace, and some find terror. The silence presses upon us ever more heavily until Death comes with his cajoling voice and promises us the key. Then we run after him into the stillness, and are heard no more.

Hazel and her father practised hard through the dark, wet evenings. She was to sing "Harps in Heaven," a song her mother had taught her. He was to accompany the choir, or glee-party, that met together at different places, coming from the villages and hillsides of a wide stretch of country.

"Well," said Abel on the morning of their final rehearsal, "it's a miserable bit of a silly song, but you mun make the best of it. Give it voice, girl! Dunna go to sing it like a mouse in milk!"

His musical taste was offended by Hazel's way of being more dramatic than musical. She would sink her voice in the sad parts almost to a whisper, and then rise to a kind of keen.

"You'm like nought but Owen's old sheep-dog," he said, "wowing the moon!"

But Hazel's idea of music continued to be that of a bird. She was a wild thing, and she sang according to instinct, and not by rule, though her good ear kept her notes true.

They set out early, for they had a good walk in front of them, and the April sun was hot. Hazel, under the pale green larch-trees, in her bright dress, with her crown of tawny hair, seemed to be an incarnation of the secret woods.

Abel strode ahead in his black cut-away coat, snuff-coloured trousers, and high-crowned felt hat with its ornamental band. This receded to the back of his head as he grew hotter. The harp was slung from his shoulder, the gilding looking tawdry in the open day. Twice during the walk, once in a round clearing fringed with birches, and once in a pine-glade, he stopped, put the harp down and played, sitting on a felled tree. Hazel, quite intoxicated with excitement, danced between the slender boles till her hair fell down and the long plait swung against her shoulder.

"If folks came by, maybe they'd think I was a fairy!" she cried.

"Dunna kick about so!" said Abel, emerging from his abstraction. "It inna decent, now you're an 'ooman growd."

"I'm not an 'ooman growd!" cried Hazel shrilly. "I dunna want to be, and I won't never be."

The pine-tops bent in the wind like attentive heads, as gods, sitting stately above, might nod thoughtfully over a human destiny. Someone, it almost seemed, had heard and registered Hazel's cry, "I'll never be an 'ooman," assenting, sardonic.

They came to the quarry at the mountain; the deserted mounds and chasms looked more desolate than ever in the spring world. Here and there the leaves of a young tree lipped the grey-white steeps, as if wistfully trying to love them, as a child tries to caress a forbidding parent.

They climbed round the larger heaps and skirted a precipitous place.

"I canna bear this place," said Hazel; "it's so drodsome."

"Awhile since, afore you were born, a cow fell down that there place, hundreds of feet."

"Did they save her?"

"Laws, no! She was all of a jelly."

Hazel broke out with sudden passionate crying. "Oh, dunna, dunna!" she sobbed. So she did always at any mention of helpless suffering, flinging herself down in wild rebellion and abandonment so that epilepsy had been suspected. But it was not epilepsy. It was pity. She, in her inexpressive, childish way, shared with the love-martyr of Galilee the heartrending capacity for imaginative sympathy. In common with him and others of her kind, she was not only acquainted with grief, but reviled and rejected. In her schooldays boys brought maimed frogs and threw them in her lap, to watch, from a safe distance, her almost crazy grief and rage.

"Whatever's come o'er ye?" said her father now. "You're too nesh, that's what you be, nesh-spirited."

He could not understand; for the art in him was not

that warm, suffering thing, creation, but hard, brightly polished talent.

Hazel stood at the edge of the steep grey cliff, her hands folded, a curious fatalism in her eyes.

"There'll be summat bad'll come to me hereabouts," she said—"summat bad and awful."

The dark shadows lying so still on the dirty white mounds had a stealthy, crouching look, and the large soft leaves of a plane-tree flapped helplessly against the shale with the air of impotent people who whisper "Alas!"

Abel was on ahead. Suddenly he turned round, excited as a boy.

"They've started!" he cried. "Hark at the music! They allus begin with the organ."

Hazel followed him, eager for joy, running obedient and hopeful at the heels of life as a young lamb runs with its mother. She forgot her dark intuitions; she only remembered that she wanted to enjoy herself, and that if she was a good girl, surely, surely God would let her.

CHAPTER VIII

THE chapel and minister's house at God's Little Mountain were all in one—a long, low building of grey stone surrounded by the graveyard, where stones, flat, erect, and askew, took the place of a flower-garden. Away to the left, just over a rise, the hill was gashed by the grey steeps of the quarries. In front rose another curve covered with thick woods. To the right was the batch, down which a road—in winter a water-course—led into the valley. Behind the house God's Little Mountain sloped softly up and away apparently to its possessor.

Not the least of the mysteries of the place, and it was tense with mystery, was the Sunday congregation, which appeared to spring up miraculously from the rocks, woods and graves.

When the present minister, Edward Marston, came there with his mother he detested it; but after a time it insinuated itself into his heart, and gave a stronger character to his religion. He had always been naturally religious, taking on trust what he was taught; and he had an instinctive pleasure in clean and healthy things. But on winter nights at the mountain, when the tingling stars sprang in and out of their black ambush and frost cracked the tombstones; in summer, when lightning crackled in the woods and ripped along the hillside like a thousand devils, the need of a God grew ever more urgent. He spoke of this to his mother.

"No, dear, I can't say I have more need of our Lord here than in Crigton," she said. "In Crigton there was the bus to be afraid of, and bicycles. Here I just cover my ears for wind, put on an extra flannel-petticoat for frost, and sit in the coal-house for thunder. Not that I'm forgetting God. God with us, of course, coal-house or elsewhere."

"But don't you feel something ominous about the place, mother? I feel as if something awful would happen here, don't you?"

"No, dear. Nor will you when you've had some magnesia. Martha!" (Martha was the general who came in by the day from the first cottage in the batch) —"Martha, put on an extra chop for the master. You aren't in love, are you, my dear?"

"Gracious, no! Who should I be in love with, mother?"

"Quite right, dear. There is no one about here with more looks than a Brussels-sprout. Not that I say anything against sprouts. Martha, just go and see if there are any sprouts left. We'll have them for dinner."

Edward looked at the woods across the batch, and wondered why the young fresh green of the larches and the elm samaras was so sad, and why the cry of a sheep from an upper slope was so forlorn.

"I hope, Edward," said Mrs. Marston, "that it won't be serious music. I think serious music interferes with the digestion. Your poor father and I went to the 'Creation' on our honeymoon, and thought little of it; then we went to the 'Crucifixion,' and though it was very pleasant, I couldn't digest the oysters afterwards. And then, again, these clever musicians allow themselves to become so passionate, one almost thinks they are inebriated. Not flutes and cornets, they have to think of their breath, but fiddlers can wreak their feelings on the instrument without suffering for it."

Edward laughed.

"I hope the gentleman that's coming to-day is a nice quiet one," she went on, as if Abel were a pony. "And I hope the lady singer is not a contralto. Contralto, to my mind," she went on placidly, stirring her porter in preparation for a draught, "is only another name for roaring, which is unseemly." She drank her porter gratefully, keeping the spoon in place with one finger.

If she could have seen father and daughter as they set forth, hilarious, to superimpose tumult on the peace of God's Little Mountain, she would have been a good deal less placid.

It was restful to sit and look at her kind old face, soft and round beneath her lace cap, steeped in a peace deeper than lethargy. She was one of nature's opiates, and she administered herself unconsciously to everyone who saw much of her. Edward's father, having had an overdose, had not survived. Mrs. Marston always spoke of him as "my poor husband who fell asleep," as if he had dozed in a sermon. Sleep was her fetish, panacea, and art. Her strongest condemnation was to call a person "a stirring body." She sat to-day, while preparations raged in the kitchen, placidly knitting. She always knitted—socks for Edward and shawls for herself. She had made so many shawls, and she so felt the cold, that she wore them in layers—pink, grey, white, heather mixture, and a purple cross-over.

When Martha and the friend who had come to help

quarrelled shrilly, she murmured, "Poor things! putting themselves in such a pother!" When, after a crash, Martha was heard to say, "There's the cream-jug now! Well, break one, break three!" she only shook her head, and murmured that servants were not what they used to be. When Martha's friend's little boy dropped the urn—presented to the late Mr. Marston by a grateful congregation, and as large as a watering-can—and Martha's friend shouted, "I'll warm your buttons!" and proceeded to do so, Mrs. Marston remained self-poised as a sun.

At last supper was set out, the cloths going in terraces according to the various heights of the tables; the tea-sets—willow and Coalport, the feather pattern, and the seaweed—looking like a china-shop; the urn, now rakishly dinted, presiding. People paid for their supper on these occasions, and expected to have as much as they could eat. Mrs. Marston had rashly told Martha that she could have what was left as a perquisite, which resulted later in stormy happenings.

From the nook on the hillside where the chapel stood, as Abel ran hastily down the slope—the harp jogging on his shoulders, and looking like some weird demon that clung round his neck and possessed him—came a roar of sound. The brass band from Black Mountain was in possession of the platform. The golden windows shone comfortably in the cold spring evening, and Hazel ran towards them as she would have run towards the wide-flung onyx doors of faery.

They arrived breathless and panting in the graveyard, where the tombstones seemed to elbow each other outside the shining windows, looking into this cave of saffron light and rosy joy as sardonically as if they knew that those within its shelter would soon be without, shelterless in the storm of death; that those who came in so gaily by twos and threes would go out one by one without a word. Hazel peered in.

"Fine raps they're having!" she whispered. "All the band's there, purple with pleasure, and sweating with the music like chaps haying."

Abel looked in.

"Eh, dear," he said, "they're settled there for the neet. We'll ne'er get a squeak in. There's nought the Black Mountain Band'll stop at when they're elbow to elbow; they eggs each other on cruel, so they do! Your ears may be dinned and deafened for life, and you lost to the bee-keeping (for hear you must, or you'm done, with bees), but the band dunna care! There! Now they've got a hencore—that's to say, do it agen; and every time they get one of them it goes to their yeads, and they play louder."

"Ah, but you play better," said Hazel comfortingly; for Abel's voice had trembled, and Hazel must comfort grief wherever she found it, for grief implied weakness.

"I know I do," he assented; "but what can I do agen ten strong men?"

At the mountain, as in the world of art and letters, it seemed that the artist must elbow and push, and that if he did not often stop his honeyed utterance to shout his wares he would not be heard at all.

"Dunna they look funny!" said Hazel with a giggle. "All sleepy and quiet, like smoked bees. Is that the Minister? Him by the old sleepy lady—she's had more smoke than most!"

"Where?"

"There. He's got a black coat on and a kind face, sad-like."

"Maybe if you took and axed him, he'd marry you —when the moon falls down the chapel chimney and rabbits chase the bobtailed sheep-dog!"

"I'm not for marrying anybody. Let's go in," said Hazel.

She took off her hat and coat, to enter more splendidly. On her head, resting softly among the coils of ruddy hair, she put a wreath of violets, which grew everywhere at the Callow; a big bunch of them was at her throat like a cameo brooch.

When she entered the band faltered, and the cornet, a fiery young man whom none could tire, wavered into silence. Edward, turning to find out what had caused this most desirable event, saw her coming up the room with the radiant fatefulness of a fairy in a dream. His heart went out to her, not only for her morning air, her vivid eyes, her coronet of youth's rare violets, but for the wistfulness that was not only in her face, but in her poise and in every movement. He felt as he would to a small bright bird that had come, greatly daring, in at his window on a stormy night. She had entered the empty room of his heart and from this night onwards his only thought was how to keep her there.

When she went up to sing, his eyes dwelt on her. She was the most vital thing he had ever seen. The tendrils of burnished hair about her forehead and ears curled and shone with life; her eyes danced with life; her body was taut as a slim arrow ready to fly from life's bow.

Abel sat down in the middle of the platform and

began to play, quite regardless of Hazel, who had to start when she could.

"Harps in heaven played for you;
Played for Christ with his eyes so blue;
Played for Peter and for Paul,
But never played for me at all!

"Harps in heaven, made all of glass,
Greener than the rainy grass.
Ne'er a one but is bespoken,
And mine is broken—mine is broken!

"Harps in heaven play high, play low;
In the cold, rainy wind I go
To find my harp, as green as spring—
My splintered harp without a string!"

She sang with passion. The wail of the lost was in her voice. She had not the slightest idea what the words meant (probably they meant nothing), but the sad cadence suited her emotional tone, and the ideas of loss and exile expressed her vague mistrust of the world. Edward imagined her in her blue-green dress and violet crown playing on a large glass harp in a company of angels.

"Poor child!" he thought. "Is it mystical longing or a sense of sin that cries out in her voice?"

It was neither of those things; it was nothing that Edward could have understood at that time, though later he did. It was the grief of rainy forests and the moan of stormy water; the muffled complaint of driven leaves; the keening—wild and universal—of life for the perishing matter that it inhabits.

Hazel expressed things that she knew nothing of, as a blackbird does. For, though she was young and fresh, she had her origin in the old, dark heart of earth, full of innumerable agonies, and in that heart she dwelt, and ever would, singing from its gloom as a bird sings in a yew-tree. Her being was more full of echoes than the hearts of those that live further from the soil; and we are all as full of echoes as a rocky wood—echoes of the past, reflex echoes of the future, and echoes of the soil (these last reverberating through our filmiest dreams, like the sound of thunder in a blossoming orchard). The echoes are in us of great voices long gone hence, the unknown cries of huge beasts on the mountains; the sullen aims of creatures in the slime; the love-call of the bittern. We know, too, echoes of things outside our ken—the thought that shapes itself in the bee's brain and becomes a waxen box of sweets; the tyranny of youth stirring in the womb; the crazy terror of small slaughtered beasts; the upward push of folded grass, and how the leaf feels in all its veins the cold rain; the ceremonial that passes yearly in the emerald temples of bud and calyx—we have walked those temples; we are the sacrifice on those altars. And the future floats on the current of our blood like a secret argosy. We hear the ideals of our descendants, like songs in the night, long before our firstborn is begotten. We, in whom the pollen and the dust, sprouting grain and falling berry, the dark past and the dark future, cry and call—we ask, Who is this Singer that sends his voice through the dark forest, and inhabits us with ageless and immortal music, and sets the long echoes rolling for evermore?

The audience, however, did not notice that there were echoes in Hazel, and would have gaped if you had proclaimed God in her voice. They looked at her with critical eyes that were perfectly blind to her real

self. Mrs. Marston thought what a pity it was that she looked so wild; Martha thought it a pity that she did not wear a chenille net over her hair to keep it neat; and Abel, peering up at her through the strings of the harp, and looking—with his face framed in wild red hair—like a peculiarly intelligent animal in a cage, did not think of her at all.

But Edward made up for them, because he thought of her all the time. Before the end of the concert he had got as far as to be sure she was the only girl he would ever want to marry. His ministerial self put in a faint proviso, "If she is a good girl"; but it was instantly shouted down by his other self, who asserted that as she was so beautiful she must be good.

During the last items on the programme—two vociferous glees rendered by a stage-full of people packed so tightly that it was marvellous how they expanded their diaphragms—Edward was in anguish of mind lest the cornet should monopolize Hazel at supper. The said cornet had become several shades more purple each time Hazel sang, so Edward was prepared for the worst. He was determined to make a struggle for it, and felt that though his position denied him the privilege of scuffling, he might at least use finesse—that has never been denied to any Church.

"My dear," whispered Mrs. Marston, "have you an unwelcome guest?"

This was her polite way of indicating a flea.

"No, mother."

"Well, dear, there must be something preying on your mind; you have kept up such a feeling of uneasiness that I have hardly had any nap at all."

"What do you think of her, mother?"

"Who, dear?"

"The beautiful girl."

"A pretty tune, the first she sang," said Mrs. Marston, not having heard the others. "But such wild manners and such hair! Like pussy stroked the wrong way. And there is something a little peculiar about her, for when she sings about heaven it seems somehow improper, and that," she added drowsily, "heaven hardly *should* do."

Edward understood what she meant. He had been conscious himself of something desperately exciting in the bearing of Hazel Woodus—something that penetrated the underworld which lay like a covered well within him, and, like a ray of light, set all kinds of unsuspected life moving and developing there.

As supper went on Edward kept more and more of Hazel's attention, and the quiet grey eyes met the restless amber ones more often.

"If I came some day—soon—to your home, would you sing to me?" he asked.

"I couldna. I'm promised for the bark-stripping."

"What's that?"

Hazel looked at him pityingly.

"Dunna you know what that is?"

"I'm afraid not."

"It's fetching the bark off'n the falled trees ready for lugging."

"Where are the felled trees?"

"Hunter's Spinney."

"That's close here."

"Ah."

Edward was deep in thought. The cornet whispered to Hazel:

"Making up next Sunday's sermon!"

But Edward turned round disconcertingly.

"As it's on your way, why not come to tea with

mother? I might be out, but you wouldn't mind that?"

"Eh, but I should! I dunna want to talk to an old lady!"

"I'll stop at home, then," he replied, very much amused, and with a look of quiet triumph at the cornet. "Which day?"

"Wednesday week's the first."

"Come Wednesday, then."

"What'll the old sleepy lady say?"

"My mother," he said with dignity, "will approve of anything I think right."

But his heart misgave. So far he had only "thought right" what her conventions approved. He had seldom acted on his own initiative. She therefore had a phrase, "Dear Edward is always right." It was possible that when he left off his unquestioning concordance with her, she would leave off saying "Dear Edward is always right." So far he had not wanted anything particularly, and as it was as difficult to quarrel with Mrs. Marston as to strike a match on a damp box, there had never been any friction. She liked things, as she said, "nice and pleasant." To do Providence justice, everything always had been. Even when her husband died it had been, in a crape-clad way, nice and pleasant, for he died after the testimonial and the urn, and not before, as a less considerate man would have done. He died on a Sunday, which was "so suitable," and at dawn, which was "so beautiful"; also (in the phrase used for criminals and the dying) "he went quietly." Not that Mrs. Marston did not feel it. She did, as deeply as her nature could. But she felt it, as a well-padded boy feels a whacking, through layers of convention. Now, at her age, to find out that life was not so pleasant as she thought would be little short of tragedy.

"Ah, I'll come, and I'm much obleeged," said Hazel.

"I'll meet you at Hunter's Spinney and see you home," Edward decided.

To this also Hazel assented so delightedly that the cornet pushed back his chair and went to another table with a sardonic laugh. But his remarks were drowned by a voice which proclaimed:

"All the years I've bin to suppers I've 'ad tartlets! To-night they wunna go round. I've paid the same as others. Tartlets I'll 'ave!"

"But the plate's empty," said Martha, flushed and determined.

"I've had no finger in the emptying of it. More must be fetched." Other voices joined in, and Mrs. Marston was heard to murmur, "Unpleasant."

Edward was oblivious to it all.

"Shall you," he asked earnestly, "like me to come to the Spinney?"

"Ah, I shall that!" said Hazel, who already felt an aura of protection about him. "It'll be so safe—like when I was little, and was used to pick daisies round grandad."

Edward knew more definitely than before the relation in which he wished to stand towards Hazel. It was not that of grandad.

Any reply he might have made was drowned by the uproar that broke forth at the cry, "She's hidden 'em! Look in the kitchen!"

Martha's cousin—in his spare time policeman of a distant village—felt that if Martha was detected in fraud it would not look well, and therefore put his sinewy person in the kitchen doorway. Edward seized the moment, when there was a hush of surprise, to say grace, during which the invincible voice murmured:

"I've not received tartlets. I'm not thankful."

"Mother," Edward said, when the last unruly guest had disappeared in the wild April night, and Hazel's vivid presence and violet fragrance and young laughter had been taken by the darkness, "I've asked Hazel Woodus to tea on Wednesday."

"She is not of your class, Edward."

"What does class matter?"

"Martha's brother calls you 'sir,' and Martha looks down on this young person."

"Don't call her 'young person,' mother."

"Whether it is mistaken kindness, dear, or a silly flirtation, it will only do you harm with the congregation."

"Bother the congregation!"

"Young men and women," soliloquized Mrs. Marston, as she hoisted herself upstairs with the candlestick very much aslant in a torpid hand, "are not what they used to be."

CHAPTER IX

HUNTER'S SPINNEY, a conical hill nearly as high as God's Little Mountain, lay between that range and Undern. It was deeply wooded; only its top was bare and caught the light redly. It was a silent and deserted place, cowled in ancient legends. Here the Black Huntsman stalled his steed, and the death-pack, coming to its precincts, ceased into the hill. Here, in November twilights, when the dumb birds cowered in the dark pines, you might hear from the summit a horn blown very clearly, with tuneful devilry, and a scattered sound of deep barking like the noise of sawing timber, and then the blood-curdling tumult of the pack at feeding time.

To-day, as Hazel began her work, the radiant woods were full of pale colour, so delicate and lucent that Beauty seemed a fugitive presence from some other world trapped and panting to be free. The small patens of the beeches shone like green glass, and the pale spired chestnuts were candelabras on either side of the steep path. In the bright breathless glades of larches the willow-wrens sang softly, but with boundless vitality. On sunny slopes the hyacinths pushed out close-packed buds between their covering leaves; soon they would spread their grave blue like a prayer-carpet. Hazel, stooping in her old multi-coloured pinafore, her bare arms gleaming like the stripped trees, seemed to Edward as he came up the shady path to be the spirit of beauty. He quite realized that her occupation was not suited to a minister's future wife. "But she may never be that," he thought despairingly.

"Have you ever thought, Hazel," he said later, sitting down on a log—"have you ever thought of the question of marriage?"

"I ne'er did till Foxy took the chicks." Edward looked dazed. "It's like this," Hazel went on. "Father (he's a rum 'un, is father!), he says he'll drown Foxy if she takes another."

"Who is Foxy?"

"Oh! Fancy you not knowing Foxy! Her's my little cub. Pretty! you ne'er saw anything so pretty."

Edward thought he had.

"But she canna get used to folks' ways." (This was a new point of view to Edward.) "She'm a fox, and she can't be no other. And I'd liefer she'd *be* a fox."

"Foxes are very mischievous," Edward said mildly.

"Mischievous!" Hazel flamed on him like a little thunderstorm. "Mischievous! And who made 'em mischievous, I'd like to know? They didna make theirselves."

"God made them," Edward said simply.

"What for did He, if He didna like 'em when they were done?"

"We can't know all His reasons; He walks in darkness."

"Well, that's no manner of use to me and Foxy," said Hazel practically. "So all as I can see to do is to get married and take Foxy where there's no chicks."

"So you think of marrying?"

"Ah! And I told father I'd marry the first as come. I swore it by the Mountain."

"And who came?" Edward had a kind of faintness in his heart.

"Never a one."

"Nobody at all?"

"Never a one."

"And if anyone came and asked for you, you'd take him?"

"Well, I'm bound to, seemingly. But it dunna matter. None'll ever come. What for should they?"

She herself answered her own question fully as she stood aureoled in dusky light. His eyes were eloquent, but she was too busy to notice them.

"And should you like to be married?" he asked gently.

He expected a shy affirmative. He received a flat negative.

"My mam didna like it. And she said it'd be the end of going in the woods and all my gamesome days. And she said tears and torment, tears and torment was the married lot. And she said, 'Keep yourself to yourself. You wunna made for marrying any more than me. Eat in company, but sleep alone'—that's what she said, Mr. Marston."

Edward was so startled at this unhesitating frankness that he said nothing. But he silently buried several sweet hopes that had been pushing up like folded hyacinths for a week. The old madness was upon him, but it was a larger, more spiritual madness than Reddin's, as the sky is larger and more ethereal than the clouds that obscure it. He was always accustomed to think more of giving than receiving, so now he concentrated himself on what he could do for Hazel. He felt that her beauty would be an ample return for anything he could do as her husband to make her happy. If she would confide in him, make demands on his time, run to him for refuge, he felt that he could ask no more of life. The strength of the ancient laws of earth was as yet hidden from him. He did not know the fierceness of the conflict in which he was engaging for Hazel's sake—the world-old conflict between sex and altruism.

If he had known, he would still not have hesitated.

Suddenly Hazel looked round with an affrighted air.

"It's late to be here," she said.

"Why?"

"There's harm here if you bide late. The jeath pack's about here in the twilight, so they do say."

They looked up into the dark steeps, and the future seemed to lower on them.

"Maybe summat bad'll come to us in this spinney," she whispered.

"Nothing bad can come to you when you are in God's keeping."

"There canna be many folk in His keeping, then."

"Do you say your prayers, Hazel?" he asked rather sadly.

"Ah! I say:

> "Keep me one year, keep me seven,
> Till the gold turns silver on my head;
> Bring me up to the hill o' heaven,
> And leave me die quiet in my bed."

That's what I allus say."

"Who taught you?"

"My mam."

"Ah, well, it must be a good prayer if she taught it you, mustn't it?" he said.

Suddenly Hazel clutched his arm affrightedly.

"Hark! Galloping up yonder! Run! run! It's the Black Huntsman!"

It was Reddin, skirting the wood on his way home from a search for Hazel. If he had come into the spinney he would have seen them, but he kept straight on.

"It's bringing harm!" cried Hazel, pulling at Edward's arm; "see the shivers on me! It's somebody galloping o'er my grave!"

Edward resolved to combat these superstitions and replace them by a sane religion. He had not yet fathomed the ancient, cruel, and mighty power of these exhalations of the soil. Nor did he see that Hazel was enchained by earth, prisoner to it only a little less than the beech and the hyacinth—bond-serf of the sod.

When Edward and Hazel burst into the parlour, like sunshine into an old garden, they were met by a powerful smell of burnt merino. Mrs. Marston had been for some hours as near Paradise as we poor mortals can hope to be. Her elastic-sided cloth boots rested on the fender, and her skirt, carefully turned up, revealed a grey stuff petticoat with a hint of white flannel beneath. The pink shawl was top, which meant optimism. With Mrs. Marston, optimism was the direct result of warmth. Her spectacles had crept up and round her head, and had a rakishly benign appearance. On her comfortable lap lay the missionary *Word* and a large roll of brown knitting which was intended to imitate fur. Edward noted hopefully that the pink shawl was top.

"Here's Hazel come to see you, mother!"

Mrs. Marston straightened her spectacles, surveyed Hazel, and asked if she would like to do her hair. This ceremony over, they sat down to tea.

"And how many brothers and sisters have you, my dear?" asked the old lady.

"Never a one. Nobody but our Foxy."

"Edward, too, has none. Who is Foxy?"

"My little cub."

"You speak as if the animal were a relation, dear."

"So all animals be my brothers and sisters."

"I know, dear. Quite right. All animals in conversation should be so. But any single animal in reality is only an animal, and can't be. Animals have no souls."

"Yes, they have, then! If they hanna, *you* hanna!"

Edward hastened to make peace.

"We don't know, do we, mother?" he said. "And now, suppose we have tea?"

Mrs. Marston looked at Hazel suspiciously over the rim of her glasses.

"My dear, don't have ideas," she said.

"There, Hazel!" Edward smiled. "What about your ideas in the spinney?"

"There's queer things doing in Hunter's Spinney, and what for shouldna you believe it?" said Hazel. "Sometimes more than other times, and midsummer most of all."

"What sort of queer things?" asked Edward, in order to be able to watch her as she answered.

Hazel shut her eyes and clasped her hands, speaking in a soft monotone as if repeating a lesson.

"In Hunter's Spinney on midsummer night there's things moving as move no other time; things free as was fast; things crying out as have been a long while hurted." She suddenly opened her eyes and went on dramatically. "First comes the Black Huntsman, crouching low on his horse and the horse going belly to earth. And John Meares o' the public, he seed the red froth from his nostrils on the brakes one morning when he was ketching pheasants. And the jeath pack's with him, great hound-dogs, real as real, only no eyes, but sockets with a light behind 'em. Ne'er a one knows what they'm after. If I seed 'em I'd die," she finished hastily, taking a large bite of cake.

"Myths are interesting," said Edward, "especially nature myths."

"What's a myth, Mr. Marston?"

"An untruth, my dear," said Mrs. Marston.

"This inna one, then! I tell you John seed the blood!"

"Tell us more." Edward would have drunk in nonsense rhymes from her lips.

"And there's never a one to gainsay 'em in all the dark 'oods," Hazel went on, "except on Midsummer Eve."

"Midsummer!"—Mrs. Marston's tone was gently wistful—"is the only time I'm really warm. That is, if the weather's as it should be. But the weather's not what it was!"

"Tell us more, Hazel!" pleaded Edward.

"What for do you want to hear, my soul?"

Edward flushed at the caressing phrase, and Mrs. Marston looked as indignant as was possible to her physiognomy, until she realized that it was a mere form of speech.

"Because I love—old tales."

"Well, if so be you go there, then"—Hazel leant forward, earnest and mysterious—"after the pack's gone you'll hear soft feet running, and you'll see faces look out and hands waving. And gangs of folks come galloping under the leaves, not seen clear, hastening above a bit. And others come quick after, all with trouble on 'em. And the place is full of whispering and rustling and voices calling a long way off. And my mam said the trees get free that night—or else folk out of the trees—creeping and struggling out of the boles like a chicken from the egg—getting free like lads out of school; and they go after the jeath-pack like birds after a cuckoo. And last comes the lady of Undern Coppy, lagging and lonesome, riding in a troop of shadows, and sobbing, 'Lost—alost! Oh, my green garden!' And they say the brake flowers on the eve of that night, and no bird sings and no star falls."

"What a pack of nonsense!" murmured Mrs. Marston drowsily.

"That it inna!" cried Hazel; "it's the bloody truth!"

Mrs. Marston's drowsiness forsook her. Hazel became conscious of tension.

"Mother!"—Edward's voice shook with suppressed laughter, although he was indignant with Hazel's father for such a mistaken upbringing—"mother, would you give Hazel the receipt for this splendid cake?"

"And welcome, my dear." The old lady was safely launched on her favourite topic. "And if you'd like a seed-cake as well, you shall have it. Have you put down any butter yet?"

Hazel never put down or preserved or made anything. Her most ambitious cooking was a rasher and a saucepan of potatoes.

"I dunna know what you mean," she said awkwardly.

Edward was disappointed. He had thought her

such a paragon. Well, well, cooking was, after all, a secondary thing. Let it go.

"You mean to say you don't know what putting down butter is, my poor child? But perhaps you go in for higher branches? Lemon-curd, now, and bottled fruit. I'm sure you can do those?"

Hazel felt blank. She thought it best to have things clear.

"I canna do nought," she said defiantly.

"Now, mother"—Edward came to the rescue again—"see how right you are in saying that a girl's education is not what it used to be! See how Hazel's has been neglected! Think what a lot you could teach her! Suppose you were to begin quite soon?"

"A batter," began Mrs. Marston, with the eagerness of a philosopher expounding his theory, "is a well-beaten mixture of eggs and flour. Repeat after me, my dear."

"Eh, what's the use? *He* dunna know what he eats no more than a pig! I shanna cook for 'im."

"Who's that, dear?" Mrs. Marston inquired.

"My dad."

Mrs. Marston held up her hands with the mock-fur knitting in them, and looked at Edward with round eyes.

"She says her father's a—a pig, my dear!"

"She doesn't mean it," said he loyally, "do you, Hazel?"

"Ah, and more!"

The host and hostess sighed.

Then Edward said: "Yes, but you won't always be keeping house for your father, you know," and found himself so confused that he had to go and fetch a pipe.

Afterwards he walked part way home with Hazel, and coming back under the driving sky—that seemed to move all in a piece like a sliding window, and showed the moon as a slim lady waiting for unlooked-for happenings—he could have wept at the crude sweetness of Hazel. She was of so ruthless an honesty towards herself as well as others; she had such strange lights and shadows in her eyes, her voice, her soul; she was so full of faults, and so brimming with fascination.

"Oh, God! if I may have her to keep and defend, to glow in my house like a rose, I'll ask no more," he murmured.

The pine-tops bowed in as stately a manner as they had when Hazel cried, "I'll never be a woman!" They listened like grown-ups to the prattle of a child. And the stars, like gods in silver armour sitting afar in halls of black marble, seemed to hear and disdain the little gnat-like voice, as they heard Vessons' defiant "Never will I!" and Mrs. Marston's woolly prayers, and Reddin's hoof-beats. All man's desires—predatory, fugitive, or merely negative—wander away into those dark halls, and are heard no more. Among the pillars of the night is there One who listens and remembers, and judges the foolishness of man, not by effects, but by motives? And does that one, in the majesty of everlasting vitality and resistless peace, ever see how we run after the painted butterflies of our desires and fall down the dark precipice? And if He sees and hears the wavering, calamitous life of all creatures, and especially of the most beautiful and the most helpless, does He ever sigh and weep, as we do when we see a dead child or a moth's wing impaled on a thorn?

Our heavy burden is that we cannot know. For all our tears and prayers and weary dreaming, we cannot know.

Edward lay awake all night, and heard the first blackbird begin, tentatively, his clear song—a song to bring tears by its golden security of joy in a world where nothing is secure.

The old madness surged in upon Edward more strongly as the light grew, and he tried to read the Gospel of St. John (his favourite), but the words left no trace on his mind. Hazel was there, and like a scarlet-berried rowan on the sky she held the gaze by the perfection of the picture she made. The bent of Edward's mind and upbringing were set against the rush of his wishes and of circumstance. She had said, "The first that came," and he was sure that in her state of dark superstition she would hold by her vow. Suppose some other—some farm-hand, who would never see the real Hazel—should have been thinking over the matter, and should go to-day and should be the first? It was just how things happened. And then his flower would be gone, and the other man would never know it was a flower. He worked himself into such a fever that he could not rest, but got up and went out into the lively air, and saw the sun come lingeringly through aery meadows of pale green and primrose. He saw the ice slip from the bright pointed lilac buds, and sheep browsing the frosty grass, and going to and fro in the unreserved way that animals have in the early hours before the restraint of human society is imposed on them. He saw, yet noticed nothing, until a long scarlet bar of cloud reminded him of Hazel by its vividness, and he found a violet by the graveyard gate.

"Little Hazel!" he whispered. He pondered on the future, and tried to imagine such an early walk as this with Hazel by his side, and could not for the glory of it. Then he reasoned with himself. This wild haste was not right, perhaps. He ought to wait. But that vow! That foolish, childish vow!

"I could look after her. She could blossom here like a violet in a quiet garden."

Giving was never too early.

"And I am asking nothing—not for years. She shall live her own life, and be mother's daughter and my little sister for as long as she likes. My little sister!" he repeated aloud, as if some voice had contradicted him. And, indeed, the whole wide morning seemed to contradict his scheme—the mating birds, the sheep suckling their lambs, the insistent neighing and bellowing that rose from the fields and farms, the very tombstones, with their legends of multitudinous families, and the voice that cried to man and woman, not in words, but in the zest of the earth and air, "Beget, bring forth, and then depart, for I have done with you!"

A sharp cold shower stung his cheeks, and he saw a slim rosebush beating itself helplessly against the wet earth, broken and muddy. He fetched a stake and tied it up. "I think," he said to himself, "that I was put into the world to tie up broken roses, and one that is not yet broken yet, thank God! It is miraculous that she has never come to harm, for that great overgrown boy, her father, takes no care of her. Yes, I was meant for that. I can't preach." He smiled ruefully as he remembered how steadfastly the congregation slept through his best sermons. "I can't say the right things at the right time. I'm not clever.

But I can take care of Hazel. And as that is my life-work," he added naïvely, "perhaps I'd better begin at once, and go to see her to-day."

Ah! the gold and scarlet morning as he came home after finding that resolve, which, as a matter of fact, he had taken with him! How the roof of the parsonage shone like the new Jerusalem! And how the fantail pigeons, very rotund denizens of that city, cooed as they walked gingerly—tiles being cold to pink feet on a frosty morning—up and down in the early sun!

Edward so much wanted to keep the violet he had found that he decided he ought to give it to his mother. So he put it on her plate, and looked for a suitable passage to read at prayers.

The Song of Solomon seemed the only thing really in tune with the morning, but he decided rather sadly that "something in Corinthians" might please his mother better. So he read, "The greatest of these is love," and his voice was so husky and so unmanageable that Mrs. Marston, who did not notice the golden undertones that matched their beauty with the blackbird's song, went straight from the chair she knelt at in the prayers to her store-room, and produced lemon and honey, which Edward loathed.

"You're very throaty, my dear, and you must take a level spoonful," she said.

It is only in poetry that all the world understands a lover. In real life he is called throaty, and given a level spoonful of that nauseous compound known as common sense.

CHAPTER X

THE garden at the Callow was full of old, sad-coloured flowers that had lost all names but the country ones. Chief among them, by reason of its hardihood, was a small plant called virgin's pride. Its ephemeral petals, pale and bee-haunted, fluttered like banners of some lost, forgotten cause. The garden was hazy with their demure, faintly scented flowers, and the voices of the bees came up in a soft roar, triumphantly as the voices of victors returning with hard-won spoil.

Abel had been putting some new sections on the hives, and, as usual, after a long spell of listening to their low, changeless music, he rushed in for his harp. He sat down under the hawthorn by the gate, and looked like a patriarch beneath a pale green tent. As day declined the music waxed; he played with a tenderness, a rage of delight, that did not often come to him except on spring evenings. He almost touched genius. Hazel came out, leaving the floor half scrubbed, and began to dance on the potato flat.

"Dunna stomp the taters to jeath, 'Azel!" said he.

"They binna up!" she replied, continuing to dance.

He never wasted words. He continued the air with one hand and threw a stone at her with the other. He hit her on the cheek.

"You wold beast!" she screamed.

"Gerroff taters!" He continued to play.

She went, hand to cheek, and frowning, off the potato patch. But she did not stop dancing. Neither of them ever let such things as anger, business, or cleanliness interfere with their pleasures. So Hazel danced on, though in a smaller area among the virgin's pride.

The music, wild, crude, and melancholy, floated on the soft air to Edward as he approached. The sun slipped lower; leaf shadows began to tremble on Hazel's pinafore, which, with its faded blue and its many stains, was transmuted in the vivid light, and looked like the flowers of virgin's pride.

" 'The Ash Tree'!" said Abel, who always announced his tunes in this way, as singers do at a choir supper.

The forlorn music met Edward at the gate. He stopped, startled at the sight of Hazel dancing in the shadowy garden with her hair loose and her abandon tempered by weariness. He stood behind the hedge until Abel brought the tune to an early end with the laconic remark, "Supper," and went indoors with his harp.

Edward opened the gate and went in.

"Eh, mister! what a start you give me!" said Hazel breathlessly.

"So this is your home?"

"Ah!"

Edward found her more disturbing to-night than at the concert; the gulf between them was more obvious; she had been comparatively tidy before. Now her disreputableness contrasted strongly with his correct black coat and general air of civilized well-being.

Hazel came nearer.

"He inna bad to live along of," she confided, with a nod towards the cottage. "O' course, he's crossways time and agen, and a devil's temper."

"You mustn't speak of your father like that, Hazel."

"What for not? He *be* like that."

"Are all these apple-trees yours?" he asked, to change the subject.

"No, they'm father's. But I get the windfa'ls and the bruised 'uns. I allus see"—she smiled winningly —"as there's plenty of them. Foxy likes 'em. He found me at it once bruising of 'em. God a'mighty! what a hiding he give me!"

Edward felt depressed. He could not harmonize Hazel's personality with his mother's; he was shocked at her expressions; he was sufficiently fastidious to recoil from dirt; the thought of Abel as a father-in-law was little short of appalling. Yet, in spite of all these things, he had felt such elation, such spring rapture when Hazel danced; the world took on such strange new colours when she looked at him that he knew he must love her for ever. He felt that as his emotions grew stronger—and they were becoming more and more like a herd of young calves out at grass—his ways of expression must increase in correctness.

"Hazel——" he began.

"I like the way you say it," she interrupted. "Ah! I like it right well! Breathin' strong, like folk coming up the Monkey's Ladder."

"Whatever's that?"

"Dunna you know Monkey's Ladder? It's that road there. Somebody's coming up it now on a horse."

They both looked down at Reddin climbing slowly,

and still some way off. They did not know who it was, nor what destiny was pacing silently towards them with his advancing figure, nor why he rode up and down this road and other roads every day; but an inexplicable sense of urgency came upon Edward. To his own surprise, he suddenly said:

"I came to ask if you'd marry me, Hazel Woodus?"

"Eh?" said she, dazed with surprise.

"Will you marry me, Hazel? I can give you a good home, and I will try to be a good husband, and—and I love you, Hazel, dear."

Hazel put her head on one side like a willow-wren singing. She liked to be called dear.

"D'you like me as much as I like Foxy?"

"Far more."

"You've bin very quick about it."

"I'm afraid I have."

"Will you buy me a green gown with yellow roses on?"

"If you like." He spoke doubtfully, wondering what his mother would think of it.

"And shall we sit down to our dinners at a table with a cloth on like at——" She stopped. She could not tell him about Undern. "Like the gentry?" she finished.

"Yes, dear."

"And will you tell that sleepy old lady as lives along of you——"

("Oh, poor mother!" thought Edward.)

"—Not to stare and stare at me over the top of her spectacles like a cow at a cornfield over the fence?"

"Yes—yes," said Edward hastily, feeling that his mother must wait to be reinstated until he had made sure of Hazel.

"All right, then; I'll come."

Edward took her hand; then he kissed her cheek gently. She accepted the kiss placidly. There was nothing in it to remind her of Reddin's.

"And you'll do always as you like," Edward went on, "and be my little sister." Then, to make matters clearer, he added: "And you shall have a room papered with buttercups and daisies for your very own."

"Eh! how grand!"

"You'll like that?" His voice was wistful in its eagerness for a denial.

"Ah! I shall like it right well."

Edward made no reply. He was never any good at putting in a word for himself. He was usually left out of things, and stood contentedly in the background while inferior men pushed in front of him.

"And now," he said, "I'll give you a token till I can get you a ring." He picked a spray of the faint pink and blue flowers.

"What's its name?" he asked.

"Virgin's pride."

Edward gave her a quick look. Then he realized that she was as innocent as her little fox, and as free from artifice. That was its name, so she told it to him.

"A very pretty little flower, and a very sweet name," he said. "And, now, where's your father?"

"Guzzling his supper."

Edward frowned. Then the humour of the situation struck him, and he laughed. Abel rose as they came to the door.

"Well, mister," he inquired glumly, "what'n you after? Money for them missions to buy clothes for savages as 'd liefer go bare? Or money for them poor clergy? I'm poorer nor the clergy."

"I want to marry Hazel."

Abel flung back his head and roared. Then he jerked his thumb over his shoulder towards Hazel.

"What?—'er?" he queried in ecstasies of mirth. "'Er? Look at the floor, man! Look at the apern she's got on! Laws, man! you surely dunna want our 'Azel for your missus?"

"Yes." Edward was nettled and embarrassed.

"Well, 'er's only eighteen." He looked Hazel over appraisingly, as he would have looked at a heifer. "Still, I suppose she's an 'ooman growed. Well, you can take her. I dunna mind. When d'you want her?"

"I shall ask her when she will wish to marry me."

Abel laughed again.

"Lord love us!" he said. "You unna take and ax her? Tell her, that's what! Just tell her what to do, and she'll do it if you give her one for herself now and agen. So you mean marrying, do yer?"

Edward was angry. Abel's outlook and manner of expression rawed his nerves.

"I leave all the arrangements to her," he said stiffly.

"Then the devil aid you," said Abel, "for I canna!"

Hazel stood with downcast face, submissive, but ill at ease. She wanted to spring at her father and scream, "Ho'd yer row!" for she hated him for talking so to Edward. Somehow it made her flushed and ashamed for Edward to be told to "give her one for herself." She looked at him under her lashes, and wondered if he would. There was something not altogether unpleasant in the idea. She felt that to be ordered about by young lips and struck by a young man's hand would be, as business men say, "quite in order." She appraised Edward, and decided that he would not. Had she been able to decide in the affirmative, she would probably have fallen in love with him there and then.

Edward came over to her and took her hand.

"When will you be my wife, Hazel?" he asked.

"I dunno. Not for above a bit."

"Haw! haw!" laughed Abel. "Hark at her! Throw summat at 'er, man!"

"I should prefer your absence," said Edward, stung to expression at last.

"Eh?"

"Go away!" said Edward rudely. He was surprised at himself afterwards. Abel withdrew open-mouthed. Hazel laughed with delight.

"But why didna you hit 'un?" she asked wistfully.

"My dear girl! What a thing to say!"

"Be it?"

"Yes. But, now, when shall we be married?"

"Not for years and years," said Hazel, pleased at the dismay on his face, and enjoying her new power. Then she reflected on the many untried delights of the new life.

"Leastways, not for days an' days," she amended. "Will you gi' me pear-drops every day?"

"Pear-drops! My dear Hazel, you must think of better things than pear-drops!"

"There's nought better," said she, "without its bulls-eyes."

"But, dear," Edward reasoned gently, "don't you want to think of helping me, and going with me to chapel?"

Hazel considered.

"D'you preach long and solemn?" she asked.

"No," said Edward rather curtly. "But if I did, you ought to like it."

Hazel took his measure again. Then she said naughtily:

"Tell you what I'll do if you preach long and solemn, mister. I'll put me tongue out!"

Edward laughed in spite of himself, and thought for the twentieth time, "Poor mother!" But that did not prevent his being anxious to have Hazel safely at the Mountain. It seemed to him that every man in the county must want to marry her.

"What would you say to May, Hazel, early May—lilac-time?"

"I'd like it right well."

"And suppose we fix it the day after the spring flower-show at Evenwood, and go to it together?"

"I'm going with father to sing."

"Well, when you've sung, you can have tea with me."

"Thank you kindly, Mr. Marston."

"Edward."

"Ed'ard."

Abel came round the house.

"You can come and see the bees, if you've a mind," he said forgivingly. In his angers and his joys he was like a child. He was, in fact, what he looked—a barbaric child, prematurely aged. He was aged and had lines on his face because he enjoyed life so much, for joy bites as deep as sickness or grief or any other physical strain. Hazel would age soon, for she lived in an intenser world than most people, as if she saw everything through magnifying-glass and coloured glass.

Edward went to the bees as he would have gone to

the dogs—sadly. He disliked the bees even more than he disliked Abel, who in his expansive mood was much less attractive than in his natural sulkiness. Abel did not know how near he came once or twice to frustrating an end that he thought very desirable. A less steadfast man than Edward, with a less altruistic object in view, would have been frightened away from Hazel by Abel's crudeness.

"What about the bitch?" he asked Edward when they had seen the bees. "Will you take her, or shall I drown her?"

Rage flamed in Hazel's face—rage all the more destructive because it was caused by pity. Her father's calm taking for granted that Foxy's fate (and her own) depended on his whim and Edward's, the picture of Foxy tied up in a bag to be drowned—Foxy, who had all her love—infuriated her.

Edward was troubled at the look in her eyes. He had not yet had much opportunity for seeing those wild red lights that burn in the eyes of the hunter, and are reflected in those of the hunted, and make life a lurid nightmare. The scene set his teeth on edge.

"Of course," he said, and the recklessness of it was quite clear to him when he thought of his mother—"of course, the little fox shall come."

"And the one-eyed cat and the blind bird and the old ancient rabbit, I'll wager?" queried Abel. "Well, minister, you can set up a menagerie and make money."

"They could go in bits of holes and corners," Hazel put in anxiously, "and nobody'd ever know they were there! And the bird chirrups lovely, fine days."

Abel shouted with laughter.

"Tuthree feathers and a beak!" he said. "And the rabbit 'd be comforbler a muff."

Edward hastily ended the discussion.

"Of course, they shall all come," he said.

Somehow, Hazel made the sheltering of these poor creatures a matter of religion. He found himself connecting them with the great "Inasmuch as ye have done it unto these——" He had never seen the text in that light before. But he was dubious about the possibility of making his mother see it thus.

"They'll be much obleeged," Hazel said. "Come and see 'em."

She spoke as one conferring the freedom of a city.

Foxy—very clean in her straw, smoothly white and brown, and dignified, and golden of eye—looked mistrustfully at Edward, and showed her baby-white teeth.

"She'll liven the old lady up," said Hazel.

"I'm afraid——" began Edward; and then—"she shows her teeth a good deal."

"Only along of being frit."

"She needn't be frightened. I'll take care of her and of you, and see that no harm comes to you."

The statement was received by the night—critical, attent—in a silence so deep that it seemed quizzical.

On his way home he felt rather dismayed at his task, because he saw that in making Hazel happy he must make his mother unhappy.

"Ah, well, it'll all come right," he thought, "for He is love, and He will help me."

The sharp staccato sound of a horse cantering came up behind him. It was Reddin returning from a wide détour. He pulled up short.

"Is there any fiddler in your parish, parson?" he inquired.

Edward considered.

"There is one man on the far side of the mountain."

"Pretty daughter?"

"No. He is only twenty."

"Damn!"

He was gone.

Hazel, in the untidy room at the Callow, fed her pets and had supper in a dream of coming peace for them all. She would not have been peaceful if she had seen the meeting of the two men in the dusk, both wanting her with a passion equal in suddenness and force, but different in quality. She wanted neither. Her passion, no less intense, was for freedom, for the wood-track, for green places where soft feet scudded and eager eyes peered out and adventurous lives were lived up in the tree-tops, down in the moss.

She was fascinated by Reddin; she was drawn to confide in Edward; but she wanted neither of them. Whether or not in years to come she would find room in her heart for human passion, she had no room for it now. She had only room for the little creatures she befriended and for her eager, quickly growing self. For, like her mother, she had the egoism that is more selfless than most people's altruism—the divine egoism that is genius.

CHAPTER XI

WHEN Edward got home his mother was asleep in the armchair. Her whole person rose and fell like a tropical sea. Her shut eyes were like those of a statue, behind the lids of which one knows there are no pupils. Her eyebrows were slightly raised, as if in expostulation at being obliged to breathe. Her figure expressed the dignity of old age, which may or may not be due to rheumatism.

Edward, as he looked at her, felt as one does who has been reading a fairy-tale and is called to the family meal. All the things he had meant to say, that had seemed so eloquent, now seemed foolish. He awoke her hastily in case his courage should fail before that most adamantine thing—an unsympathetic atmosphere.

"I've got some news for you, mother."

"Nothing unpleasant, dear?"

"No. Pleasant. It makes me very happy."

"The good are always happy," replied Mrs. Marston securely.

Before the bland passivity of this remark it seemed that irony itself must soften.

"I am engaged, mother."

"What in, dear?"

"I am going to bring home a wife."

She was deaf and very sleepy.

"What kind of a knife, dear?" she asked.

"I am going to marry Hazel Woodus."

"You can't do that, dear." She spoke with unruffled calm, as if Edward were three years old.

"I can and shall, mother."

"Ah, well, it won't be for a long, long time," she said, thinking aloud as she often did, and adding with the callousness that sometimes comes with age—arising not from hardness, but from atrophy of the emotions—"and, of course, she may die before then."

"Die!" Edward's voice surprised himself, and it made his mother jump.

"The young do die," she went on; "we all have to go. Your poor father fell asleep. I shall fall asleep."

She began to do so. But his next words made her wide awake again.

"I'm going to be married in May, next month."

Her whole weight of passive resistance was set against his purpose.

"Such unseemly haste!" she murmured. "So inordinate—such a hurried marriage!"

But, Edward's motives being what they were, he was proof against this.

"What will the congregation think?"

"Bother the congregation!"

"That's the second time you've said that, Edward. I'm afraid you are going from bad to worse."

"No. Only going to be married, mother."

"But a year's engagement is the least, the very least I could countenance," she pleaded, "and a year is so soon gone. One eats and sleeps, and Lord's Day breaks the week, and time soon passes."

"Oh, can't you understand, mother?" He tried illustration. "Suppose you saw a beautiful shawl out on a hedge in the rain, shouldn't you want to bring it in?"

"Certainly not. It would be most unwise. Besides, I have seven."

"Well, anyway, I can't put it off. Even now something may have happened to her."

He spoke with the sense of the inimical in life that all lovers feel.

"But things will have to be bought," she said helplessly, "and things will have to be made."

"There is plenty of time, several weeks yet. Won't you," he suggested tactfully, "see after Hazel's clothes for her? She is too poor to buy them herself. Won't you lay out a sum of money for me, mother?"

"Yes, I think," she said, beginning to recover her benignity—"I think I could lay out a sum of money."

Mrs. Marston had what she called "not a wink of sleep"—that is to say, she kept awake for half an hour after getting into bed. The idea of a wedding, although it was offensive by reason of being different from every day, was still quite pleasant. It would be an opportunity for using the multitude of things that were stored in every cupboard and never used, being thought too good for every day. Mrs. Marston was one of those that, having great possessions, go sadly all their days. It is strange how generation after generation spend their fleeting years in this fetish-worship, never daring to make life beautiful by the daily use of lovely things, but for ever being busy about them.

Mrs. Marston's china glowed so, and was so stainless and uncracked, that it seemed as if the lives of all the beautiful young women in her family must have been sacrificed in its behalf.

They had all drunk of the cup of death long ago,

and their beauty had long ago been broken and defaced; but the beautiful old china remained. There were still the two dozen cups and saucers, the cream-jug, sugar-basin, and large plates of the feather-cups, just as when they were first bought. Their rich gilding, which completely covered them outside, was hardly worn at all, nor were the bright birds' feathers and raised pink flowers. It would be very pleasant, Mrs. Marston reflected wistfully, to use it again. There were all the bottled fruits, too, and lemon-curd and jellies; and a wedding would be a very pleasant, suitable opportunity for making one of her famous layer cakes and for wearing her purple silk dress. Mingled with these ideas was the knowledge that Edward wanted it, would be "vexed" if it had to be put off. "I have never known him to be so reckless," she pondered. "But still, he'll settle down once he's married. And she'll sober down, too, when the little ones come. It will be pleasant when they come. A grandmother has all the pleasures of a mother and none of the pains. And she will not want to manage anything. Edward said so. I should not have liked a managing daughter-in-law. Edward was wise in his choice. For, though noisy, she'll quiet down a little with each of the dear babies, and there will be plenty of them, I think and hope."

It was characteristic of Mrs. Marston's class and creed (united with the fact that she was Edward's mother) that she did not consider Hazel in the matter. Hazel's point of view, personality, hopes, and fears were non-existent to her. Hazel would be absorbed into the Marston family like a new piece of furniture. She would be provided for without being consulted; it would be seen to that she did her duty, also without being consulted. She would become, as all the other women in this and the other families of the world had, the servant of the china and the electro-plate and the furniture, and she would be the means by which Edward's children came into the world. She would, when not incapacitated, fetch shawls. At all times she would say "Yes, dear" or "As you wish, Edward." With all this before her, what did she want with personality and points of view? Obviously nothing. If she brought all the grandchildren safely into the world, with their due complement of legs and arms and noses, she would be a satisfactory asset. But Mrs. Marston forgot, in this summing up, to find out whether Hazel cared for Edward more than she cared for freedom.

Mrs. Marston came down to breakfast with an air of resignation.

"I have decided to make the best of it, my dear Edward," she said; "of course, I had hoped there would never be anyone. But it doesn't signify. I will lay out the money and be as good a grandmother as I can. And now, dear" (she spoke passively, shifting the responsibility on to Edward's shoulders) "—and now, how will you get me to town?"

Here was a problem. The little country station was several miles away, far beyond her walking limit, and no farmer in the neighbourhood had a horse quiet enough to please her.

"In my day, dear, I can remember horses so quiet, so well-bred, so beautifully trained, and, above all, so fat, that an accident was, apart from God's will, impossible. Now, my dear father, in the days when he travelled for Jeremy's green tea (and very good tea it was, and a very fine flavour, and a picture of a black man on every canister). Where was I? Oh yes; he always used to allow a day for a ten-mile round. Very pleasant it was, but horses are not——"

Here Edward cut in with a suggestion.

"Why shouldn't you go by the traction trailer? You enjoyed it that one time?"

The traction engine, belonging to a stone quarry, passed two or three times a week, and was never—the country being hilly—so full that it could not accommodate a passenger.

It was therefore arranged that Edward should go and see the driver, and afterwards see Hazel, and arrange for her to go to town also. He was to stay at home. Mrs. Marston would never leave the house, as she said, "without breath in it," though she could give no reason for this idea, and prided herself on having no superstitions. She would not trust Martha by herself; so Edward was ruefully obliged to undertake the office of "breathing," like a living bellows to blow away harm.

It was settled that they were to go on the day before the flower-show, and Hazel was to stay the night. It would be the last night but one before the wedding.

Meanwhile, the bark-stripping continued, and fate went on leading Jack Reddin's horse in every direction but the right one. Edward went to Hunter's Spinney every day. He began to find a new world among the budding hyacinths, on the soft leafy soil, breaking up on every side with the push of eager lives coming through, and full of those elusive, stimulating scents that only come in spring.

When the day came for going to Silverton, and Hazel arrived fresh and rosy from her early walk, he felt very rebellious. Still, it was ordained that someone must breathe, and only his mother could choose the clothes.

It took Mrs. Marston several hours to get ready, and Edward and Martha were kept busy running up and down. Not that Mrs. Marston's clothes had to be hunted for or mended—far from it. But there were so many cupboards to be locked, their keys hidden in drawers, the keys of which, in their turn, went into more cupboards. When such an inextricable tangle as no burglar could tackle had been woven, Mrs. Marston always wanted something out of the first cupboard, and all had to be done over again. But at last she was achieved. Edward and Martha stood back and surveyed her with pride, and looked to Hazel for admiration of their work; but Hazel was too young and too happy to see either the pathos or the humour of old ladies.

She danced down the steep path with an armful of wraps, at the idea of wearing which she made faces.

The path led in a zigzag down one side of the quarry cliff, where Abel had told Hazel of the cow falling, and where she had felt drodsome. Once more, as she came down with a more and more lagging step, the same horror came over her.

"I'm frit!" she cried; "canna we be quick?"

But speed was not in Mrs. Marston. She came, clinging to Edward's arm, very cautiously, like a cat on ice.

Martha, her stout red arms bare, her blue gingham dress and white apron flying in the wind, was directed to hold on to Mrs. Marston's mantle behind—as one tightens the reins downhill—to keep her on her feet.

Edward was carrying a kitchen chair for his mother to sit on during the journey.

Hazel felt that they were none of them any good; they none of them knew what it was like to be frit. So she ran away, and left the hot, secretive, omniscient place with its fierce white and its crafty shadows.

She reached a tiny field that ran up to the woods, and there, among the brilliantly varnished buttercups, the bees sounded like the tides coming in on the coasts of faery. Hazel forgot her dread—an inexplicable, sickening dread of the quarry. She chased a fat bumble-bee all across the golden floor—one eager, fluffy, shining head after the other. They might have been, in the all-permeating glory on their hill terrace, with the sapphire-circled plain around—they might have been the two youngest citizens of Paradise, circled in for ever from bleak honeyless winter, bleak honeyless hearts.

The slow cortège came down the path, Martha being obliged, as the descent grew steeper, to fling herself back like a person in a tug-of-war, for Mrs. Marston gathered way as she went, and uttered little helpless cries.

"I'm going, Martha! I'm losing control! Not by the bugles, Martha! Not by the braid!"

When they reached the road, the traction engine was not in sight, so they sat in the bank and waited, Mrs. Marston regal in the chair; and Hazel held a buttercup under Edward's chin to see if he liked butter.

"Very warm and pleasant," murmured Mrs. Marston, and dropped into a doze.

Edward listened to the thrushes; they were flinging their voices—as jugglers fling golden balls—against the stark sides of the quarry. Up went a rush of bright notes, pattered on the gloomy wall, and returned again defeated.

To Edward, as he watched Hazel, they seemed like people thanking God for blessings, and being heard and blessed again. To Hazel, they seemed so many other Hazels singing because it was a festal day. To Mrs. Marston they were "noisy birds, and very disturbing." Martha crocheted. She was making edging, hundreds of yards of it, for wedding garments. This was all the more creditable, as it was an act of faith, for no young man had as yet seemed at all desirous of Martha.

At last the traction engine appeared, and Mrs. Marston was hoisted into the trailer—a large truck with scarlet-painted sides, and about half full of stone. This had been shovelled away from the front to make room for Mrs. Marston and Hazel. A flap in the scarlet side was let down, and with the help of one of the traction men Edward and Martha got her safely settled. She really was a very splendid old lady. Her hat, a kind of spoon-shape, was trimmed lavishly with black glass grapes, that clashed together softly when she moved. There was also a veil with white chenille spots. The hat was tied under her chin with black ribbons, and her kind old face, very pink and plump and charming, looked out pleasantly upon the world. She wore her best mantle, heavily trimmed with jet bugles, and her alpaca skirt was looped up uncompromisingly with an old-fashioned skirt-hook made like a butterfly. Hung on one arm was her umbrella, and she carried her reticule in both hands for safety. So, with all her accoutrements on, she sat, pleasantly aware that she was at once self-respecting and adventurous.

They started in a whirl of good-byes, shrieks of delight from Hazel, and advice of Mrs. Marston to the driver to put the brake on and keep it on. Hazel was perched on the side of the truck near her. They rounded a turn with great dignity, the trailer, with Mrs. Marston as its figure-head—wearing an expression of pride, fear, and resignation—swinging along majestically.

"Please, Mrs. Marston, can I buy a green silk gown wi' yellow roses on?"

"Certainly not, my dear. It would be most unsuitable. So very far from quiet."

"What's quiet matter?"

"Quietness is the secret of good manners. The quieter you are, the more of a lady you'll be thought. All truly good people are quiet in manners, dress, and speech, just as all the best horses are advertised as quiet to ride and drive, but few are really so."

"Han you got to be ever and ever so quiet to be a lady?"

"Yes."

"What for have you?"

"Because, dear, it is the proper thing. Now my poor husband was quiet, so quiet that you never knew if he was there or not. And Edward is quiet, too—as quiet as——"

"Oh! dunna, dunna!" wailed Hazel.

"Is a pin sticking into you, dear?"

"No. Dunna say Ed'ard's quiet!"

Mrs. Marston looked amicably over her spectacles.

"My dear, why not?" she asked.

"I dunna like that sort."

"Could you explain a little, dear?"

"I dunna like quiet men—nor quiet horses. My mam was quiet when she was dead. Everybody's quiet when they're dead."

"Very, very quiet," crooned Mrs. Marston. "Yes, we all fall asleep in our turn."

"I like," went on Hazel in her rather crude voice, harsh with youth like a young blackbird's—"I like things as go quick and men as talk loud and stare hard and drive like the devil!"

She broke off, flushing at Mrs. Marston's expression, and at the sudden knowledge that she had been describing Reddin.

"It doesn't signify very much," said Mrs. Marston (severely for her), "what you like, dear. But I suppose"—she softened—"that you do really like Edward, since he has chosen you and you are pledged?"

Hazel shook her shoulders as if she wanted to get rid of a yoke. They fell into silence, and as Mrs. Marston dozed, Hazel was able to fulfil a desire that had sprung into being at the moment of seeing Mrs. Marston's hat—namely to squash one of those very round and brittle grapes.

Her quick little hand, gleaming in the sun, hovered momentarily above the black hat like a darting dragonfly, and the mischief was done—bland respectability smashed and derided.

CHAPTER XII

THEY went gallantly, if slowly, on through narrow ways, lit on either side by the breath-taking freshness of new hawthorn leaves. Primroses, wet and tall, crisply pink of stalk and huge of leaf, eyed them, as madonnas might, from niches in the aisles of grass and weed.

Carts had to back into gates to let them go by, and when they came into the main-road horses reared and had to be led past. Hazel found it all delightful. She liked, when the driver pulled up outside little wayside inns, to peer into the brown gloom where pewter-pots and rows of china jugs shone, and from which, over newly washed floors of red tiles, landlords advanced with foaming mugs.

Mrs. Marston strongly disapproved of these proceedings, but did not think it polite to expostulate, as she was receiving a favour.

In Silverton Mrs. Marston lingered a long while before any shop where sacred pictures were displayed. The ones she looked at longest were those of that peculiarly seedy and emasculated type which modern religion seems to produce. Hazel, all in a fidget to go and buy her clothes, looked at them, and wondered what they had to do with her. There was one of an untidy woman sitting in a garden of lilies—evidently forced—talking to an anæmic-looking man with uncut hair and a phosphorescent head. Hazel did not know about phosphorus or haloes, but she remembered how she had gone into the kitchen one night in the dark and screamed at sight of a sheep's head on the table, shining with a strange greenish light. This picture reminded her of it. She hastily looked at the others. She liked the one with sheep in it best, only the artist had made them like bolsters, and given the shepherd saucer eyes. Then she came to one of the Crucifixion, a subject on which the artist had lavished all the slumbering instincts of torture that are in so many people.

"Oh! what a drodsome un! I dunna like this shop," said Hazel tearfully. "What'n they doing to 'im? Oh, they'm great beasts!"

Perhaps she had seen in her dim and childish way the everlasting tyranny of the material over the abstract; of bluster over nerves; strength over beauty; States over individuals; churches over souls; and fox-hunting squires over the creatures they honour with their attention.

"What is it, my dear?" Mrs. Marston looked over her spectacles, and her eyes were like half moons peering over full moons.

"That there picture! They'm hurting Him so cruel. And Him fast and all."

"Oh!" said Mrs. Marston wonderingly, "that's nothing to get vexed about. Why, don't you know that's Jesus Christ dying for us?"

"Not for me!" flashed Hazel.

"My dear!"

"No. What for should He? There shall none die along of me, much less be tormented."

"Needs be that one Man die for the people," quoted

Mrs. Marston easily. "Only through blood can sin be washed white."

"Blood makes things raddled, not white; and if so be any's got to die, I'll die for myself."

The old gabled houses, dark and solemn with heavy carved oak, the smart plate-glass windows of the modern shops, the square dogmatic church towers and the pointed insinuating spires, all seemed to listen in surprise to this being who was not content to let another suffer for her. For civilization as it now stands is based solely on this one thing—vicarious suffering. From the central doctrine of its chief creed to the system of its trade; from the vivisection-table to the consumptive genius dying so that crowds of fat folk may get his soul in a cheap form, it is all built up on sacrifice of other creatures.

"What'd you say if Ed'ard died for yer?" queried Hazel crudely.

"My dear! How unseemly! In the street!"

"And what'd I do if Foxy died for me?"

"Well, well, Foxy's only an animal."

"So're you and me animals!" said Hazel so loudly that poor Mrs. Marston flushed all over her gentle old face.

"So indecent!" she murmured. "My dear," she said, when she had steered Hazel past the shop, "you want a nice cup of tea. And I do hope," she went on softly, putting a great deal of cream in Hazel's cup as she would have put lubricating oil on a stiff sewing-machine—"I do hope, my dear, you'll become more Christian as time goes on."

"If Foxy died along of me," said Hazel stubbornly, for, although grateful for the festive meal, she could not let her basic rule of life slip—"if Foxy died along of me, I'd die, too. I couldna do aught else."

"Things are very different," said Mrs. Marston, flustered, flushed, and helpless—"very different from what they used to be."

"What for are they, Mrs. Marston?"

But that question Mrs. Marston was quite unable to answer. If she had known the answer—that the change was in herself, and that the world was not different, but still kept up its ancient war between love and respectability, beauty and mass—she would not have liked it, and so she would not have believed it.

It was seven o'clock when they were put down, tired and laden with parcels, at the quarry half-way up God's Little Mountain. Edward had been there for more than an hour, tormented with fears for Hazel's safety, angry with himself for letting her go. All afternoon he had fidgeted, worried Martha with suggestions about tea, finally gone to the shop several miles away for some of Hazel's favourite cake, quite forgetting that he ought to be in the house breathing. It all resulted in a most beautiful tea, as Hazel thought when they had pushed and pulled Mrs. Marston home.

What with the joy of staying the night and the wonder of her new clothes, Hazel was so radiant and talked so fast that Edward could do nothing but watch her.

In her short life there had not been many moments of such rose and gold. It was the happiest hour of Edward's life also; for she looked to him as flowers to warm heaven, as winter birds to a fruited tree. As he watched her opening parcel after parcel with frank innocence and little bird-like cries of rapture, he knew the intolerable sweetness of bestowing delight on the beloved—a sweetness only equalled by the intolerable agony of seeing helpless and incurable pain on the loved face.

"And what's that one?" he asked, like a mother helping in a child's game. He pointed to a parcel which contained chemises and nightdresses.

"That," said Mrs. Marston, frowning portentously at Hazel, who was tearing it open—"that is other useful garments."

"What for canna I show 'em Ed'ard? I want to show all. The money was his'n."

It was a tribute to Edward's self-control that she was so entirely lacking in shyness towards him.

"My dear! A young man!" whispered Mrs. Marston.

Suddenly, by some strange necromancy, there was conjured in Hazel's mind a picture of Reddin—flushed, hard-eyed, with an expression that aroused in her misgiving and even terror. So she had seen him just before she fled to Vessons. At the remembrance she flushed so deeply that Mrs. Marston congratulated herself on the fact that her daughter-in-law had *some* modesty and right feeling.

If she had known who caused the flush, who it was that had awakened the love of pretty clothes which Edward was satisfying, she would have thought very different thoughts, and would have been utterly miserable. For her love for Edward was deep enough to make her wish him to have what he wanted, and not what she thought he ought to want, as long as he did not clash with her religion. For Edward to know it, though so early in his love for Hazel, would have meant a rocking of heaven and earth around him. Even she with her childish egotism like a shell about her, realized that this was a thing that could not be.

"But it be all right," she thought, as she curled up luxuriously in the strangely clean and comfortable bed, "it'll be all right. Him above'll see as Mr. Reddin ne'er shows his face here; for the old lady said Him above looked after good folk, and Ed'ard's good. But I wish some un 'ud look after the bad uns," she thought, gazing across the room to the north where Undern lay.

"My dear, wait a moment!" said Mrs. Marston to Edward downstairs, as he was lighting her candle. "I have something to tell you. I fear you must brace yourself."

"Well, mother?" Edward smiled.

"Hazel's not a Christian!" She spoke in a sepulchral whisper, and looked at him afterwards, as if to say, "There now, I *have* surprised you!"

"And how do you make that out, mother?"

Edward found in his heart this fact, that it made no difference to his love whether Hazel were a Christian or not; this troubled him.

"No. She's not a Christian, my dear," said Mrs. Marston in a kind of gasp; "she refuses to be died for!"

Upstairs, Hazel was saying her orisons at the window.

"If there's anybody there," she murmured, staring out into the consuming darkness that had absorbed every colour, every form, except the looming outline of God's Little Mountain against a watery moon-rise —"if there's anybody there, I'd be obleeged if you'd give an eye to our Foxy, as is lonesome in tub. It dunna matter about me, being under Ed'ard's roof."

Hazel had never felt so like a child in its mother's

lap. Her own mother had not made her feel so. She had been a vague, abstracted woman with an air of bepuzzlement and lostness. She looked so long out of the door—never shut, except when Abel insisted on it—that there was no time for Hazel. Only occasionally she would catch her by the shoulders and look into her eyes and tell her strange news of faery. But now she felt cared for as she looked round the low room with its chair-bed and little dressing-table hung with pink glazed calico. There was a text over the fireplace.

'Not a hair of thy head shall perish.'

It seemed particularly reassuring to Hazel as she brushed her long shining coils before the hanging mirror. There was a bowl of double primroses—red, mauve and white—on the window-sill, and a card "with Edward's love."

Flowers in a bedroom were something very new. To her, as to so many poor people, a bedroom was a stuffy place to crawl into at night and get out of as quickly as possible in the morning.

"Eh! it'll be grand to live here," she thought drowsily, as she lay down in the cool clean sheets and heard the large clock on the wall of the landing ticking slumbrously in a measured activity that deepened the peace. She heard Mrs. Marston slide past in her soft slippers with her characteristic walk, rather like skating. Then Edward came up (evidently in stocking feet, for he was only heralded by creakings). Hazel never dreamt that he had taken his shoes off for her sake.

The moon, riding clear of cloud, flung the shadow of Edward's primroses on the bed—a large round posy like a Christmas-pudding with outstanding leaves and flowers clearly defined, all very black on the counterpane.

Undern seemed very far off.

"I like this better'n that old dark place, green dress or no green dress," she thought, "and I'll ne'er go back there. It inna true what he said, 'Have her he will, for certain sure,' for I'm going to live along of Ed'ard, and the old sleepy lady'll learn me to make batter for ever and ever. Batter's a well-beaten mixture of eggs and summat."

She fell asleep.

In his room Edward walked up and down, too happy to go to bed.

"My little one! my little one!" he whispered. And he prayed that Hazel might have rosy and immortal happiness, guarded by strong angels along a path of flowers all her life long, and at last running in through the celestial gates as a child runs home.

The spring wind, rainy and mournful, came groping out of the waste places and cried about the house like a man mourning for his love. The cavern of night, impenetrable and vast, was full of echoes, as if some voice, terrible and violent, had shouted there a long while since, and might, even before the age-long reverberations had died away, be uplifted again, if it was the will of the Power (invisible but so immanent that it pressed upon the brain) that inhabited the obscure, star-dripping cavern.

CHAPTER XIII

NEXT morning Mrs. Marston came in from the kitchen with the toast, which she would not trust anyone but herself to make, with a face portending great happenings.

"Mind you see that they are all properly placed, Edward; they should be all together in one part of the room."

"Who'd that be?" Hazel inquired.

"1906, plums; 1908, gooseberries; 1909, cherries, sugarless. The sugared ones are older." Mrs. Marston spoke so personally that Hazel stared.

"Its mother's exhibits, Hazel," explained Edward.

"Yes. They've been to shows year by year, and very well they've stood it. I only hope the constant travelling won't set up fermentation. I should like those Moreilas to outlive me. A receipt I had of Jane Thorn, and she died of the dropsy, poor thing, and bottled to the end."

"Dunna you ever eat 'em?" asked Hazel.

This was blasphemy. To eat the 1909 Morellas! It was passed over in tense silence, allowances being made for a prospective bride. "Poor thing! she's upset."

The exhibits, packed in a great bed of the vivid star-moss that grew in the secret recesses of the woods, were waiting on the front step in their usual box. There were some wonderful new jellies that made

Hazel long to be Mrs. Marston and have control of the storeroom. This was a dim place where ivy leaves scraped the cobwebby window, and tall green canisters stood on shelves in company with glass jars, neatly labelled, and barrels of home-made wine; where hams hung from the ceiling, and herbs in bunches and on trays sent out a pungent sweetness. In there the magic was now heightened by the presence—dignified even in deshabille—of a wedding-cake which was being slowly but thoroughly iced.

People often wondered how Mrs. Marston did it. No one ever saw her hurried or busy, yet the proofs of her industry were here. She worked like the coral insect, in the dark, as it were, of instinct unlit by intellect, and, like the coral insect, she raised a monumental structure that hemmed her in.

They had to start early, driven by Edward's one substantial parishioner, who was principal judge, chief exhibitor, and organizer of the show. The exhibits must be there by ten; but Edward did not care in the least how many hours he spent there. The day was only darkened for him by one thing.

When the trap came round, and Hazel climbed in joyously, Edward forgot the exhibits. He would have gone off without them had not Martha come flying down the path shouting:

"Mr. Ed'ard! Mr. Ed'ard! Nineteen six! Nineteen nine! Jam!"

"What for's Martha cursing?" asked Hazel.

Edward, looking round, saw his mother's face in the doorway, dismayed, surprised, wounded. He jumped out and ran up the path.

"Oh, mother! How could I?" he said miserably.

Mrs. Marston looked up; her mouth, that had fallen

in a little, trembling pitifully, and her eyes smarting with the thick, painful tears of age.

"It wasn't you, my dear," she said; "you never forget; it was—the young woman."

One's gods must at all hazards go clear of blame.

Edward kissed her, but with reserve, and when he got into the trap he put an arm protectingly round Hazel.

"What a fool I am!" he thought. "Now everything's spoilt."

In the silent store-room, hour by hour, Mrs. Marston propelled the mixture of sugar and egg through her icing syringe, building complex designs of frosty whiteness.

Her back ached, and it seemed a long way round the cake, but she went on until Martha, with a note of sympathetic understanding in her voice, announced:

"Yer dinner's in, mum, and a cup of tea along of it."

Mrs. Marston sighed gratefully.

"How nice and pleasant!" she said; "but not as nice and pleasant as it was—before."

"Not by a long mile!" said Martha heartily. For Hazel had "taken the eye" of all the eligibles at the concert, and was altogether disturbing.

"Perhaps, Martha," said Mrs. Marston wistfully, "when she's been here a long while, and we're used to her, and she's part of the house—perhaps it'll be as nice and pleasant as before?"

"When the yeast's in," said Martha pessimistically, "the dough's leavened!"

As Edward and Hazel drew near the show-ground they passed people walking and were overtaken by traps.

A man passed at full gallop, and Hazel was reminded of Reddin. Later, she said:

"How'd you like it, Ed'ard, if somebody was after you, like a weazel after a rabbit or a terrier at a fox-earth? What'd you do?"

"What morbid things you think of, dear!"

"What'd you do?"

"I don't know."

"There's nought to do."

Edward remembered his creed.

"I should pray, Hazel."

"What good'd that do?"

"God answers prayers."

"That He dunna! Or where'd the fox-hunting gents be, and who'd have rabbit-pie? I dunna see as He *can* answer 'em."

"Little girls mustn't bother their pretty heads."

"If you'd found as many creatures in traps as me, and loosened 'em, and seed their broken legs, and eyes as if they'd seed ghosses, and onst a dog caught by the tongue—eh! you'd bother! You would that! And feyther killing the pig Good Fridays."

"Why Good Friday, of all days?"

"That was the day. Ah! every Good Friday I was used to fight feyther!"

"My dear child!"

"You would if you'd seed the pig that comforble and contented, and know'd what it'd look like in a minute. I'd a killed feyther if I could."

"But why? Surely it was worse of you to want to kill your father than of him to want to kill the pig?"

"I dunno. But I couldn't abear it. I bit him awful one time, and he hit me on the head with the rake, and I went to sleep."

Edward's forehead was damp with sweat.

"Merciful God!" he thought, "that such things should be!"

"And when I've heard things screaming and crying to be loosed, and them in traps, and never a one coming to 'em but me, it's come o'er me to won'er who 'd loose *me* out if I was in a trap."

"God would."

"I dunna think so. He ne'er lets the others out."

Edward was silent. The radiant day had gone dark, and he groped in it.

"What for dunnot He, my soul? What for dun He give 'em mouths so's they can holla, and not listen at 'em? I listen when Foxy shouts out."

At this moment Edward saw Abel approaching, swaggering along with the harp. He had never been glad to see him so far; now he was almost affectionate.

"Laws, Ed'ard!" said Abel, straining the affection to breaking-point, "you'm having a randy, and no mistake! Dancing and all, I s'pose?"

"No. I shall go before the dancing."

"You won't get our 'Azel to go along of you, then. Dance her will, like a leaf in the fall."

"You'd rather come home with me on your wedding-eve, Hazel, wouldn't you?"

Abel, seeing Hazel's dismayed face, laughed loudly. Edward hated him as only sensitive temperaments can, and was conscience-stricken when he realized the fact.

"Well, Hazel?" he asked gently, and created a situation.

"I dunno," said Hazel awkwardly. A depressed silence fell between them; both were so bitterly disappointed. Abel, like an ancient mischievous gnome, went off, calling to Hazel:

"Clear your throat agen the judgin's over!"

The judges were locked into the barn where the exhibits were. They took a long while over the judging, presumably because they tasted everything, even to the turnips (Mr. James was partial to early turnips). Edward and Hazel passed a window and looked in.

"Look at 'em longing after the old lady's jam!" said Hazel. "It's a mercy the covers are well stuck on, or they'd be in like wasps! Look at Mr. Frodley wi' the eggs! Dear now, he's sucking one like a lad at a throstle's nest! Oh! Father'd ought to be there! He ne'er eats a cooked egg. Allus raw. Oh! Mr. James has unscrewed a bottle of father's honey and dipped! Look at 'im sucking his fingers!"

"Do people buy the remnants?" asked Edward, amused and disgusted.

"Ah! What for not?"

The judges were now making a hearty meal off some cheeses.

"I wonder whose cheeses they are?" Edward mused.

They were, in fact, Vessons'. He always insisted on making cheeses for some obscure reason; possibly it was the pride of the old-fashioned servant in being worth more than his wages. Vessons certainly was. He made stacks of cheeses, and took them to fairs and shows without the slightest encouragement from his master, who, when Vessons returned, red with conflict, and said planking down the money with intense pride —" 'Ere it is! I 'ad to labour for the thre'pences, though," would merely nod uninterestedly. But still the Undern cheeses went to shows labelled "John Reddin, Esquire, per A. Vessons."

At last the judges came out. The mere judging did

not take long, for Mr. James usually considered his exhibit the best, and said so; the others, being only small holders, were generally too polite to gainsay him.

Edward and Hazel went into the barn where the exhibits were set out with stern simplicity, looking brave and beautiful with their earthy glamour. There were rolls of golden butter, nut-brown eggs, snowy bouquets of broccoli, daffodils with the sun striking through their aery petals, masses of dark wallflower where a stray bee revelled. There was Abel's honey, with a large placard drawn by himself proclaiming in drunken capitals:

ABEL WOODUS. BEE-MAN.
COFFINS. HONEY. WREATHS.

OPEN TO ENGAGEMENTS TO PLAY THE HARP AT
WEDDINGS, WAKES AND CLUB-DAYS.

The golden jars shone; the sections in their lace-edged boxes, whitely sealed, were provocative as the reserve of a fair woman.

Edward bought one for Hazel. "To open on your wedding-day," he said. But the symbolism, so apparent to him, was lost on Hazel.

Between the judging and the tea hour was a dull time. The races had not begun, and though an ancient of benign aspect announced continually, "I'll take two to one!" no one responded.

The people stood about, taking their pleasure like an anæsthetic, and looking like drugged bees. Now and then an old man from a far hillside would meet another old man from a farther one, and there would be handshaking lasting, perhaps, a quarter of an hour.

When Abel played, they remained stoical and silent,

however madly or mournfully the harp cried. They took good music as their right.

Then Hazel sang, gazing up at the purple ramparts of the hills that hung above the show-ground, and Edward's eyes were full of tears.

A very old man, smooth-faced and wondering as a baby, came, leaning on his stick, and stood before Hazel, gazing into her mouth with the steadfast curiosity of a dog at a gramophone. If she moved, he moved, absorbed, his jaw dropped with interest. Hazel did not notice him. She was free on the migratory wings of music. She did not see Vessons looking across the crowd with dismay, nor know that he edged away, muttering, "That gel agen! Never will I!"

Edward was glad when the singing and collection were over, and he could take Hazel into the shilling tent, where sat the élite, and give her tea. People remained in a sessile state over tea for a long time while the chief race of the afternoon was begun by the ringing of a dinner-bell. The race took so long, the riders having to go round the course so many times, that people went on complacently with their tea, only looking out occasionally to see how things progressed, watching the riders go by—one with bright red braces, one in a blue cotton coat, two middle-aged men in their best bowlers, and one, obviously too well mounted for the rest, in correct riding-dress. They came round each time in the same order—the correct one, red braces, blue coat, and the bowlers last. Evidently the foremost one knew he could easily win, and the others had decided that "it was to be." In the machine-like regularity of their advent, their unaltered positions, and leisured pace, they were like hobby-horses.

"How many times have they bin round?" Hazel asked the waitress, who poured tea and made conversation in a sociable manner.

"It'll be the seventh. They might as well give over. They're only labouring to stay in the same place."

"I want to see 'em come in," said Hazel. They went out, but Abel waylaid them, and took Edward off to show him a queen bee in a box from Italy. Edward loathed bees in or out of boxes, but he was too kind-hearted to refuse. Abel was so unperceptive that he touched pathos.

Hazel found a place some distance down the course where she could look along the straight to the winning-post; she loved to hear them thunder past. She leaned over the rail and watched them come, still fatalistic, but gallant, bent on a dramatic finish, stooping and "cutting" their horses. The first man was on her side of the course. She stared at him in amazed consternation as he came towards her. His strong blue eyes, caught by the fixity of her glance or by her bright hair, saw her, and became triumphant. He pulled the horse in sharply, and within a few yards of the winning-post wheeled and went back, amid the jeers and howls of the crowd, who thought he must be drunk.

"You've given me a long enough chase," he said, leaning towards her. "Where the devil *do* you live?"

"Oh, dunna stop! He's coming."

"Who?"

"Mr. Marston, the minister."

"What do I care if he's a dozen ministers?"

"But he'll be angered."

"I'll make his nose bleed if he's got such cheek."

"Oh, he's coming, Mr. Reddin! I mun go." She turned away. Reddin followed.

"Why should he be angry?"

"Because we're going to be wed to-morrow."

Reddin whistled.

"And Foxy's coming, and all of 'em. And there's a clock as tick-tacks ever so sleepy, and a sleepy old lady, and Ed'ard's bought me a box full of clothes."

"I gave you a box full too," he said with a note of pleading. "You little runaway!"

Hazel was annoyed because he disturbed her so. She wanted to get rid of him, and she desired to exercise her power. So she looked up and said impishly:

"Yours were old 'uns. His be new—new as morning."

He was too angry to swear.

"You've got to come and talk to me while they're dancing to-night," he said.

"I wunna."

"You must. If you don't, I'll tell the parson you stopped the night at Undern. Surely you know that he wouldn't marry you then?"

He was bluffing. He knew Vessons would tell Marston the truth if he spoke. But it served his turn.

"You wouldna!" she pleaded.

He laughed.

"A'right, then," she said, "if you wunna tell 'un."

"Will he stay for the dancing?"

"No. I mun go along of him."

"You know better."

He turned away sharply as Edward came up. He knew him for the minister he had met near the Callow.

Edward was tying up some daffodils for Hazel, and did not see Reddin.

Scarlet braces, a fatalist no more, came trotting up.

"What went wrong?" he asked with thinly veiled triumph.

"Everything," snapped Reddin, and calling Vessons, he went off to the beer-tent to wait till the dancing began.

"These are for your room, Hazel," Edward was saying, "because the time of the singing of birds is come."

He was thinking that God was indeed leading him forth by the waters of comfort.

Hazel said nothing. She was wondering what excuse she could make for staying.

"Don't frown, little one. There are no more worries for you now."

"Binna there?"

No. You are coming to God's Little Mountain. What harm can come there? Now look up and smile, Hazel."

She met his grey eyes, very tender and thoughtful. What she saw, however, were blue eyes, hard, and not at all thoughtful.

CHAPTER XIV

PRIZE-GIVING time came, and the younger Miss Clomber, who was to present them, tried to persuade Reddin to go up on the platform, a lorry with chairs on it. There already were Mr. James and the secretary, counting the prize-money. Below stood the winners, Vessons conspicuous in his red waistcoat. Miss Clomber felt that she looked well. She was dressed in tweeds to show that this was not an occasion to her as to the country damsels.

"No. I shall stay here," said Reddin, answering her stare, intended to be inviting, with a harder stare of indifference.

"As the last representative of such an old family——"

"Oh, damn family!" he said peevishly, having lost sight of Hazel.

As Miss Clomber still persisted, he quenched the argument.

"Young families are more in my line than old 'uns."

She blushed unbecomingly, and hastily got on to the lorry.

Reddin went in search of Hazel, while Mr. James began to read the names.

"Mr. Thomas. Mr. James. Mrs. Marston. Mr. James——"

He handed the piles of shillings to Miss Clomber, who presented them with the usual fatuous remarks. When he had won the prize he received it back from her with a bow, taking off his hat. As his own name occurred more frequently than usual, he began to get rather self-conscious. He looked round the ring of faces, and translated their stodginess as self-consciousness dictated.

Perhaps it would be well to carry it off as a jest? So his hat came off with a flourish, and he said jocosely as he took the next heap, "Keeping-apples, Mr. James. I'll put it in me pocket!"

This attitude wearing thin, he took refuge in that of unimpeachable honesty. "Fair and square! The best man wins!" This lasted for some time, but was not proof against "Swedes, Mr. James. Mangolds, Mr. James. Stewing pears, Mr. James." He began to get in a panic. His bow was cursory. He pocketed the money furtively and read his name in a low, apologetic tone. But this would never do! He must pull himself together. He tried bravado.

"Mr. Vessons. Mr. James."

Vessons stood immovable within arm's reach of Miss Clomber. When he got a prize, which he did three times, no one else having sent any cheeses, he extended his arm like one side of a pair of compasses, and vouchsafed neither bow nor smile. He disliked Miss Clomber because he knew that she meant to be mistress of Undern. Mr. James was getting on well with the bravado.

"What do I care what people think? Dear me! All the world may see me get my prize."

Then he caught Abel's satiric eye, and went all to pieces. He clutched at his first attitude—the business-like—and so began all over again, and managed to get through by not looking in Abel's direction, being upheld by the knowledge that his pockets were getting very full.

When he read out, "Cherries, bottled. Mrs. Marston," and Edward went to receive the prize, Reddin shouldered up to Hazel and asked:

"What time's he going?"

"I dunno."

"Don't forget, mind."

"Oh, Mr. Reddin, I mun go! What for wunna you let me be?"

But Reddin, finding Miss Clomber's eye on him, was gone.

Mr. James had come to the end of the list. He read out Abel's name and that of an old bent man with grey elf-locks, a famous bee-master. Mr. James looked at Abel as much as to say, "You've got your prize, you see! It's quite fair."

"Thank yer," said Abel to Miss Clomber, and then to James with fine irony: "You dunna keep bees, do yer, Mr. James?"

The hills loomed in the dusk over the show-ground. They were of a cold and terrific colour, neither purple nor black nor grey, but partaking of all. Kingly, mournful, threatening, they dominated the life below as the race dominates the individual. Hazel gazed up at them. She stood in the attitude of one listening, for in her ears was a voice that she had never heard before, a deep inflexible voice that urged her to do—she knew not what. She looked up at the round wooded hill that hid God's Little Mountain—so high, so cold for a poor child to climb. She felt that the life there would be too righteous, too well-mannered. The thought of it suddenly made her homesick for dirt and the Callow.

She thought of Undern crouched under its hill like

a toad. She remembered its echoing rooms and the sound as of dresses rustling that came along the passages while she put on the green gown. Undern made her more homesick than the parsonage.

Edward had gone. She had said she wanted to stay with her father, and Edward had thought her a sweet daughter and had acquiesced, though sadly.

Now she was awaiting Reddin. The dancing had not begun, though the tent was ready. Yellow light flowed from every gap in the canvas, and Hazel felt very forlorn out in the dark; for light seemed her natural sphere. As she stood there, looking very small and slight, she had a cowering air. Always, when she stood under a tree or sheltered from the rain, she had this look of a refugee, furtive and brow-beaten. When she ran she seemed a fugitive, fleeing across the world with no city of refuge to flee into.

Miss Clomber's approach made her start.

"A word with you!" said Miss Clomber in her brisk, unsympathetic voice. "I saw you with Mr. Reddin twice. I just wanted to say in a sisterly and Christian spirit"—she lowered her voice to a hollow whisper—"that he is *not a good man.*"

"Well," said Hazel, with a sigh of relief in the midst of her shyness and her oppression about the mountain, "that's summat, anyway!"

Miss Clomber, outraged and furious, strode away.

Hazel was again left to the hills. The taciturnity of winter was upon them still, and in the sky beyond was the cynical aloofness that comes with frost after sunset.

She turned from them to the lighted tent. The golden glow was like some bright creature imprisoned. Abel had prorogued an interminable argument with the old man with the elf-locks, and now began thrumming inside the tent.

Young men and women converged upon it at the sound of the music, as flies flock to the osier blossom. They went in, as the blessed to Paradise. The canvas began to sway and billow in the wind of the dancing. Hazel felt that life was going on gaily without her—she shut away in the dark. Her feet began to dance.

"I'll go in!" she said defiantly. "What for not?"

But just as she was lifting the flap she heard Reddin's voice at her elbow.

"Hazel, why did you run away?"

"I dunno."

"Why didn't you tell me your name? Here have I been going hell-for-leather up and down the country."

"Ah! That's gospel! That's righteous! I seed you."

Reddin was speechless.

"Me and father was in the public, and you came. I thought it was the Black Huntsman."

"Thanks. Not a pin to choose, I suppose."

"Not all that."

"We're wasting time. What's all this about the parson?"

"I told 'ee."

"But it isn't true. You and the parson!"

He laughed. Hazel looked at him with disfavour.

"You're like a hound-dog when you laugh like to that," she said, "and I dunna like the hound-dogs."

He stopped laughing.

Abel's harping beat upon them, and the soft thudding of feet on turf, like sheep stamping, had grown in volume as the shyest were gradually drawn into the revelry.

A rainstorm, shaped like a pillar, walked slowly along the valley, skirting the base of the hills. It was like a grey god with folded arms and head aloof in the sky. As it drew slowly nearer to the two who stood there like lovers and were not lovers, and as it lashed them across the eyes, it might have been fate.

"Hazel, can't you see I'm in love with you?"

"What for are you?" There was a wailing note in Hazel's voice, and the rain ran down her face like tears. "There's you and there's Ed'ard! Oh, what for are you?"

Reddin looked at her in astonishment. A woman not to like a man to be in love with her! It was uncanny. He stood square-set against the darkening sky, his fine massive head slightly bent, looking down at her.

"I never thought," he said helplessly—"I never thought, when I had come to forty years without the need of women" ("of love," he corrected himself), "that I should be like this."

He looked at Hazel accusingly; then he gazed up at the coming night as a lion might at the sound of thunder.

"Be you forty?" Hazel's voice was on the top note of wonder. "Laws! what an age!"

"It's not really old," he pleaded, very humbly for him.

She laughed.

"The parson, now, I suppose he's young?" His voice was wistful.

"He'm the right age."

Reddin's temper flamed.

"I'll show you if I'm old! I'll show you who makes the best lover, me or a silly lad!"

"Hands off, Mr. Reddin!"

But her words went down the lonely wind that had begun to drag at the lighted tent.

"There!" said Reddin, pleased with his kisses. "Now come and dance, and you'll see if a chap of forty can't tire you. Afterwards we'll settle the parson's hash."

He lifted the tent-flap, and they went in and were taken by the bright, slow-whirling life.

Hazel was glad to dance with him or anyone, so that she might dance. Reddin held his head high, for he was a lover to-night, and he had never been that before in any of his amours.

He was angry and enthralled with Hazel, and the two emotions together were intoxicating.

Hazel was a flower in a gale when she danced, a slim poplar tremulous and swaying in the dawn, a young beech assenting to the wind's will.

Abel watched her with pride. She was turning out a credit to him, after all. It was astonishing.

"It's worth playing for our 'Azel's feet. The others just stomps," he thought. "Who's the fellow she's along with? I'd best keep an eye. A bargain's a bargain."

"You'm kept your word," said Hazel suddenly to Reddin.

"H'm?"

"Tired me out."

"Come outside, then, and I'll get you a cup of tea."

He fetched it and sat down by her on an orange-box.

"Now look here," he said, "fair and square, will you marry me?"

He was surprised at himself.

Andrew Vessons, who had tip-toed after them from the tent, spread out his hands and gazed at heaven with a look of supreme despair, all the more intense because he could not speak. He returned desolately to the tent, where he stood with a cynical smile, leaning a little forward with his arms behind him, watching the dancing, an apotheosis of sex, to him not only silly and pitiful, but disgusting. Now and then he shook his head, went to the door to see if his master was coming, and shook it again. A friend came up.

"Why did the gaffer muck up the race?" he asked.

"Why," asked Vessons, with a far-off gaze, "did 'Im as made the 'orld put women in?"

Outside, things were going more to his liking than he knew.

"What's the good of keeping on, Mr. Reddin? I told 'ee I was promised to Ed'ard."

"But you like me a bit? Better than the parson?"

"I dunno."

"Come off with me now. I swear I'll play fair."

"*I* swore!" she cried. "I swore by the Mountain, and that can ne'er be broke."

"What did you swear?"

"To marry the first as come. That's Ed'ard. If I broke that oath, when I was jead, my cold soul 'ud wander and find ne'er a bit of rest, crying about the Mountain and about, nights, and Ed'ard thinking it was the wind."

"If you chuck him, he'll soon get over it; if you chuck me, I shan't. He's never gone after the drink and women."

It was a curious plea for a lover.

"Miss Clomber said you wunna a good man."

"Well, I'm blowed! But look here. If he loses you, he'll be off his feed for a bit; but if I lose you, there'll be the devil to pay. Has he kissed you?"

"Time and agen."

"I won't have it!"

"'Azel!" called her father.

"You won't go?"

"I mun. It's father."

"And I shan't see you again—till you're married? Oh, marry *me,* Hazel! Marry *me!*"

His voice shook. At the mysterious grief in his face—a grief that was half rage, and the more pitiful for that—she began to sob. Abel came up.

"A mourning-party, seemingly," he said, holding his lantern so as to light each face in turn.

"I want to marry your daughter."

Abel roared.

"Another? First 'er bags a parson and next a squire!"

"Farmer."

"It'll be the king on his throne next. Laws, girl! you're like beer and treacle."

"You've not answered me," said Reddin.

"She's set."

"Eh?"

"Set. Bespoke. Let."

"She's a right to change her mind."

"Nay! A bargain's a bargain. Why, they've bought the clothes, mister, and the furniture and the cake!"

"If she comes with me, you'll go home with a cheque for fifty pounds, and that's all I've got," said Reddin naïvely.

"I tell you, sir, she's let," Abel repeated. "A bargain's a bargain!"

It occurred to him that the Callow garden might, with fifty pounds, be filled with beehives from end to end.

"Mister," he said, almost in tears, "you didn't ought to go for to 'tice me! Eh! dear 'eart, the wood I could buy, and the white paint and a separator and queens from foreign parts!" He made a gesture of despair and his face worked.

"You could have a new harp if you wanted one," Reddin suggested.

Abel gulped.

"A bargain's a bargain!" he repeated. "And I promised the parson." He turned away.

" 'Azel," he said over his shoulder, "you munna go along of this gent. Many's the time," he added, turning round and surveying her moodily, "as you've gone agen me and done what I gainsayed."

With a long imploring look he hitched the harp on his back and trudged away.

Hazel followed. But Reddin stepped in front of her.

"Look here, Hazel! You say you don't like hurting things. You're hurting me!"

Looking at his haggard face, she knew it was true. She wiped her tears away with her sleeve.

"It inna my fault. I'm allus hurting things. I canna set foot in the garden nor cook a cabbage but I kill a lot of little pretty flies and things. And when we take honey there's allus bees hurted. I'm bound to go agen you or Ed'ard, and I canna go agen Ed'ard; he sets store by me, does Ed'ard. You should 'a seen the priminyroses he put in my room last night; I slep' at the parsonage along of us being late."

Reddin frowned as if in physical pain.

"And he bought me stockings, all thin, and a sky-blue petticoat."

Reddin looked round. He would have picked her

up then and there and taken her to Undern, but the road was full of people.

"I couldna go agen Ed'ard! He'm that kind. Foxy likes him, too; she'd ne'er growl at 'im."

"Perhaps," Reddin said hoarsely, "Foxy 'd like me if I gave her bones."

"She wouldna! You'm got blood on you."

She drew away coldly at this remembrance, which had been obliterated by Reddin's grief.

"You'm got the blood of a many little foxes on you," she said, and her voice cut him like sharp sleet, "little foxes as met have died quick and easy wi' a gunshot. And you've watched 'em minced alive."

"I'll give it up if you'll chuck the parson."

"I won'er you dunna see 'em, nights, watching you out of the black dark with their gold eyes, like king-cups, and the look in 'em of things dying hard. I won'er you dunna hear 'em screaming."

His cause was lost, and he knew it, but he pleaded on.

"No. If I hadna swore by the mountain I wouldna come," she said. "You've got blood on you."

At that moment a neighbour passed and offered Hazel a lift. Now that she was marrying a minister, she had become a personality. Hazel climbed in and drove off, and Reddin's tragic moment died, as great fires die, into grey ash.

He went home heavily. His way lay past the parsonage where Edward and his mother slept peacefully. The white calm of unselfish love wrapped Edward, for he felt that he could make Hazel happy. As he fell asleep that night he thought:

"She was made for a minister's wife."

Reddin, leaning heavily on the low wall, staring at

the drunken tombstones and the quiet moon-silvered house, thought:

"She was made for me."

Both men saw her as what they wanted her to be, not as she was.

Many thoughts darkened Reddin's face as he stood there hour after hour in the cold May night. The rime whitened his broad shoulders as he leaned on the wall, and in the moonlight the sprinkling of white hairs at his temples shone out from the black as if to mock this young passion that had possessed him.

God's Little Mountain lay shrugged in slumber; the woods crouched like beaten creatures under the night; the small soft leaves hung limply in the frost.

Still Reddin stood there, chilled through and through, brooding upon the house.

Not until dawn, like a knife, gashed the east with blood did he stir.

He sighed. "Too late!" he said.

Then he laughed. "Beaten by the parson!"

A demoniac rage surged in him. He picked up a piece of rock, and lifting it in both arms, flung it at the house. It smashed the kitchen window. But before Edward came to his window Reddin was out of sight in the batch.

"My dear," said Mrs. Marston tremulously, "I always feared disaster from this strange match."

"How *can* Hazel have anything to do with it, mother?"

"I think, dear, it is a sign from God. On your wedding-morning! Broken glass! Yes, it is a sign from God. I wish it need not have been quite so violent. But, of course, He knows best!"

CHAPTER XV

AT the parsonage everything was ready early. Edward, restless after his rough awakening, had risen at three and finished his own preparations, being ready to help Mrs. Marston when she came down, still a good deal upset. Whenever she passed Hazel's room, or saw Edward take flowers there, she said, "Oh, my dear!" and shook her head sadly. For the kind of life that seemed to be mapped out by Edward would, she feared, not include grandchildren. And grandchildren had acquired, through long cogitations, the glamour of the customary. She was also ruffled by Martha, who, unlike her own pastry, was "short." What with the two women angry and grieved, and the fact that his wedding-day held only half the splendour that it should have held, Edward's spirits might have been expected to be low; but they were not. He ran up and down, joked with Martha, soothed his mother, and sang until Martha, who thought that a minister's deportment at a wedding should be only a little less grandiloquent than at a funeral, said:

"He'm less like a minister than a nest of birds."

She and Mrs. Marston were setting out the feather-cups in the best parlour.

At that moment Edward stood at the door of Hazel's room and realized that he would enter it no more. He must not see the sweet disarray of her unpacking, nor rest night by night in the charmed circle of her presence. Almost he felt, in this agony of loss—loss of things never possessed, the most bitter loss of all—that, if he could have had these things, even the ruddy-haired, golden-eyed children of his dreams might go. He knelt by Hazel's bed and laid his dark head on the pillow, torn by physical and spiritual passion. His hair was clammy, and a new line marked his forehead from that day. Anyone seeing him would have thought that he was praying; he was so still. It was Edward's fate to be thought "so quiet," because the fires within him made no sound, burning at a still white-heat.

He was not praying. Prayer had receded to a far distance, like a signpost long passed. Perhaps he would come round to it again; but now he was in the trackless desert. It is only those that have suffered moderately that speak of prayer as the sufferer's refuge. By that you know them. Those that have been tortured remember that the worst part of the torture was the breaking of prayer in their hands, piercing, and not upholding.

Edward knew, kneeling there with his eyes shut, how Hazel's hair would flow sweetly over the pillow; how her warm arm would feel about his neck; how wildly sweet it would be, in some dark hour, to allay dream-fears and hush her to sleep. Never before had the gracious intimacy of marriage so shone in his eyes. And he was going to have just the amount of intimacy that his mother would have, perhaps rather less. Every night he would stand on the threshold, kiss Hazel with a brotherly kiss, and turn away. His life would be a cold threshold. Month by month, year by year, he would read the sweet, frank love-stories of the

Bible—stories that would, if written by a novelist, be banned, so true are they; year by year he would see nests and young creatures, and go into cottages where babies in fluffy shawls gazed at him anciently and caught his finger in a grip of tyrannous weakness. And always there would be Hazel, alluring him with an imperishable magic even stronger than beauty, startling him from his hard-won calm by the turn of a wrist, the curve of a waist-ribbon, a wave of her hair. And then the stern hour of crisis rode him down, and a great voice cried, not with the cunning that he would have expected of a tempter, but with the majesty of morning on the heights:

"Take her. She is yours."

He knew that it was true. Who would gainsay him? She was his. In a few hours she would be his wife, in his own house, given him by every law of creed and race. In fact, by not pleasing himself he would be outraging creed and race. The latch of her door was his to lift at any time. That chamber of rose and gold, rainbows and silver cries like the dawn-notes of birds, was there for him like the open rose for the bee. His mother, too, would be pleased. She had expostulated gelatinously about "this marriage which was no marriage." He would be that companionable and inspiring thing—the norm. He would be one of the world-wide company of men that work, marry, bring up children, maybe see their grandchildren, and then, in the glory of fulfilment, lay their silver heads on the pillow of sleep. He had always loved normal things. He was not one of those who are set apart by the strange aloofness of genius, whose souls burn with a wild light, instead of with the comfortable glow of the hearth fire. He was an ordinary man, loving ordinary things. Neither was he effeminate or a celibate by instinct, though he had not Reddin's fury of masculinity. Sex would never have awakened in him but at the touch of spiritual love. But the touch had come; it had awakened; it threatened to master him.

Pictures came dimly and yet radiantly before him: Hazel as she would stand to-night brushing out her hair; this room as it would be when she had put the light out and only starlight illumined it; the flowery scent, the sound of her soft breathing; and then, in a tempestuous rush, the emotions he would feel as he laid his hand on the latch—love, triumph, intoxication.

How would she look? What would she say? She could not forbid him. She would, perhaps, when she awoke to the sweetness of marriage, love him as passionately as he loved her.

A wild mastery possessed him. He would have what he wanted of life. What need was there to renounce? And then, like a minor chord, soft and plaintive, he heard Hazel's voice in bewildered accents murmur:

"What for do you, my soul?" and, "I'm much obleeged, I'm sure."

What stood between him and his desire was Hazel's helplessness, her personality, like a delicate glass that he would break if he stirred. Creed and convention pushed him on. For Church and State are for material righteousness, the letter of the law. Spiritual flowerings, high motives clad in apparent lawlessness—these are hardly in their province, since they are for those who still need crude rules. To the scribes, and still more to them that sold doves, Christ was a brawler.

Rather than break that glass he would not stir. What were the race and public opinion to him compared with her spirit? His tenets must make an exception for her. These things were negligible. All that mattered was himself and Hazel; his passion, Hazel's freedom; his longing for husbandhood and fatherhood, her elvish incapacity for wifehood and motherhood. He suddenly detested himself for the rosy pictures he had seen. He was utterly abased at the knowledge that he had really meant at one moment to enforce his rights, to lift the latch. The selfish use of strength always seemed to him a most despicable thing. From all points he surveyed his crisis with shame. He had made his decision; but he knew how easy it would have been to make the opposite one. How easy and how sweet! He stayed where he was for a long time, too tired to get up, weary with a conflict that was hardly yet begun. Then he heard his mother calling, and got up, closing the door as one surrenders a dream. He still held in one hand the bunch of rosy tulips he had bought for Hazel at the show. They hung their heads.

"Oh, my dear boy," said Mrs. Marston, "I've called and better called, and no answer! Where were you?"

Edward might have said with truth, "In hell." He only said: "In a valley of this restless mind."

"What valley, dear? Oh, no valley, only a poem? How very peculiar! Dear, dear!" she thought; "I hope all this isn't turning his brain; it seemed so like nonsense what he said. You look so pale, my dear, and so distraught," she went on; "I think you want a——"

"No, mother. Thank you, I want nothing."

He was half-conscious of the bitter irony of it as he said it.

Mrs. Marston was looking at his knees.

"Oh, my dear, I know now," she said; "I beg your pardon for saying you wanted a powder. You were with the Lord. You could not have been better occupied on your wedding-morning!"

She was very much touched. Edward flushed darkly, conscious of how he had been occupied.

"There!" cried she; "now you're as flushed as you were pale. It's the fever. I'll mix you something that will soon put you all right."

"I only wish you could," he sighed.

"And what I wanted," said she, catching at her previous thought in the same blind way as she caught at her skirts on muddy days—"what I wanted, dear, was—it's so heavy, the cake——"

"You want me to lift it, mother?"

"Yes, my dear. How well you know! And mind not to spoil the icing; it's so hard not to, it being so white and brittle."

"No, I won't spoil the white," he said earnestly, "however hard it is."

She did not notice that the earnestness was unnatural; intense earnestness in household matters was her normal state.

CHAPTER XVI

THE stately May morning, caparisoned in diamonds, full of the solemnity that perfect beauty wears, had come out of the purple mist and shamed the hovel where Hazel dressed for her bridal. The cottage had sunk almost out of recognition in the foam of spring. Ancient lilacs stood about it and nodded purple-coroneted heads across its one chimney. Their scent bore down all other scents like a strong personality, and there was no choice but to think the thoughts of the lilac. Two laburnums, forked and huge of trunk, fingered the roof with their lower branches and dripped gold on it. The upper branches sprang far into the blue.

The may-tree by the gate knew its perfect moment, covered with crystal buds that shone like rain among the bright green leaves. From every pear-tree—full-blossomed, dropping petals—and from every shell-pink apple-tree came the roar of the bees.

Abel rose very early, for he considered it the proper thing to make a wreath for Hazel, being an artist in such matters. The lilies-of-the-valley were almost out; he had put some in warm water overnight, and now he sat beneath the horse-chesnut and worked at the wreath. The shadows of the leaves rippled over him like water, and often he looked up at the white spires of bloom with a proprietory eye, for his bees were working there with a ferocity of industry.

He was moody and miserable, for he thought of the township of hives that Hazel might have won for him. He comforted himself with the thought that there would be something saved on her keep. It never occurred to him to be sorry to lose her; in fact, there was little reason why he should be. Each had lived a lonely, self-sufficing life; they were entirely unsuitable companions for each other.

He wove the wet lilies, rather limp from the hot water, on to a piece of wire taken from one of his wreath-frames.

So Hazel went to her bridal in a funeral wreath.

She awoke very tired from the crisis yesterday, but happy. She and Foxy and the one-eyed cat, her rabbit, and the blackbird, were going to a country far from troublous things, to the peace of Edward's love on the slope of God's Little Mountain.

The difficulties of the new life were forgotten. Only its joys were visible to-day. Mrs. Marston seemed to smile and smile in an eternal loving-kindness, and Martha's heavy face wore an air of good-fellowship. The loud winds, lulled and bearing each its gift of balm, would blow softly round Edward's house. Frost, she thought, would not come to God's Little Mountain as to the cold Callow.

She had not seen Reddin's rimy shoulders, nor the cold glitter of the tombs.

She sang as she dressed with the shrill sweetness of a robin. She had never seen such garments; she hardly knew how to put some of them on. She brushed her hair till it shone like a tiger-lily, and piled it on her small head in great plaits. When her white muslin frock was on, she drew a long breath, seeing herself in bits in the small glass.

"I be like a picture!" she gasped. Round her slim sunburnt neck was a small gold chain holding a topaz pendant, which matched her eyes.

When she came forth like a lily from the mould, Abel staggered backwards, partly in clownish mirth, partly in astonishment. He was so impressed that he got breakfast himself, and afterwards went and sand-papered his hands until they were sore. Hazel, en-throned in one of the broken chairs, fastened on Foxy's wedding-collar, made of blue forget-me-not.

Foxy, immensely dignified, sat on her haunches, her chin tucked into the forget-me-nots, immovably bland. She was evidently competent for her new rôle; she might have been ecclesiastically connected all her life. The one-eyed cat was beside her, blue-ribboned, purr-ing her best, which was like a broken bagpipe on ac-count of her stormy youth.

"Ah! you'd best purr!" said Hazel. "Sitting on cushions by the fireside all your life long you'll be, and Foxy with a grand new tub!"

Not many brides think so little of themselves, so much of small pensioners, as Hazel did this morning. Breakfast was a sociable meal, for Abel made several remarks. Now and then he looked at Hazel and said, "Laws!" Hazel laughed gleefully. When she stood by the gate watching for the neighbour's cart that was to take them, she looked as full of white budding promise as the may-tree above her.

She did not think very much about Edward, except as a protecting presence. Reddin's face, full of strong, mysterious misery; the feel of Reddin's arm as they danced; his hand, hot and muscular, on hers—these claimed her thoughts. She fought them down, con-scious that they were not suitable in Edward's bride.

At last the cart appeared, coming up the hill with the lurching deportment of market-carts. The pony had a bunch of marigolds on each ear, and there was lilac on the whip. They packed the animals in—the cat giving ventriloquist mews from her basket, the rabbit in its hutch, the bird in its wooden cage, and Foxy sitting up in front of Hazel. The harp completed the load. They drove off amid the cheers of the next-door children, and took their leisurely way through the resinous fragrance of larch-woods.

The cream-coloured pony was lame, which gave the cart a peculiar roll, and she was tormented with hunger for the marigolds, which hung down near her nose, and caused her to get her head into strange contortions in the effort to reach them. The wind sighed in the tall larches, and once again, as on the day of the concert, they bent attentive heads towards Hazel. In the glades the widespread hyacinths would soon be paling towards their euthanasia, knowing the art of dying as well as that of living, fortunate, as few sentient creatures are, in keeping their dignity in death.

When they drove through the quarry, where deep shadow lay, Hazel shivered suddenly.

"Somebody walking over your grave," said Abel.

"Oh, dunna say that! It be unlucky on my wedding-day," she cried. As they climbed the hill she leaned forward, as if straining upwards out of some deep horror.

When their extraordinary turn-out drew up at the gate, Abel boisterously flourishing his lilac-laden whip and shouting elaborate but incomprehensible witticisms, Edward came hastily from the house. His eyes rested on Hazel, and were so vivid, so brimful of tenderness, that Abel remained with a joke half expounded.

"My Hazel," Edward said, standing by the cart and looking up, "welcome home, and God bless you!"

"You canna say fairer nor that," remarked Abel. "Inna our 'Azel peart? Dressed up summat cruel, inna she?"

Edward took no notice. He was looking at Hazel, searching hungrily for a hint of the same overwhelming passion that he felt. But he only found childlike joy, gratitude, affection, and a faint shadow for which he could not account, and from which he began to hope many things.

If in that silent room upstairs he had come to the opposite decision; if he had that very day told Hazel what his love meant, by the irony of things she would have loved him and spent on him the hidden passion of her nature.

But he had chosen the unselfish course.

"Well," he said in a business-like tone, "suppose we unpack the little creatures, Hazel first?"

Mrs. Marston appeared.

"Oh, are you going to a show, Mr. Woodus?" she asked Abel. "It would have been so nice and pleasant if you would have played your instrument."

"Yes, mum. That's what I've acome for. I inna going to no show. I've come to the wedding to get my belly-full."

Mrs. Marston, very much flustered, asked what the animals were for.

"I think, mother, they're for you." Edward smiled.

She surveyed Foxy, full of vitality after the drive; the bird, moping and rough; the rabbit, with one ear inside-out, looking far from respectable. She heard the ventriloquist mews.

"I don't want them, dear," she said with great decision.

"It's a bit of a cats' 'ome you're starting, mum," said Abel.

Mrs. Marston found no words for her emotions.

But while Edward and Abel bestowed the various animals, she said to Martha:

"Weddings are not what they were, Martha."

"Bride to groom," said Martha, who always read the local weddings: "a one-eyed cat; a foolish rabbit as'd be better a pie; an ill-contrived bird; and a filthy, smelly fox!"

Mrs. Marston relaxed her dignity so far as to laugh softly. She decided to give Martha a rise next year.

CHAPTER XVII

HAZEL sat on a large flat gravestone with Foxy beside her. They were like a sculpture in marble on some ancient tomb. Coming, so soon after her strange moment of terror in the quarry, to this place of the dead, she was smitten with formless fear. The crosses and stones had, on that storm-beleaguered hill-side, an air of horrible bravado, as if they knew that although the winds were stronger than they, yet they were stronger than humanity; as if they knew that the whole world is the tomb of beauty, and has been made by man the torture-chamber of weakness.

She looked down at the lettering on the stone. It was a young girl's grave.

"Oh!" she muttered, looking up into the tremendous dome of blue, empty and adamantine—"oh! dunna let me go young! What for did she dee so young? Dunna let me! dunna!"

And the vast dome received her prayer, empty and adamantine.

She was suddenly panic-stricken; she ran away from the tombs calling Edward's name.

And Edward came on the instant. His hands were full of cabbage which he had been taking to the rabbit.

"What is it, little one?"

"These here!"

"The graves?"

"Ah. They'm so drodsome."

Edward pointed to a laburnum-tree which had rent a tomb, and now waved above it.

"See," he said. "Out of the grave and gate of death——"

"Ah! But her as went in hanna come out. On'y a new tree. I'll be bound she wanted to come out."

At this moment Edward's friend, who was to marry them, arrived.

"Now I shall go and wait for you to come," Edward whispered.

Waiting in the dim chapel, with its whitewashed walls and few leaded windows half covered with ivy, his mind was clear of all thoughts but unselfish ones.

His mother, trailing purple, came in, and thought how like a sacred picture he looked; this, from her, was superlative praise. Martha's brother was there, ringing the one bell, which gave such a small fugitive sound that it made the white chapel seem like a tinkling bell-wether lost on the hills.

Mr. James was there, and several of the congregation, and Martha, with her best dress hastily donned over her print, and a hat of which her brother said "it 'ud draw tears from an egg."

Mr. James' daughter played a voluntary, in the midst of which an altercation was heard outside.

"Her'll be lonesome wi'out me!"

"They wunna like it. It's blasphemy."

Then the door opened, and Abel, very perspiring, and conscious of the greatness of the occasion, led in Hazel in her wreath of drooping lilies. The green light touched her face with unnatural pallor, and her eyes, haunted by some old evil out of the darkness of life, looked towards Edward as to a saviour.

She might have been one of those brides from Faery, who rose wraith-like out of pool or river, and had some mysterious ichor in their veins, and slipped from the grasp of mortal lover, melting like snow at a touch. Edward, watching her, was seized with an inexplicable fear. He wished she had not been so strangely beautiful, that the scent of the lilies had not brought so heavy a faintness, reminding him of death-chambers.

It was not till Hazel reached the top of the chapel that the congregation observed Foxy, a small red figure, trotting willingly in Hazel's wake—a loving though incompetent bridesmaid.

Mr. James arose and walked up the chapel.

"I will remove the animal," he said; then he saw that Hazel was leading Foxy. This insult was, then, deliberate. "A hanimal," he said, "hasn't no business in a place o' worship."

"What for not?" asked Hazel.

"Because——" Mr. James found himself unable to go on. "Because not," he finished blusterously. He laid his hand on the cord, and Foxy prepared for conflict.

Edward's colleague turned away, hand to mouth. He was obliged to contemplate the ivy outside the window while the altercation lasted.

"Whoever made you," Hazel said, "made Foxy. Where you can come, Foxy can come. You'm deacon, Foxy's bridesmaid!"

"That's heathen talk," said Mr. James.

"How very naughty Hazel is!" thought poor Mrs. Marston. She felt that she could never hold up her head again. The congregation giggled. The black grapes and the chenille spots trembled. "How very unpleasant!" thought the old lady.

Then Edward spoke, and his voice had an edge of masterfulness that astonished Mr. James.

"Let be," he said. "'Other sheep I have which are not of this fold. Them also will I bring.' She has the same master, James."

Silence fell. The other minister turned round with a surprised, admiring glance at Edward, and the service began. It was short and simple, but it gathered an extraordinary pathos as it progressed.

The narcissi on the window-sills eyed Hazel in a white silence, and their dewy golden eyes seemed akin to Foxy's and her own. The fragrance of spring flowers filled the place with wistful sadness. There are no scents so tearful, so grievous, as the scents of valley-lilies and narcissi clustered ghostly by the dark garden hedge, and white lilac, freighted with old dreams, and pansies, faintly reminiscent of mysterious lost ecstasy.

Edward felt these things, and was oppressed. A great pity for Hazel and her following of forlorn creatures surged over him. A kind of dread grew up in him that he might not be able to defend them as he would wish. It did seem that helplessness went to the wall. Since Hazel had come with her sad philosophy of experience, he had begun to notice facts.

He looked up towards the aloof sky as Hazel had done.

"He is love," he said to himself.

The blue sky received his certainty, as it had received Hazel's questioning, in regardless silence.

Mrs. Marston observed Edward narrowly. Then she wrote in her hymn-book: "Mem: Maltine; Edward."

The service was over. Edward smiled at her as he

passed, and met Mr. James' frown with dignified good-humour.

Foxy, even more willing to go out than to come in, ran on in front, and as they entered the house they heard from the cupboard under the stairs the epithalamium of the one-eyed cat.

"Oh, dear heart!" said Hazel tremulously, looking at the cake, "I ne'er saw the like!"

"Mother iced it, dear."

Hazel ran to Mrs. Marston and put both her thin arms round her neck, kissing her in a storm of gratitude.

"There, there! quietly, my dear," said Mrs. Marston. "I'm glad it pleases." She smoothed the purple silk smilingly. Hazel was forgiven.

"I'd a brought the big saw if I'd 'a thought," said Abel jocosely.

Only Mr. James was taciturn.

Foxy was allowed in, and perambulated the room, to Mrs. Marston's supreme discomfort; every time Foxy drew near she gave a smothered scream. In spite of these various disadvantages, it was a merry party, and did not break up till dusk.

After tea Abel played, Mr. James being very patronizing, saying at the end of each piece, "Very good"; till Abel asked rudely, "Can yer play yerself?"

Edward came to the rescue by offering Mr. James tobacco. They drew round the fire, for the dusk came coldly, only Abel remaining in his corner playing furiously. He considered it only honest, after such a tea, to play his loudest.

Hazel, happy but restless, played with Foxy beside the darkening window, low and many-paned, and cumbered with bits of furniture dear to Mrs. Marston.

Edward was showing his friend a cycle map of the country.

Mrs. Marston was sleepily discussing hens—good layers, good sitters, good table-fowl—with Mr. James. Hazel, tired of playing with Foxy, knelt on the big round ottoman with its central peak of stuffed tapestry and looked idly from the window.

Suddenly she cried out. Edward was alert in a moment.

"What is it, dear?"

Hazel had sunk back on the ottoman, pale and speechless; but she realized that she must pull herself together.

"I stuck a pin in me," she said.

"Pins in a wedding-dress? Oh, fie!" said Mrs. Marston. "Pricked at your wedding, pricked for aye."

"Oh, dear, dearie me!" cried Hazel, bursting into tears, and flinging herself at Edward's feet.

Wondering, he comforted her.

Mrs. Marston called for the lamp; the blinds were drawn, and all was saffron peace.

Outside, in the same attitude as before, bowed and motionless, stood Reddin. He saw Hazel, watched her withdraw, and knew that she had seen him. When the windows suddenly shone like daffodils, he recoiled as if at a lash, and, turning, went heavily down the batch. He turned into the woods, and made his way back till he was opposite the house. Thence he watched the guests depart, and later saw Martha go to her cottage. The lights wavered and wandered. He saw one go up the stairs.

Inside the house Mrs. Marston, confronted with a bridal which she did not quite know how to regard, very tactfully said good-night, and left them together in the parlour. They sat there for a time, and Edward tried not to realize how much he was missing. He got up at last and lit Hazel's candle. At her door he said good-night hastily. Hazel took the arrangements for granted, partly because she had slept in this same room two nights ago, partly because Edward had never shown her a hint of passion.

The higher the nature, the more its greatness is taken for granted. Edward turned and went to his room.

Reddin, under his black roof of pines, counted the lights, and seeing that there were three, turned homewards with a sigh of relief. But as he went through the fields he remembered how Hazel had looked last night; how she had danced like a leaf; how slender and young she was. He was a man everlastingly maddened by slightness and weakness. As a boy, when his father and mother still kept up their position a little, he had broken a priceless Venetian glass simply because he could not resist the temptation to close his hand on it. His father had flogged him, being of the stupid kind who believe that corporal punishment can influence the soul. And Reddin had done the same thing next day with a bit of egg-shell china.

So now, as he thought of Hazel's lissom waist, her large eyes, rather scared, her slender wrists, he cursed until the peewits arose mewing all about him. In the thick darkness of the lonely fields he might have been some hero of the dead, mouthing a satanic recitative amid a chorus of lost souls.

The long search for Hazel, begun in a whim, had ended in passion. If he had never looked for her, never felt the nettled sense of being foiled, or if he had found her at once, he would never have desired her so fiercely. Now, for the first time in his life impassioned, he felt something mysterious and unwelcome to him begin to mingle with his desire. Above all, life without her meant dullness, lack of vitality, the swift onset of middle-age. He saw this with shrinking. He walked wearily, looking older than he was in the pathos of loss.

Life with her meant an indefinitely prolonged youth, an ecstasy he had not dreamt of, the well-being of his whole nature. He walked along moodily, thinking how he would have started afresh, smartened up Undern, worked hard, given his children—his and Hazel's—a good education, become more sober.

But he had been a fortnight too late. A miserable fortnight! He, who had raved over the countryside, had missed her. Marston, who had simply remained on his mountain, had won her.

"It's damned unfair!" he said, and pathos faded from him in his rage. All the vague thoughts, dark and turgid, of the last two nights took shape slowly. He neither cursed nor brooded any more. He thought keenly as he walked. His face took a more powerful cast—it had never been a weak face at the worst—and he looked a man that it would not be easy to combat. Bitter hatred of Edward possessed him, silent fury against fate, relentless determination to get Hazel whether she would or not. He had a purpose in life now. Vessons was surprised at his quick, authoritative manner.

"Make me some sandwiches early to-morrow," he said, "and you'll have to go to the auction. I shan't go myself."

"'Ow can I go now? Who's to do the cheeses?"

"Give 'em to the pigs."

"Who's to meet the groom from Farnley? Never will I go!"

"If you're so damned impudent, you'll have to leave."

"Who's to meet the groom?" Vessons spoke with surly, astonished meekness.

"Groom? Groom be hanged! Wire to him."

"It'll take me the best part of two hour to go and telegrapht. And it cosses money. And dinner at the auction cosses money."

"Oh!" cried Reddin with intense irritation, "take this, your fool!"

He flung his purse at Vessons.

"Well, well," thought Vessons, "I mun yumour 'im. He's fretched along of her marrying the minister. 'Long live the minister!' says Andrew."

Is he going to kill Edward?

Take Hazel?

CHAPTER XVIII

NEXT morning Vessons went off in high feather; Hazel was so safely disposed of. Reddin left at the same time, and all the long May day Undern was deserted, and lay still and silent as if pondering on its loneliness. Reddin did not return until after night-fall.

He spent the day in a curious manner for a man of his position, under a yew-tree, riven of trunk, gigantic, black, commanding Edward's house. He leant against the trunk that had seen so many generations, shadowed so many fox-earths, groaned in so many tempests.

Above his tent sailed those hill-wanderers, the white clouds of May. They were as fiercely pure, as apparently imperishable, as a great ideal. With lingering majesty they marched across the sky, first over the parsonage, then over Reddin, laying upon each in turn a hyacinth shadow.

Reddin watched the house indifferently, while Martha went to and fro cleaning the chapel after the wedding.

Then Mrs. Marston came to the front door and shut it.

After that, for a long time, nothing moved but the slow shadows of the gravestones, shortening with the climbing sun. The laburnum waved softly, and flung its lacy shadow on the graves where the grass was long and daisied.

A wood-pigeon began in its deep and golden voice a low soliloquy recollected as a saint's, rich as a lover's.

Reddin stirred disconsolately, trampling the thin leaves and delicate flowers of the sorrel.

At last the door opened, and Edward came out carrying a spade.

Hazel followed. They went round to the side of the house away from the graveyard, and Edward began to dig, Hazen sitting on the grass and evidently making suggestions. With the quickness of jealousy, Reddin knew that Edward was making a garden for Hazel. It enraged him.

"I could have made her a garden, and a deal better than that!" he thought. "She could have had half an acre of garden at Undern; I could have it made in no time."

He uttered an exclamation of contempt. "The way he fools with that spade! He's never dug in his life."

Before long Hazel brought out the bird-cage and hung it in the sun. And surprisingly, almost alarmingly, the ancient bird began to sing. It was like hearing an old man sing a love-song. The bird sat there, rough and purblind, and chanted youth with the magic of a master.

Hazel and Edward stood still to hear it, holding each other's hands.

"He's ne'er said a word afore," breathed Hazel. "Eh! but he likes the Mountain!"

In the little warm garden with Hazel, among the thick daisies, with the mirth of the once desolate ringing in his ears, Edward knew perfect happiness.

He stood looking at Hazel, his eyes dark with love. She seemed to blossom in the quiet day. He stooped and kissed her hand.

To Reddin in his deep shadow every action was clear, for they stood in sunlight. He ground the sorrel into the earth. After a time Martha rang the dinner-bell, not because she could not both see and hear her master, but because it was the usual thing. To Reddin the bell's rather cracked note was sardonic, for it was summoning another man to eat and drink with Hazel. He ate his sandwiches, not being so much in love that he lost his appetite. Then he sat down and read the racing news. There was no danger of anyone seeing him, for the place was entirely solitary with the double loneliness of hill and woodland. There were no children in the batch except Martha's friend's little boy, and he was timid and never went bird's-nesting. The only sound, except the intermittent song of birds, was the far-away noise of a woodman's axe, like the deep scattered barking of hungry hounds. Nothing else stirred under the complex arches of the trees except the sunlight, moving like a ghost.

These thick woods, remote on their ridges, were to the watchful eye rich with a half-revealed secret, to the attentive ear full of urgent voices. The solving of all life's riddles might come to one here at any moment. In this hour or in the next, from a grey ash-bole or a blood-red pine-trunk, might come the naked spirit of life with a face fierce or lovely. Coiled in the twist of long honeysuckle ropes that fell from the dead yews; curled in a last year's leaf; embattled in a mailed fir-cone, or resting starrily in the green moss, it seemed that God slumbered. At any moment He might wake, to bless or curse.

Reddin, not having a watchful eye or an attentive ear for such things, was not conscious of anything but a sense of loneliness. He read the paper indefatigably. In an hour or so Edward and Hazel came out again, she in her new white hat. They went up God's Little

Mountain where it sloped away in pale green illuminated vistas till it reached the dark blue sky. They disappeared on the skyline, and Reddin impatiently composed himself for more waiting. Was he never to get a chance of seeing Hazel alone?

"That fellow dogs her steps," he said.

The transfigured slopes of the mountain were, it seemed to Edward, a suitable place for a thing he wished to tell Hazel.

"Hazel," he said, "if you ever feel that you would rather have a husband than a brother, you have only to say so."

Hazel flushed. Although it was such a muted passion that sounded in his voice, it stirred her. Since she had known Reddin, her ignorance had come to recognize the sound of it, and she had also begun to flush easily.

If Edward had understood women better, he would have seen that this speech of his was a mistake; for even if a woman knows whether she wishes for a husband, she will never tell him so.

They turned home in a constrained silence. Foxy, frightened by a covey of partridges, created a diversion by pulling her cord from Hazel's inattentive hand and setting off for the parsonage.

"Oh! she'll be bound to go to the woods!" cried Hazel, beginning to run. "Do 'ee see if she's in tub, Ed'ard, and I'll go under the trees and holla."

Reddin was startled when he saw Hazel, who had out-distanced Edward, making straight for his hiding-place. She came running between the boles with an easy grace, an independence that drove him frantic. A pretty woman should not have that easy grace; she should have exchanged it for a matronly bearing by this time, and independence should have yielded to subservience—to the male, to him. With her vivid hair and eyes and her swift slenderness, Hazel had a fawn-like air as she traversed the wavering shadows. She passed his tree without seeing him, and stood listening. Then she began to plead with the truant.

"What for did you run away, Foxy, my dear? Where be you? Come back along with me, dear 'eart, for it draws to night!"

Reddin stepped from his tree and spoke to her.

With a stifled scream she turned to run away, but he intercepted her.

"No. I've waited long enough for this. So you're married to the parson, after all?"

"Ah."

"You'll be sorry."

"What for do you come tormenting of me, Mr. Reddin?"

"You were meant for me. You're mine."

"Folk allus says I'm theirs. I'd liefer be mine."

"As you wouldn't marry me, Hazel, the least you can do is to come and talk to me sometimes."

"Oh, I canna!"

"You must. Any spare time, come to this tree. I shall generally be here."

"But why ever? And you a squire with a big place and fine ladies after you!"

"Because I choose."

"Leave me be, Mr. Reddin. I be comforble, and Foxy be, and they're all settling so nice. The bird's sung."

"The parson, too, no doubt. If you don't come often enough, I shall walk past the house and look in. If you go on not coming, I shall tell the parson you stayed the night with me, and he'll turn you out."

"He wouldna! You wouldna!"

"Yes, I would. He would, too. A parson doesn't want a wife that isn't respectable. So as you've got to"—he dropped his harshness and became persuasive —"you may as well come with a good grace."

"But it wunna my fault as I stayed the night over. It was Aunt Prowde's. What for should folk chide me and not auntie?"

"Lord, I don't know! Because you're pretty."

"Be I?"

"Hasn't that fellow told you so?"

"No. He dunna say much."

"You could make such a good chap of me if you liked, Hazel."

"How ever?"

"I'd give up the drink."

"And fox-hunting?"

"Well, I might give up even that—for you. Be my friend, Hazel."

He spoke with an indefinable charm inherited from some courtly ancestor. Hazel was fascinated.

"But you've got blood on you!" she protested.

"So have you!" he retorted unexpectedly. "You say you kill flies, so you're as bad as I am, Hazel. So be my friend."

"I mun go!"

"Say you'll come to-morrow."

"Not but for a minute, then."

Edward's voice came from the house.

"I've found her!"

Hazel ran home. But as she left the wood she turned and looked down the shadowy steeps of green at Reddin as he strode homewards. She watched him until he passed out of sight; then, sighing, she went home.

CHAPTER XIX

NEXT day Hazel did not go into the woods. In the evening, sitting in the quiet parlour while Edward read aloud and Mrs. Marston knitted, she felt afraid as she remembered it. Yet she had been still more afraid at the idea of going.

She had helped Mrs. Marston to cover rhubarb-jam in the dim store-room while Edward visited a sick man at some distance. It had been delightful, gumming on the clean tops, and then writing on them. She had dipped freely into the biscuit-box. Then Edward had returned, and they had gardened again. Now they were settled for the evening, and she was learning to knit, twisting obdurate wool round anarchic needles, while Mrs. Marston—the pink shawl top—chanted: "Knit, pearl! Knit, pearl!"

"Will it come to ought ever?" queried Hazel. "It's nought but a tail o' string now!"

"It will come to anything you like to make, dear," said the old lady.

"Is knitting so like life, mother?" Edward spoke amusedly.

"But it wunna," said Hazel. "It'll only come a tanglement."

Edward suggested that he should help: there was great laughter over this interlude, while Mrs. Marston still chanted, "Knit, pearl!"

Reddin, walking lingeringly past the house in the dark, heard it, and was very angry and miserable.

Hazel heard his step on the rough stones, and was alarmedly sure that it was he. She was terribly afraid he would tell Edward. Then a new idea occurred to her. Should she tell Edward herself?

She sat in the firelight with her head bent, and turned this new thought about in her brain as incompetently as she twisted the blue wool round the needles. And from the silent shadows, as she played with the thread of destiny, two presences eyed each other across her bright head—one armed, the other bearing roses. Neither Mrs. Marston, with her antiphonal "Double knit, double pearl!" nor Edward, reading in his pleasant voice—he rather fancied his reading, and tried not to—saw those impalpable figures, each with a possessive hand outstretched to Hazel pending her decision.

"Why shouldna I say? There was no harm!" she thought. Then she remembered that there had been something—a queer feeling—that had sent her out of the glass door into the snow.

She had never wanted to tell anyone of the episode. She glanced at Edward through her lashes—a look that always made him think of the pool above the parsonage, where lucent brown water shone through rushes. He saw the look, for he always glanced round as he read, having gathered from his book on elocution that this was correct. He smiled across at her, and went on reading.

The book was one of those affected by Mrs. Marston and her kind. It had no relation whatever to life. Its ideals, characters, ethics, and crisis made up an unearthly whole, which being entirely useless as a tonic or as a balm, was so much poison. It was impossible to imagine its heroine facing any of the facts of life, or engaging in any of those physical acts to which all humanity is bound, and which need more than resignation—namely, open-eyed honesty—to raise them from a humiliation to a glory. It was impossible to imagine also how the child, which appeared discreetly and punctually on the last page, could have come by its existence, since it certainly, with such unexceptionable parents, could not have been begotten.

Hazel listened anxiously to hear if the heroine ever drove on a winter night with a man who stared at her out of bold blue eyes, and whether she got frightened and took refuge in a bedroom full of white mice. But there were no mice, nor dark roads, nor bold men in all its pages. By the time the reading came to an end, Hazel had quite made up her mind that she could not possibly tell Edward. The blue wool was inextricably tangled, and one of the shadowy presences had vanished.

Followed what Mrs. Marston called "a little chat"; the evening tray, containing cake and cocoa, was brought from its side-table; the kettle was put on, and soon the candles were lit.

The presence that remained was with Hazel as she went up to her little room, as she undressed, and when she lay down to sleep. From the mantlepiece in the faint moonlight shone the white background of the text, "Not a hair of thy head shall perish."

But the promising words were obliterated by night.

Next morning, and sometime during every subsequent day, Hazel met Reddin under the dark yew-tree.

"You're very fond of the woods, my dear," said

Mrs. Marston one morning. "It must be very nice and pleasant there just now."

"No, it inna, Mrs. Marston. It's drodsome."

"If I could start very early," Mrs. Marston went on, "please God I'd go with you. For you always go while Edward is visiting, and it's lonely for you."

Hazel fled down the batch that morning, and back up a shadowed ride to Reddin.

"You munna come never no more, Mr. Reddin!" she cried. "The old lady's coming to-morrowday, her says."

Reddin swore. He was getting on so nicely. Already Hazel went red and white at his pleasure, and though he had not attempted to kiss her, he had gained a hold on her imagination.

Whenever he saw himself as others would see him if they knew, he hastily said, "All's fair in love," and shut his eyes. Also, he felt that he was doing evil in order to bring Hazel good.

"For how a girl can live in that stuffy hole with that old woman and that die-away fellow, Lord only knows!" he thought. "She'll be twice the girl she is when she lives with a man that *is* a man, and she can do as she likes with Undern so long as she's not stand-off with me. No, by ——! I'll have no nonsense after this! Here I am, sitting under a tree like a dog with a treed cat!"

So now he was very angry. His look was like a lash as he said: "You made that up to get rid of me."

"I didna!" cried Hazel, trembling, "But oh! Mr. Reddin, canna you leave me be? There's Ed'ard reading the many mansions bit to old Solomon Bache, as good as gold, and you'd ought to let me bide along of the old lady and knit."

"I'll give you something better to do than knit soon."

"What for will you?"

"Oh! you women! Are you a little innocent, Hazel? Or are you a d—d clever woman?"

"I dunno. But I canna come no more."

"Won't, you mean. Very well."

"What'n you mean, saying 'very well' so choppy?"

"I mean that if a man chooses to see a woman, see her he will. It's his place to find ways. It's her privilege to hide if she likes, or do any d—d thing she likes. That only makes it more exciting. "Now go back to your knitting. Fff! knitting!"

The startled pigeons fled up with a steely clatter of wings at his sudden laughter.

"Oh! hushee! They'll hear and come out."

"I don't care. If the dead heard and came out and stood between us, I shouldn't care! What are you whispering?"

Hazel had said, "Whoever she be, have her he will, for certain sure."

She would not repeat it, and he turned sharply away in a huff.

She also turned away with a sigh of relief, but almost immediately looked back, and watched his retreating figure until he was lost in the trees.

CHAPTER XX

ON Lord's Day more than on any other at the mountain Hazel was like a small derelict boat beached on a peaceful shore. There was a hypnotic quiet about the place, with no sound of Martha's scrubbing, no smell of cooking. There was always cold meat on Lord's Day, with pickled cabbage, that concomitant of mysterious Sabbath blessedness. A subdued excitement prevailed about service-time, and sank again afterwards like a wind in the tree-tops.

Hazel felt very proud of Edward in chapel, and a little awed at his bearing and his abstracted air. She came near to loving him on the lilac-scented Sundays when he read those old fragrant love-stories that he had dreaded. His voice was pleasant and deep.

" 'And he took unto him his wife, and she bare him a son.' "

It may have been that the modulations of Edward's voice spoke as eloquently as words to her, or that Reddin had destroyed her childish detachment, but she began to bring these old tales into touch with her own life. She envied these glamorous women of the ancient world. They were so tall, so richly clad, dwelling under their golden-fruited trees beneath skies for ever blue. It was all so simple for them. There were no Reddins, no old ladies.

Their stories went smoothly with unravelled thread,

not like her knitting. She began to long to be one of that dark-eyed company, clear and changeless as polished ivory, moving with a slow and gliding stateliness across the rose-coloured dawn, bearing on their heads with effortless grace beautiful pitchers of water for a thirsty world.

Edward had shown her just such a picture in his mother's illustrated Bible. Instinctively she fell back on the one link between herself and them.

"Ed'ard's took *me* to wife," she thought. The sweetest of vague new ideas stirred in her mind like leaf-buds within the bark of a spring tree. They brought a new expression to her face.

Edward's eyes strayed continually to the bar of dusky sunlight where she sat, her down-bent face mysterious as all vitality is when seen in a new aspect. The demure look she wore in chapel was contradicted by a nascent wildness hovering about her lips.

Edward tried to keep his attention on the prayers, and wished he was an Episcopalian, and had his prayers ready-made for him. He once mentioned this to his mother, who was much shocked. She said home-made prayers and home-made bread and home-made jam were the best.

"As for manufactured jam, it's a sloven's refuge, and no more to be said. And prayer's the same. The best printed prayer's no better than bought mixed at fourpence the pound, and a bit gone from keeping."

Edward stumbled on, as Mr. James said afterwards, "like my old mare Betsy, a step and a stumble, a nod and a flop, and home in the Lord's own time—that's to say, the small hours."

The chapel was still hot, though cool green evening brooded without and the birds had emerged from their day-long coma. Wood-pigeons spoke in their deep voices from the dark pines across the batch a language older than the oldest script of man. Cuckoos shouted in the wind-riven larches, green beyond imagining, at the back of the chapel. A blackbird meditated aloud in high rhapsody, very leisured, but very tireless, on matters deeper than the Coppice Pool far below, deep as the mystery of the chipped, freckled eggs in his nest in the thorn. In and out of the yellow broom-coverts woodlarks played, made their small flights, and sang their small songs. Bright orange wild bees and black bumblebees floated in through the open windows. Mrs. Marston's black and white hens and the minorca cockerel pecked about the open door and came in inquiringly, upon which Martha, who sat near the door for that purpose, swept them softly out with the clothes-prop, which she manipulated in a masterly manner.

Mrs. Marston, eyeing Hazel at all the "Amens," when, as she always said, one *ought* to look up, like fowls after a drink, thought it was a pity. What was a pity she did not divulge to herself. She concluded with "Well, well, the childless father no sinners," and hastily shut her eyes, realizing that another "Amen" had nearly come. Edward's voice had taken a tone of relief which meant the end of a prayer.

Mrs. Marston glanced at him, and decided to put some aniseed in his tea. "High thinking's as bad as an embolus," she thought. But Edward was not thinking. He was doing a much more strenuous thing—feeling. Hazel wondered at the vividness of his eyes when he rose from his knees.

"I'm glad I'm Ed'ard's missus, and not Mr. Reddin's," she thought.

She had not seen Reddin for a week, having, since their last meeting in the wood, been so much afraid of encountering him that she had scarcely left the house. The days were rather dull without her visits to the woods, but they were safe.

Edward gave out his text.

"Of those that Thou hast given me have I lost none."

All his tenderness for Hazel and her following crept into his sermon. He spoke of the power of protection as almost the greatest good in life, the finest work. He said it was the inevitable reward of self-sacrifice, and that, if one were ready for self-denial, one could protect the beloved from all harm.

There was a crunching of gravel outside, and Reddin walked in. He sat down just behind Hazel. Edward glanced up, pleased to have so important an addition to the congregation, and continued his sermon. Hazel, red and white by turns, was in such a state of miserable embarrassment that Reddin was almost sorry for her. But he did not move his gaze from her profile.

At last Mrs. Marston, ever watchful for physical symptoms, whispered, "Are you finding it oppressive? Would you like to go out?"

Hazel went out with awkward haste, and Mrs. Marston followed, having mouthed incomprehensible comfort to Edward.

He went on stumblingly with the service.

Reddin, realizing that he had been femininely outwitted, smiled. Edward wondered who this distinguished-looking man with the merciless mouth might be. He thought the smile was one of amusement at his expense. But Reddin was summing him up with a good deal of respect.

Here was a man who would need reckoning with.

"The parson's got a temper," he reflected, looking at him keenly, "and, by the Lord, I'm going to rouse it!"

He smiled again as he always did when breaking horses.

He got up suddenly and went out. Mrs. Marston, administering raspberry cordial in the parlour, heard him knock, and went to the front door.

"Can I help?" he asked in his pleasantest manner. "A doctor or anything?"

Mrs. Marston laughed softly. She liked young men, and thought Reddin "a nice lad," for all his forty years. She liked his air of breeding as he stood cap in hand awaiting orders. Above all, she was curious.

"No, thank you," she said. "But come in, all the same. It's very kind of you. And such a hot day! But it's very pleasant in the parlour. And you'll have a drink of something cool. Now what shall it be?"

"Sherry," said he, with his eyes on Hazel's.

"I misdoubt if there's any of the Christmas-pudding bottle left, but I'll go and see," she said, all in a flutter. How tragic a thing for her, who so prided herself on her housewifery, to have no sherry when it was asked for!

Her steps died away down the cellar stairs.

"So you thought you'd outwitted me?" he said. "Now you know I've not tamed horses all my life for nothing."

"Leave me be."

"You don't want me to."

"Ah! I do."

"After I've come all these miles and miles to see you, day after day?"

"I dunna care how many miles you've acome," said Hazel passionately; "what for do you do it? Go back to the dark house where you come from, and leave me be!"

Reddin dropped his pathos.

She was sitting on the horsehair sofa, he in an armchair at its head. He flung out one arm and pulled her back so that her head struck the mahogany frame of the sofa.

"None of that!" he said.

He kissed her wildly, and in the kisses repaid himself for all his waiting in the past few weeks. She was crying from the pain of the bump; his kisses hurt her; his shoulder was hard against her breast. She was shaken by strange tremors. She struck him with her clenched hand. He laughed.

"Will you behave yourself? Will you do what I tell you?" he asked.

"I'd be much obleeged," she said faintly, "if you'd draw your shoulder off a bit."

Something in the request touched him. He sat quite silent for a time in Edward's armchair, and they looked at one another in a haunted immobility. Reddin was sorry for his violence, but would not say so.

Then they heard Mrs. Marston's slide, and she entered with a large decanter.

"This is some of the sparkling gooseberry," she said, "by Susan Waine's recipe, poor thing! Own cousin to my husband she was, and a good kind body.

Never a thing awry in her house, and twelve children had Susan. I remember as clear as clear how the carpet (it was green jute, reversible) was rucked up at her funeral by the bearers' feet. And George Waine said, 'That'll worry Susan,' and then he remembered, and burst out crying, poor man! And he cried till the party was quite spoilt, and our spirits *so* low. Where was I? Oh yes. It's quite up, you see, and four years old this next midsummer. But I'm sure I'm quite put out at having no sherry, on account of Martha thinking to return the bottle and finishing the dregs. And there, you asked for sherry!"

"Did I? Oh, well, I like this just as much, thanks."

He felt uncomfortable at this drinking of wine in Marston's house. It seemed unsportsmanlike to hoodwink this old lady. He had no qualms about Hazel. He was going, if Hazel would be sensible, to give her a life she would like, and things her instincts cried out for. Possibly he was right in imagining that her instincts were traitors to her personality. For Nature —that sardonic mother—while she cries with the silver cadence of ten thousand nightingales, "Take what you want, my children," sees to it, in the dark of her sorcery-chamber, that her children want what she intends.

"Is it to your liking, Mr. ——? I didn't quite catch your name," said Mrs. Marston.

"Reddin, ma'am. Jack Reddin of Undern."

The name rang in the quiet room with a startling sound, like a gunshot in a wood at night when the birds are roosting.

At that moment Edward came in, not having waited till Mr. James had affectionately counted the collection.

"Is Hazel all right, mother?" he called when he got to the front door.

"Oh yes, my dear. It was but the heat. And here's a gentleman to see you. Mr. Reddin of Undern."

Edward came forward with his hand out, and Reddin took it. Their eyes met; a curious hush fell on the room; Hazel sighed tremulously.

"Pleased to see you at our little service, Mr. Reddin," Edward said heartily.

Reddin smiled and said, "Thanks."

"Glad there's anything in our simplicity to attract you," Edward went on, wondering if his sermons were really not so bad, after all.

Reddin laughed again shortly. Edward put this down to shyness.

"I hope we shall often have you with us again."

Reddin's eyes narrowed slightly. "Yes, thanks. I shall be with you again."

"You'll stay and have some supper?"

"Thanks."

He had left off feeling unsportsmanlike. He had no compunction towards Edward. It was man to man, and the woman to the winner. This was the code avowed by his ancestors openly, and by himself and his contemporaries tacitly. He began to be as excited as he was in a steeplechase.

Edward went and sat down by Hazel, asking softly: "And how is my little girl?"

She looked up at him, quiescent, and smiled. Reddin eyed them for a moment, construing their attitudes in his own way. To the unclean mind all frankness of word or action is suspect. Then he turned sharply to Mrs. Marston.

"I can't stay, after all," he said; "I've just remembered—something. Thanks very much"—he looked reflectively at Hazel—"for the sherry."

He was gone.

"My dear"—Mrs. Marston spoke triumphantly—"didn't I always say that gooseberry wine of Susan Waine's recipe was as good as champagne? Now you see I'm right. For Mr. Reddin of Undern—and a nice pleasant young man he is, too, though a little set about the mouth—and I remember when I was a girl there was a man with just such a mouth came to the May fair with a magic wheel, and it was a curious thing that the wheel never stopped opposite one of the prizes except when he turned it himself; and there! I did so want the green and yellow tab cat—real china—and I spent every penny, but the wheel went on."

"Poor mother!"

"Yes, my dear, I cried buckets. And I've never trusted that mouth since. But, of course, Mr. Reddin's not that kind at all, and quite above fairs and such things."

"I don't care for him much," Edward said.

"No more do I," said Hazel in a heartfelt tone.

CHAPTER XXI

HAZEL was up early next morning. She could not sleep and thought she would go down into the valley and look for spring mushrooms.

She crept out of the house, still as death, except for Mrs. Marston's soft yet all-pervading snores. Out in the graveyard, where as yet no bird sang, it was as if the dead had arisen in the stark hours between twelve and two, and were waiting unobtrusively, majestically, each by his own bed, to go down and break their long fast with the bee and the grass-snake in refectories too minute and too immortal to be known by the living. The tombstones seemed taller, seemed to have a presence behind them; the lush grass, lying grey and heavy with dew, seemed to have been swept by silent passing crowds. A dank smell came up, and the place had at once the unkempt look worn by the scene of some past revelry and the expectant air of a stage prepared for a coming drama.

Foxy barked sharply, urgently alive in the stronghold of the dead, and Hazel went to explain why she could not come. They held a long conversation, Hazel whispering, Foxy eloquent of eye. Foxy had a marked personality. Dignity never failed her, and she could be hilarious, loving, or clamorous for food without losing a jot of it. She was possessed of herself; the wild was her kingdom. If she was in a

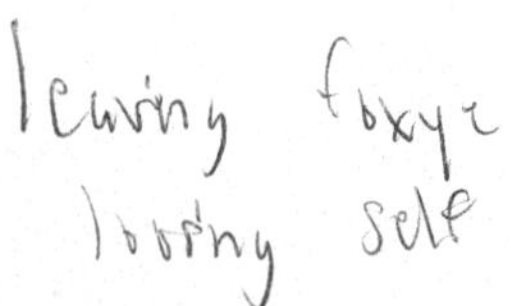

kennel—so her expression led you to understand—she was there incognito and of her own choice. Hazel, sitting at Edward's table, had the same look.

When the conversation was over, and Foxy had obediently curled herself to sleep, with one swift motion like a line of poetry, Hazel went down the hill. She felt courageous; going to the valley was braving civilization. She had Mrs. Marston's skirt-fastener—the golden butterfly, complicated by various hooks—to keep her petticoats up later on. She also had the little bag in which Edward was accustomed to take the Lord's Supper to a distant chapel. To her, mushrooms were as clean as the Lord's Supper, no less mysterious, equally incidental to human needs. In her eyes nothing could be more magical and holy than silken, pink-lined mushrooms placed for her in the meadows overnight by the fairies, or by someone greater and more powerful called God.

As she went down the mountain it seemed that the whole country was snowed over. Mist—soft, woolly, and intensely white—lay across the far plain in drifts, filled the valley, and stood about the distant hills almost to their summits. The tops of Hunter's Spinney, God's Little Mountain, and the hill behind Undern stood out, darkly green. The long rose-briars, set with pale coral buds, looked elvish against the wintry scene.

As Hazel descended the mist rose like a wall about her, shutting her off from Undern and the Mountain. She felt like a child out of school, free of everyone, her own for the pearly hours of morning. When she came to the meadows she gathered up her skirts well above her knees, took off her shoes and stockings, and pinned her sleeves to the shoulders. She ran like a tightly swathed nymph, small and slender, with her slim legs and arms shining in the fresh cold dew. She looked for nests, and called "Thuckoo!" to the cuckoos, and found a young one, savagely egotistic, not ready for flight physically, but ready for untold things psychically.

"You'm proud-stomached, you be!" said Hazel. "You'd ought to be me, with an old sleepy lady drawing her mouth down whatever you do, and a young fellow——" She stopped. She could not tell even a bird about Reddin. She danced among the shut daisies, wild as a fairy, and when the sun rose her shadow mocked her with delicate foolery. In her hand, and in that of the shadow, bobbed the little black Lord's Supper bag.

She went on, regardless of direction. At last she found an old pasture where heavy farm-horses looked round at her over their polished flanks and a sad-eyed foal rose to greet her. There she found button mushrooms to her heart's content. Ancient hedges hung above the field and spoke to her in fragrant voices. The glory of the may was just giving place to the shell-tint of wild-roses. She reached up for some, and her hair fell down; she wisely put the remaining pins in the bag for the return journey. She was intensely happy, as a fish is when it plunges back into the water. For these things, and not the God-fearing comfort of the Mountain, nor the tarnished grandeur of Undern, were her life. She had so deep a kinship with the trees, so intuitive a sympathy with leaf and flower, that it seemed as if the blood in her veins was not slow-moving human blood, but volatile sap. She was of a race that will come in the far future, when we shall have outgrown our egoism—the brainless egoism of a little boy pulling off flies' wings. We shall attain philosophic detachment and emotional sympathy. We have even now far outgrown the age when a great genius like Shakespeare could be so clumsy in the interpretation of other than human life. We have left behind us the bloodshot centuries when killing was the only sport, and we have come to the slightly more reputable times when lovers of killing are conscious that a distinct effort is necessary in order to keep up "the good old English sports." Better things are in store for us. Even now, although the most expensively bound and the most plentiful books in the stationers' shops are those about killing and its thousand ramifications, nobody reads them. They are bought at Christmas for necessitous relations and little boys.

Hazel, in the fields and woods, enjoyed it all so much that she walked in a mystical exaltation.

Reddin in the fields and woods enjoyed himself only. For he took his own atmosphere with him wherever he went, and before his footsteps weakness fled and beauty folded.

The sky blossomed in parterres of roses, frailer and brighter than the rose of the briar, and melted beneath them into lagoons greener and paler than the veins of a young beech-leaf. The fairy hedges were so high, so flushed with beauty, the green airy waters ran so far back into mystery, that it seemed as if at any moment God might walk there as in a garden, delicate as a moth. Down by the stream Hazel found tall water-plantains, triune of cup, standing each above the ooze like candelabras, and small rough-leaved forget-me-nots eyeing their liquid reflections with complaisance. She watched the birds bathe—bullfinches, smooth-coated and well-found; slim willow-wrens; thrushes, ermine-breasted; lusty blackbirds with beaks of crude yellow. They made neat little tracks over the soft mud, drank, bathed, preened, and made other neat little tracks. Then they "took off," as Hazel put it, from the top of the bank, and flew low across the painted meadow or high into the enamelled tree, and piped and fluted till the air was full of silver.

Hazel stood as Eve might have stood, hands clasped, eyes full of ecstasy, utterly self-forgetful, enchanted with these living toys.

"Eh, yon's a proper bird!" she exclaimed, as a big silken cuckoo alighted on the mud with a gobble, drank with dignity, and took its vacillating flight to a far ash-tree. "Foxy ought to see that," she added.

Silver-crested peewits circled and cried with their melancholy cadences, and a tawny pheasant led out her young. Now that the dew was gone, and cobwebs no longer canopied the field with silver, it was blue with germander speedwell—each flower painted with deepening colour, eyed with startling white, and carrying on slender stamens the round white pollen-balls—worlds of silent, lovely activity. Every flower-spike had its family of buds, blue jewels splashed with white, each close-folded on her mystery. To see the whole field not only bright with them, but brimming over, was like watching ten thousand saints rapt in ecstasy, ten thousand children dancing. Hazel knew nothing of saints. She had no words for the wonder in which she walked. But she felt it, she enjoyed it with a passion no words could express.

Mrs. Marston had said several times, "I'm almost afraid Hazel is a great one for wasting her time."

But what is waste of time? Eating and sleeping; hearing grave, sedulous men read out of grave, sedulous books what we have heard a hundred times; besieging God (whom we end by imagining as a great ear) for material benefits; amassing property—these, the world says, are not waste of time. But to drink at the stoup of beauty; to lift the leafy coverlet of earth and seek the cradled God (since here, if anywhere, He dwells), this in the world's eye is waste of time. Oh, filthy, heavy-handed, blear-eyed world, when will you wash and be clean?

Hazel came to a place where the white water crossed the road in a glittering shallow ford. Here she stayed, leaning on the wooden bridge, hearing small pebbles grinding on one another; seeing jewel-flashes of ruby, sapphire, and emerald struck from them by the low sunlight; smelling the scent that is better than all (except the scent of air on a barren mountain, or of snow)—the scent of running water. She watched the grey wagtails, neat and prim in person, but wild in bearing, racing across the wet gravel like intoxicated Sunday-school teachers. Then, in a huge silver willow that brooded, dove-like, over the ford, a blackcap began to sing. The trills and gushes of perfect melody, the golden repetitions, the heart-lifting ascents and wistful falls drooping softly as a flower, seemed wonderful to her as an angel's song. She and the bird, sheltered under the grey-silver feathers of the tree, lived their great moments of creation and receptivity until suddenly there was a sharp noise of hoofs, the song snapped, the willow was untenanted, and Reddin's horse splashed through the ford.

"Oh!" cried Hazel, "what for did you break the song? A sacred bird, it was. And now it's fled!"

He had been riding round the remnant of his estate, a bit of hill sheep-walk that faced the Mountain and overlooked the valley. He had seen Hazel wander down the road, white-limbed and veiled in tawny hair. He thought there must be something wrong with his sight. Bare legs! Bare arms! Hair all loose, and no hat! As a squire-farmer, he was very much shocked. As a man, he spurred downhill at the risk of a bad fall.

Hazel, unlike the women of civilization, who are pursued by looking-glasses, was apt to forget herself and her appearance. She had done so now. But something in Reddin's face recalled her. She hastily took the butterfly out of her skirt and put on her shoes and stockings.

"What song?" asked Reddin.

"A bird in the tree. What for did you fritten it?"

Reddin was indignant. Seeing Hazel wandering thus so near his own domain, he thought she had come in the hope of seeing him. He also thought that the strangeness of her dress was an effort to attract him. To the pure all things are pure.

"But you surely wanted to see me? Wasn't that why you came?" he asked.

"No, it wasna. I came to pick the little musherooms as come wi' the warm rain, for there's none like spring musherooms. And I came to see the flowers, and hearken at the birds, and look the nesses."

"You could have lots of flowers and birds at Undern."

"There's plenty at the Mountain."

"Then why did you come here?"

"To be by my lonesome."

"Snub for me!" He smiled. He liked opposition.

"But look here, Hazel," he reasoned. "If you'd come to Undern, I'd make you enjoy life."

"But I dunna want to. I be Ed'ard's missus."

"Be *my* missus!" At the phrase his weather-coarsened face grew redder. The phrase intoxicated him.

He slipped off his horse and kissed her.

"I dunna want to be anybody's missus!" she cried vexedly. "Not yourn nor Ed'ard's neither! But I *be* Ed'ard's, and so I mun stay." She turned away.

"Good-morning to you," she said in her old-fashioned little way. She trudged up the road. Reddin watched her, a forlorn, slight figure armed with the black bag, weary with the sense of reaction. Reddin was angry and depressed. The master of Undern had been for the second time refused.

"H'm," he said, considering her departing figure, "it won't be asking next time, my lady! And it won't be for you to refuse."

He turned home, accompanied by that most depressing companion—the sense of his own meanness. He was unable to help knowing that the exercise of force against weakness is the most cur-like thing on earth.

CHAPTER XXII

HAZEL was picking wimberry-flowers from their stalks. She sucked out the drop of honey from each flower like a bee. The blossoms were like small, rose-coloured tulips upside down, very magical and clear of colour. The sky also was like a pink tulip veined and streaked with purple and saffron. In its depth, like the honey in the flowers, it held the low, golden sun. Evening stood tiptoe upon the windy hill-top.

Hazel had eaten quite a quantity of honey, and had made an appreciable difference in the wimberry yield of half an acre, for she sipped hastily like a honey-fly. She was one of those that are full of impatience, and haste through the sunny hours of day, clamorous for joy, since the night cometh. Some prescience was with her. She snatched what her eyes desired, and wept with disappointment. For it is the calm natures, wrapt in timeless quiet, taking what comes and asking nothing, that really enjoy. Hazel ate the fairy tulips as a pixie might, sharp-toothed, often consuming them whole. So she partook of her sacrament in both kinds, and she partook of it alone, taking her wafers and her honeyed wine from hands she never saw, in a presence she could not gauge. She did not even wonder whether it meant ill or well by her. She was barely conscious of it. When she found an unusually large globe of honey in a flower, she sang. Her song was as inconsequent as those of the woodlarks, who, with their hurried ripple of notes and their vacillating flights, were as eager and as soon discouraged as she was herself. Her voice rang out over the listening pastures, and the sheep looked up in a contemplative, ancient way like old ladies at a concert with their knitting. Hazel had fastened two foxgloves round her head in a wreath, and as she went their deep and darkly spotted bells shook above her, and she walked, like a jester in a grieving world, crowned with madness.

Suddenly a shout rang across the hill and silenced her and the woodlarks. She saw against the full-blown flower of the west—black on scarlet—Reddin on his tall black horse, galloping towards her. Clouds were coming up for night. They raced with him. From one great round rift the light poured on Hazel as it does from a burning glass held over a leaf. It burned steadily on her, and then was moved, as if by an invisible hand. Reddin came on, and the thunder of his horse's hoofs was in her ears. Hurtling thus over the pastures, breaking the year-long hush, he was the embodiment of the destructive principle, of cruelty, of the greater part of human society—voracious and carnivorous—with its curious callousness towards the nerves of the rest of the world.

"I a'most thought it was the death-pack," said Hazel, speaking first, as the more nervous always does.

She stood uncomfortably looking up at him as a rabbit looks, surprised half-way out of its burrow.

"Where be going?" she asked at last.

"Looking for you."

Hazel could not enjoy the flattery of this; she was so perturbed by his nearness.

"Where's your lord and master?"

"Ed'ard inna my master. None is." A hot indignant flush surged over her.

"Yes," said he; "I am."

"That you're not, and never will be."

Reddin said nothing. He sat looking down at her. In the large landscape his figure was carved on the sky, slenderly minute; yet it was instinct with forces enough to uproot a thousand trees and became, by virtue of these, the centre of the picture. He looked his best on horseback, where his hardness and roughness appeared as necessary qualities, and his too great share of virility was used up in courage and will-power.

Hazel gazed defiantly back; but at last her eyelids flickered, and she turned away.

"I am," Reddin repeated softly.

He was as sure of her as he was of the rabbits and hares he caught in spring-traps when hunger drove them counter to instinct. A power was on Hazel now, driving her against the one instinct of her life hitherto—the wild creature's instinct for flight and self-preservation. She said nothing.

Reddin was filled with a tumultuous triumph that Sally Haggard had never roused.

"I am," he said again, and laughed as if he enjoyed the repetition. "Come here!"

Hazel came slowly, looked up, and burst into tears.

"Hello! Tears already?" he said, concerned. "Keep 'em till there's something to cry for."

He dismounted and slipped the rein over his arm.

"What's up, Hazel Woodus?" He put one arm round her.

The sheep looked more ancient than ever, less like old ladies at a concert than old ladies looking over their Prayer-Books at a blasphemer.

"My name inna Woodus. You'd ought to call me Mrs. Marston."

For answer, he kissed her so that she cried out.

"That's to show if I'll call you Mrs. Marston!"

"I'd liefer be."

"What?"

"Ed'ard's missus than yourn."

He ground a foxglove underfoot.

"And there's Foxy in a grand new kennel, and me in a seat in chapel, and a bush o' laylac give me for myself, and a garden and a root o' virgin's pride."

"I shall have that!" said Reddin, and stopped, having blundered into symbolism, and not knowing where he was. Hazel was silent also, playing with a foxglove flower.

"What are you up to?" he asked.

She was glad of something to talk about.

"Look! when you get 'un agen the light you can see two little green things standing inside like people in a tent. They think they're safe shut in!" She bent down and called: "I see yer! I see yer!" laughing.

Reddin was bent on getting back to more satisfactory topics.

"They're just two, like us," he said.

"Ah! We're like under a tent," she answered, looking at the arching sky.

"Only there's nobody looking at us."

"How d'you know?" she whispered, looking up

gravely. "I'm thinking there *be* somebody somewhere out t'other side of that there blue, and looking through like us through this here flower. And if so be he likes he can tear it right open, and get at us."

Reddin looked round almost apprehensively. Then, as the best way of putting a stop to superstition, he caught her to him and kissed her again.

"That's what tents are for, and what you're for," he said. But he felt a chill in the place, and Hazel had frightened herself so much that she could not be lured from her aloofness.

"I mun go home along," she said; "the sun's undering."

"Will you come to Hunter's Spinney on Sunday?"

"Why ever?"

"Because I say so."

"But why so far, whatever?" she asked amazedly.

"Because I want you to."

"But I mun go to chapel along of Ed'ard, and sing ymns proper wi' the folks—and me singing higher nor any of them can go, for all I'm new to it—and the old lady"—her face grew mischievous—"the old lady in a shiny silk gownd as creaks and creaks when she stirs about!"

Reddin lost patience.

"You're to start as soon as they're in church, d'you see?"

"Maybe I 'unna come."

"You've got to. Look here, Hazel, you like having a lover, don't you?"

"I dunno."

"Hazel! I'll bring you a present."

"I dunna want it. What is it?" she said in a breath.

"Something nice. Then you promise to come?"

There was a long silence.

Her eyes seemed to her to be caught by his. She could not look away. And his eyes said strange, terrific things to her, things for which she had no words, wakening vitality, flattering, commanding, stirring a new curiosity, robbing her of breath.

They stood thus for a long time, as much alone under the flaming sky as a man and woman of the stone age.

When at last he released her eyes, he swung silently into the saddle and was gone.

When he got home, Vessons came shambling to the door.

"Supper and a tot of whisky!" ordered his master.

Vessons took no notice, but eyed the horse.

"You dunna mind how much work you give me at the day's end, do you?" he inquired conversationally.

"Get on with your jobs!"

"Now, what wench'll cry for this night's work?" mused Vessons.

CHAPTER XXIII

HAZEL ran home through the dew, swift as a hare to her form. Mrs. Marston, communing with a small wood fire and a large Bible, looked over her spectacles as Hazel came in, and said:

"Draw your stocking foot along the boards, my dear. Yes, I thought so, damp."

Hazel changed her stockings by the fire, and felt very cared for and very grand. A fire to change by in the parlour! And several pairs of new stockings! She had never had more than one pair before, and those with "ladders" in them. "These here be proper stockings," she said complacently—"these with holes in 'em as Edward bought me. Holes as *ought* to be there, I mean. They show my legs mother-naked, and they look right nice."

"Don't say that word, dear."

"What 'un?"

Mrs. Marston was silent for a moment. "The sixth from the end," she said; "it's not nice for a minister's wife."

"What mun I say?"

Mrs. Marston was in a difficulty. "Well," she said at last, "Edward should not have given you any cause to say anything."

Hazel blazed into loyalty.

"I'm sure I'm very much obleeged to Ed'ard," she

said, "and I like 'em better for showing my legs. Oh, here *be* Ed'ard! Ed'ard, these be proper stockings, inna they?"

Edward glanced at them, and said indifferently that they were. As he did so, a line that had lately appeared on his forehead became very apparent.

In her room upstairs, papered with buttercups and daisies by Edward himself, and scented by a bunch of roses he had given her, Hazel thought about Hunter's Spinney. Edward would not like her to go, and Edward had been kind—kinder than anyone had ever been. He had extended his kindness to Foxy also. "I'm sure Foxy's much obleeged," she thought. No, she could never tell Edward about Hunter's Spinney. If he questioned her, she knew that she would lie. He would certainly not be pleased. He might be very angry. Mrs. Marston would not like it at all; she would talk about a minister's wife. Reddin had said she must go, but she must not. She smelt the roses.

"No," she said, "I must ne'er go to the Hunter's Spinney—not till doom breaks!" She said her prayers under the shelter of that resolve, with a supplementary one written out very neatly in gold ink by Edward, who wrote, as his mother said, "a parchment script."

But when she lay down she could not keep her mind clear of Reddin; during each meeting with him she had been more perturbed. His personality dragged at hers. Already he was stronger than her fugitive impulses, her wilding reserve. He was like a hand tearing open a triplet of sorrel leaves folded for rain, so strong in their impulse for self-protection that they could only be conquered by destruction. She was afraid of him, yet days without him were saltless food. There was a ruthlessness about him—the male instinct unaccompanied by humility, the patrician instinct unaccompanied by sympathy, the sportsman's instinct unaccompanied by pity. Whatever he began he would finish. What had he now begun?

Innocence and instinct, ignorance and curiosity, struggled in her mind. The attitude of civilization and the Churches towards sex is not one to help a girl in such an hour. For while approving of, and even insisting on, children, they treat with a secrecy that implies disapproval the necessary physical factors that result in children. Tacitly, though not openly, they consider sex disgraceful. Though Hazel had come in contact with the facts of life less than most cottage girls, she was not completely ignorant. But the least ignorant woman knows nothing at all about sex until she has experienced it. So Hazel was dependent on intuition. Intuition told her that if the peaceful life at the parsonage was to continue, she must keep away from Hunter's Spinney. But she could not keep away. It was as if someone had spun invisible threads between her and Reddin, and was slowly tightening them.

Long after Edward had locked the house up and shut his door, after the ticking of the clock had ceased to be incidental and become portentous, Hazel lay and tried to think. But she only heard two voices in endless contradiction, "I munna go. I mun go." At last she got up and fetched the book of charms, written in a childish, illiterate hand, and nearly black with use.

"I'll try a midsummer 'un, for it's Midsummer Eve come Saturday," she thought.

She searched the book and found a page headed

"The Flowering of the Brake." That one she decided to work on Saturday.

"And to-morrow the Harpers, and Friday the Holy Sign," she said. "And if they say go, I'll go, and if they say stay, I'll stay."

She fell asleep, feeling that she had shifted the responsibility.

Her mother had said that before any undertaking you should work the Harper charm. The book directed that, on a lonely hill, you must listen with your eyes shut for the fairy playing. If the undertaking was good you would hear, coming from very far away, a sound of harping. Silver folk with golden harps, so the book said, keep on a purple hill somewhere beyond seeing, and there they play the moon up and the moon down. And at sun-up they cry for those that have not heard them. If you hear them ever so faintly, you can go on to the end of your undertaking, and there'll be no tears in it. But you must never tire of waiting, nor tell anyone what you have heard.

The next night Hazel stole out in the heavy dew to a hummock of the mountain, and sat down there to wait for moon-rise. But when the moon came—the thinnest of silver half-hoops, very faint in the reflected rose from the west—there was no sound except the song of the woodlarks. They persevered, although the sun was gone. Soon they, too, were hushed, and Hazel was folded in silence.

She waited a long while. The chapel and the minister's house sank into the deepening night as into water. The longer the omen tarried, the more she wanted it to come. Then fatalism reasserted itself, and she relapsed into her usual state of mind.

"I dunna care," she said. "It inna no use to tarry.

They unna play. I'll bide along of Ed'ard at chapel on Sunday, and sing higher than last time." She turned home.

At that moment a note of music, strayed, it seemed, out of space, wandered across the hill-top. Then a few more, thin and silvery, ran down the silence like a spray of water. The air was lost in distance, but the notes were undoubtedly those of a harp.

"It's them!" whispered Hazel. "I'm bound to go." Then she remembered her mother's injunctions, and took to her heels. At home in her quiet room, she thought of the strange shining folk playing on their purple mountain.

She never knew that the harper was her father returning by devious roads from one of the many festivals at which he played in summer-time, and having frequent rests by the way, owing to the good ale he had drunk. Her bright galaxy of faery was only a drunken man. Her fate had been settled by a passing whim of his, but so had been her coming into the world.

When she went in, Edward was sitting up for her, anxious, but trying to reason himself into calm, as Hazel was given to roaming.

"Where have you been?" he asked rather sternly, for he had suffered many things from anxiety and from his mother.

"Only up to 'erts the pool, Ed'ard."

"Don't go there again."

"Canna I go walking on the green hill by my lonesome?"

"No. You can go in the woods. They're safe enough.

"Foxy's a bad dog!" came Mrs. Marston's voice

from upstairs. "She bit the rope and took the mutton!"

"Eh, I'm main sorry!" cried Hazel. "But she inna a bad dog, Mrs. Marston; she's a good fox."

"According to natural history she may be, but in my sight she's a bad dog." She shut her door with an air of finality.

"The old lady canna'd abear Foxy," said Hazel. "Nobody likes Foxy."

She was stubbornly determined that the world bore her a grudge because she loved Foxy. Perhaps she had discovered that the world has a sharp sword for the vulnerable, and that love is easily wounded.

"Don't call mother the old lady, dear."

"Well, she is. And she says animals has got no souls. She'm only got a little small 'un herself."

"Hazel!"

"Well, it's God's truth."

"Why?"

"If she'd got a nice tidy bit herself, she'd know Foxy'd got one, too. Now I've got a shimmy with lace on, I know lots of other girls sure to have 'em. Afore I couldna have believed it."

Edward could find no reply to this.

"Are you happy here, Hazel?" he asked.

"Ah! I be."

"You don't miss——"

"Father? Not likely!" She looked up with her clear golden eyes. "You'm mother and father both!"

"Only that, dear?"

"Brother."

"You've forgotten one, Hazel—husband." His eyes were wistful. "And lover, perhaps, some day," he added. "Good-night, dear."

She lifted a childish mouth, grateful and ready to be affectionate. Too ready, he thought. He looked so eagerly for shyness—a flicker of the eyelids, a mounting flush. He was no fool, nor was he in the least ascetic. In his dreamy life before Hazel came, he had thought of a sane and manly and normal future when he thought of it at all. Now he found that the reality was not like his dreams. The saneness and manliness were still needed, but the joy had gone, or at least was veiled.

"It will all come right," he told himself, and waited. His face took an expression of suspense. He was like one that watches, rapt, for the sunrise. Only the sun stayed beneath the horizon. He called Hazel in his mind by the country name for wood-sorrel—the Sleeping Beauty. He left her to sleep as long as she would. He kept a hand on himself, and never tried to waken her by easier ways than through the spirit—through the senses, or vanity, or by taking advantage of his superior intellect.

He would win her fairly or not at all. So, though to glance into her empty white room set him trembling, though the touch of her hand set his pulses going, he never schemed to touch her, never made pretexts to go into her room. A stormed citadel was in his eyes a thing spoilt in the capturing. So he waited for the gates to open. The irony was that if he had listened to sex—who spoke to him with her deep beguiling voice, like a purple-robed Sibyl—if he had for once parted company with his exacting spiritual self, Hazel would have loved him. We cannot love that in which is nothing of ourselves, and there was no white fire of spiritual exaltation in Hazel. The nearest she approached to that was in her adoration of sensuous beauty, a green flame of passionless devotion to loveliness as seen in inanimate things. But that there should be anything between a man and a woman except an obvious affection, a fraternal sort of thing, or an uncomfortable excitement such as she felt with Reddin, was quite beyond her ideas. She did not know that there could be a fervour of mind for mind, a clasp more frantic than that of the arms, a continuous psychic state more passionate than the great moments of physical passion. If Edward had told her, she could not at this time have understood it. She would have gazed up at him trustingly out of her autumn-tinted eyes; she would have embodied all the spiritual glories of which he dreamed; and she would have understood nothing. Once he tried to share with her a passage in Drummond's "Natural Law in the Spiritual World." He was reading it with young delight a good many years behind the times, for books had usually grown very out of date before they percolated through the country libraries to him. He had read it in his pleasant, half-educated voice, dramatically and tenderly; his cheeks had flushed; he had challenged her criticism with keen, attentive eyes. She had said: "I wonder if that's our Foxy barking, or a strange 'un?"

Hazel looked long from her window that night.

"Oh, I canna go! I canna go! Ed'ard setting store by me and all!" she said. "Maybe the other signs wunna come."

On Friday she waited until after the others had gone to bed, and then slipped out. She went into the silent woods as the moths went, purposeless, yet working out destiny. It was a very warm wet evening, and glow-worms shone incandescently in the long grass, each with her round, wonderful, greenish lamp at its brightest. They beckoned on to fairy, though they glowed in perfect stillness. They spoke of marvellous things, though they lit the night in silence. It was a very grave, a very remote personality, surely, that lit those lamps. A more intent eye, a more careful hand were needed, one thinks, to make these than to make the planets, and a mind more vast, big enough to include minuteness. But Hazel felt no awe of them; she was too bounded and earthly a creature to be afraid of mystery. It is the spirit that maketh afraid. She was sure that they were not the Holy Sign, for she had seen them often. The Holy Sign was quite different.

"If I be to go to Hunter's Spinney," she said, looking up through the black branches and twigs that were like great fowling-nets spread over her—"if I be to go, show me the Holy Sign."

She wandered down the narrow paths. It was very dark and warm and damp. Once the moon came out, and she saw a long pool startle the woods with its brightness, like lightning on steel. The yellow irises that stood about its marges held a pale radiance, and were like butterflies enchanted into immobility. Huge toadstools, vividly tawny as leopards, clumps of lady-fern not yet at their full height and thick with curled fronds, stood proudly on their mossy lawns.

But none of these were the Sign.

"If it dunna come soon I'll go home-along," she said.

And then, round the next bend, she saw it. At first she thought it was an angel just beginning to appear. The phantom was of a man's height, and it shone as the glow-worms did, only its light would have been enough to read by. It had a strange effect, standing there bathed in its own light in the black unbroken silence. It had a look of life—subdued, but passionate—as a spirit might have when it had just reintegrated its body out of the air. Hazel was terrified. As a rule, she was never afraid in the woods and fields, but only in the haunts of men. But from this, after one paralyzed moment, she fled in panic. So she never knew that her second sign was only a rotten tree, shining with the phosphorescence of corruption.

Next morning she asked Edward:

"Could folk see angels now?"

"Yes, if it was God's will."

"If one came, would it be a sign?"

"I suppose so, dear."

"What'd you do, Ed'ard, if you were bound to find out summat?"

Edward was thinking out heads of a discourse on the power of prayer.

"I should pray, dear," he said absently.

"Who'd answer?"

"God."

"Would you hear 'Im?"

"No, dear; of course not."

He wanted quiet to finish his sermon, but he tried to be patient.

"You would know by intuition," he said, "little signs."

"The Holy Sign!" murmured Hazel. "I saw it yesternight—a burning angel."

"I'm afraid you are too superstitious," Edward said, and returned to his remarks on ejaculatory prayer.

Some people would have found it hard to decide which was the more superstitious, the more pathetic.

CHAPTER XXIV

IN the early morning of Midsummer Eve Hazel wandered up the hill-slopes. There the sheep golden and gospelline in the early light, fed on wet lawns pale and unsubstantial as gauze. She did not, as the more self-conscious creatures of civilization would have done, envy their peace in so many words. But she did say wistfully to a particularly ample and contented one, "You'm pretty comfortable, binna you?" When she went in to breakfast she thought the same of Mrs. Marston.

Afterwards they picked black currants, Mrs. Marston seated on a camp-stool and wearing her large mushroom hat, which always tilted slightly and made her look rakish. Whenever a blackbird dashed out of the grove of half-ripe red currants, scolding with dæmonic vitality, she would look up and say, "Naughty bird." She picked with deliberation, and placed the currants in the basket with an air of benediction. The day was hot and splendid, a day to make the leaves limp and crack the flower-beds. But it was cool in the shadow of the mountain-ash that grew near the currants, and a breeze laden with wild thyme and moss fragrance played about the garden like an invisible child.

At eleven Martha appeared with cake and milk, and Edward returned from old Solomon's bedside. Then they went on picking, while Edward read them snatches of "Natural Law." Hazel was soothed by the reading, to the sense of which she paid no heed. It mingled with the drone of the hot bees falling in and out of the big red peonies, the far-off sound of grass-cutting, the grave measured soliloquy of a blackbird hidden in the flame-flowered chestnut. Hazel felt that she would like to go on picking currants for ever, growing more and more like Mrs. Marston every day, and at last becoming (possibly through sheer benignity) a grandmother. There seemed no place in her life for Reddin, no time for the Hunter's Spinney. She thought, "I wunna go. I'll stay along of Ed'ard, and no harm'll come to me." But a peremptory voice said that she must go, and once more her soul became the passive battleground of strange emotions of which she had never even dreamed. While they fought there like creatures in the dark, Hazel, sitting in the aromatic shadow of the currants, fell fast asleep; and as Mrs. Marston could never bring herself to wake anyone, she slept until Martha rang the dinner-bell. So the peaceful, golden day wore on to green evening. It was a day that Hazel always remembered.

When the shadows grew long and dew fell, and the daisies on the graves filled the house with their faint, innocent fragrance, and closed their pink-lined petals for the night, Hazel felt very miserable. This very night she was going to work the last charm—the charm of the bracken flower—and whoso she dreamed of with that flower beneath her pillow must be her lover. She felt traitorous to Edward in doing this. She and Edward were handfasted. How, then, could she have any lover but Edward? Why should she work the charm? She puzzled over this during prayers, but no answer came to her questioning. Life is a taciturn mother, and teaches not so much by instruction as by blows. Edward was reading the twenty-third Psalm, which always affected his mother to tears, and in reading which his voice was very tender, ". . . And lead thee forth beside the waters of comfort."

The room was full of a deep exaltation, a passion of trustfulness.

"I went along by the water," Hazel thought, "and watched the piefinches and the canbottlins flying about. And I thought it was the waters of comfort. Only Mr. Reddin came and frit the birds and made the water muddy." She did not feel as sure as the others did of the waters of comfort.

"So beautiful, dear," murmured Mrs. Marston, "so like your poor dear father."

Edward's good-night to Hazel was more curt than usual. She was looking so mysteriously lovely. Her stress of mind had given a touch of spirituality to her face, and there is nothing that stirs passion as spirituality does. She had on a print frock of a neat design reminiscent of old-fashioned china, and she had pinned a posy of daisies on her shoulder.

For one second, as she held up her cheek to be kissed, standing on the threshold of her moonlit room, Edward hesitated. Then he abruptly turned and shut his door. His hour had struck. His hour had passed.

Hazel stood in the window reading the charm.

"On Midsummer Eve, when it wants a little of midnight, spread your smock where the bracken grows. For this is the night of the flowering of the brake, that beareth a blue flower on the stroke of midnight. But it is withered afore morning. Come you again about the time of the first bird-call. If ought is in the smock, take it; it is the dust of the flower. Sleep above it, and he you dream of is your lover. This is a sure charm, and cannot be broke."

She took a clean chemise from the drawer, and when the landing clock struck the half hour she slipped out on to the hillside and laid it under a clump of bracken. As she stooped to set it smooth and straight, the moon swam out of cloud and flung her shadow, black and gigantic, up the hillside. Frightened, she ran home, raked the fire together, and made herself a cup of tea to keep her awake.

Sipping it in the dim parlour, where familiar things looked eerie, she thought of Reddin and his strange doings since her wedding.

"Eh, but it ud anger Ed'ard sore if he came to know," she thought. "What for does Mr. Reddin come, when he can see I dunna want him?"

A slow flush crept over neck and temples as she half guessed the answer.

She waited in the dove-grey hour that precedes dawn—an hour pregnant with the future. It is full of hope; for what great deed may not be done, what ethereal idea caged in music or poetry or colour, what rare emotion struck out of pain in the coming day? It is full of grief; for how many beautiful things will be trampled, great dreams torn, sensitive spirits crucified in the time between dusk and dusk? For the death-pack hunts at all hours, light and dark; it is no pale phantom of dreams. It is made not of spirit hounds with fiery eyes—a ghastly "Melody," a grisly "Music"—but of our fellows, all that have strength without pity. Sometimes our kith and kin, our nearest intimates, are in the first flight; give a view halloo as we slip hopefully under a covert; are in at the death.

It is not the killing that gives horror to the death-pack so much as the lack of the impulse not to kill. One flicker of merciful intention amid relentless action would redeem it. For the world is founded and built up on death, and the reality of death is neither to be questioned nor feared. Death is a dark dream, but it is not a nightmare. It is mankind's lack of pity, mankind's fatal propensity for torture, that is the nightmare. When a man or woman, confronted by helpless terror, is without the impulse to save, the world becomes hell. It was this, dimly but passionately felt, that made Hazel shrink from Reddin. For unless Reddin was without this impulse to save, and had the mind of a fiend without pity, how could he in the mere pursuit of pleasure inflict wholly unnecessary torture, as in fox-hunting?

She watched Venus shrink from a silver pool to a silver point. She was full of trouble and unrest. Would she dream of Reddin? Would she go to sleep at all? Mrs. Marston's armchair loomed in the gathering light, and she felt guilty again.

The east quickened, as if someone had turned up a light there. She opened the window, and in rushed the inexpressible sweetness of dawn. The bush of syringa by the kitchen window swept in its whole fragrance, heady and sensuous. She took long breaths of it, and thought of Reddin's green dress, of the queer look in his eyes when he stared long at her. A curious passivity quite foreign to her came over her now at the thought of Reddin. What would he look like, what would he say, would he hold her roughly, if she went to Hunter's Spinney? An unwilling elation possessed her as she thought of it. It did not occur to her to wonder why Edward did not kiss her as Reddin did. She took him as much for granted as a child takes its parents.

Suddenly the first bird called silverly, startling the dusk. It was a woodlark, and its song seemed even more vacillating than usual in the vast hush. At the first note all Hazel's thoughts of Reddin fled. It seemed that clarity, freshness, and music were bound up in her mind with Edward. She thought only of him as she ran up the hill over the minute starry carpet of mountain bedstraw.

"Maybe there'll be no flower, and then the charm's broke," she thought hopefully. "If the charm's broke, I canna dream, and I shanna go."

But when she came to the white garment lying wet and pale in the half-light she drew a sharp breath. There in the centre lay one minute blue petal. Its very smallness proved to her its magic. It was a fairy flower. She took it up reverently and went home, solemn as a child in church. When, with the blue petal under her pillow, she lay down, she fell asleep in a moment. She dreamt of Reddin, for he had more control over her thoughts than Edward, who appealed to her emotions, while Reddin stirred her instincts. sex Waking at Martha's knock, she said to herself, with mingled heart-sickness and elation:

"The signs say go. I mun go. Foxy wants me to go." -> personality

She would not have believed that her third sign was no faery flower, but only a petal of blue milkwort—little sister of the bracken—loosened by her own nervous hands the night before.

CHAPTER XXV

ON Sunday evening, as usual, the little bell began to sound plaintively in the soft air that was like a pale wild-rose. Mrs. Marston had betaken herself out of her own door into that of the chapel with a good many sighs at the disturbance of her nap, and with injunctions to Martha to put a bit of fire in the parlour. Edward had gone with his sermon to the back of the house where the tombstones were fewer and it was easier to walk while he read. Hazel ran up to her room and put on her white dress, which was considered by Mrs. Marston "too flighty" for chapel. She leant out of her window and looked away up the purple hill. Then she gathered a bunch of the tea-roses that encircled it. They were deep cream flushed with rose. She pinned them into her breast, and they matched her flushed face. She was becoming almost dainty in her ways; this enormously increased her attraction for both men. She put on her broad white wedding-hat, and slipped downstairs and out by the kitchen door while Martha was in the parlour. She shut the door behind her like a vanished life. She felt, she did not know why, a sense of excitement, of some great happening, something impending, in her appointment with Reddin.

She met no one as she ran down the Batch, for the chapel-goers were all inside. The hedges were full of white "archangel" and purple vetch. When she came to the beginning of Hunter's Spinney she felt frightened; the woods were so far-reaching, so deep with shadow; the trees made so sad a rumour, and swayed with such forlorn abandon. In the dusky places the hyacinths, broken but not yet faded, made a purple carpet solemn as a pall. Woodruff shone whitely by the path and besieged her with scent. Early wild-roses stood here and there, weighed down with their own beauty, set with rare carmine and tints of shells and snow, too frail to face the thunderstorm that even now advanced with unhurrying pomp far away beyond the horizon. She hurried along, leaving the beaten track, creeping under the broad skirts of the beeches and over the white prostrate larch-boles where the resin ran slowly like the dark blood of creatures beautiful, defeated, dying. She began to climb, holding to the grey, shining boles of mountain ash-trees. The bracken, waist-high at first, was like small hoops at the top of the wood, where the tiny golden tormentil made a carpet and the yellow pimpernel was closing her eager eyes.

Hazel came out on the bare hill-top where gnarled may-trees, dropping spent blossom, were pink-tinted as if the colours of the sunsets they had known had run into their whiteness. Hazel sat down on the hill-top and saw the sleek farmhorses far below feeding with their shadows, swifts flying with their shadows, the hills eyeing theirs stilly. So with all life the shadow lingers—incurious, mute, yet in the end victorious, whelming all. As Hazel sat there her own shadow lay darkly behind her, growing larger than herself as the sun slipped lower.

Bleatings and lowings, the evening caw of the rooks

ascended to her; a horse neighed, aggressively male. From some distance came the loud, crude voice of a man singing. He sang, not in worship, not for the sake of memory or melody or love, but for the same reason that people sing so loudly in church—in the urgent need of expending superabundant vitality. His voice rolled out under the purple sky as if he were the first man, but half emerged from brutishness, pursuing his mate in a world all fief to him, a world that revealed her as she fled through the door of morning and the door of evening, rolling its vaporous curtains back as she went through. It was Reddin, come forth from his dark house, as his foraging ancestors had done, to take his will of the weaponless and ride down the will of others. He did not confess even to himself why he had come. His thoughts on sex were so prurient that, in common with many people, he considered any frankness about it most indecent. Sex was to him a thing that made the ears red. It is hard for them that have breeding-stables to enter the kingdom of heaven. Too often the grave, the majestic significance of the meeting of the sexes—holding as it does the fate of the golden pageantry of life, sacrificially spending as it does the present for the future—is nothing to them. They see it only as a fillip to appetite. So Sally Haggard usually spent most of the money earned by Reddin's stallion "The Pride of Undern."

He put the horse to a gallop as he came up Hunter's Spinney, to quench the voice that spoke within him saying things he would not hear, that spoke of love, and the tenderness and humility of love, and of how these did not detract from the splendour of manhood, the fine rage of passion, but rather glorified them.

Something in his feeling for Hazel answered that voice, and it worried him. By heredity and upbringing he had been taught to dislike and mistrust everything that savoured of emotion or ideas, to consider unmanly all that was of the spirit. Therefore he sang more loudly as he saw on the hill-top the flutter of Hazel's white dress, to quench the voice that steadfastly spoke of mutual love as the one reason for, the one consecration of passion in man and woman. The hoof-beats thudded like a full pulse.

Hazel got up. Suddenly she was afraid of the place, more afraid than she had ever been of the death-pack, which, this evening, she had forgotten.

But before she could move away Reddin shouted to her and came up the bridle-path. Hazel hesitated, swayed like the needle of a compass, and finally stood still.

"What'n you wanting me for, Mr. Reddin?"

"Don't you know?"

"If I knew, I shouldna ask."

"What do men generally want women for?"

"I'm not a woman. I dunna want to be. But what be it, anyway?"

He felt in his pocket and drew out a small parcel.

"There! Don't say the giving's all on your side," he remarked.

She opened the parcel. It contained two heavy old-fashioned gold bracelets. Each was set with a large ruby that stared unwinkingly from its setting of pale gold.

"Eh! they'm like drops of blood!" said Hazel. "Like when feyther starts a-killing the pig. He's a hard un, is feyther, hard as b'rytes. I'm much obleeged to you, Mr. Reddin, but I dunna want 'em. I canna'd abear the sight of blood."

"Little fool!" said Reddin. "They're worth pounds."

He caught her wrists and fastened one bracelet on each. She struggled, but could not get free or undo the clasps.

She began to cry, loudly and easily, as she always did. All her emotions were sudden, transparent, and violent. She also, since her upbringing had not been refined, began to swear.

"Damn your clumsy fists and your bloody bracelets!" she screamed. "Take 'em off, oot? I 'unna stay if you dunna!"

Reddin laughed, and in his eyes a glow began; nothing could have so suited his mood.

"You've got to wear 'em," he said, "to show you're mine."

"I binna!"

"Yes."

"I won't never be!"

"Yes, you will, now."

She raved at him like a little wild-cat, pulling at the bracelets like a kitten at its neck ribbon.

He laughed again, stilly.

He knew there was not a soul near, for the people from the farm at the foot of the spinney had all gone to church.

"Look here, Hazel," he said, not unkindly; "you've got to give in, see?"

"I see nought."

"You've got to come and live with me at Undern. You can wear those fine dresses."

"I'm a-cold," said Hazel; "the sun's undering; I'd best go home-along."

"Come on, then. Up you get. We'll be there in no time. You shall have some supper and——"

"What'n I want trapsing to Undern when I live at the Mountain?"

"You'll be asking to come soon," he said, with the crude wisdom of his kind. 'You like me better than that soft parson even now."

She shook her head.

"I'm a man, anyway."

She looked him over, and owned that he was. But she did not want him; she wanted freedom and time to find out how much she liked Edward.

"Well, good-neet to you," she said. "I'm off."

She ran downhill into the wood.

Reddin hitched the reins to a tree and followed. He caught her and flung her into the bracken, and suddenly it seemed to her that the whole world, the woods, herself, were all Reddin. He was her sky, her cloak. The tense silence of the place was heavy on her.

Away at God's Little Mountain Edward preached his sermon on the power of prayer—how we could plant a hedge of prayer round the beloved to keep them from all harm.

The clock at Alderslea down the valley struck eight in muffled tones. They were burnt into Hazel's brain. The plovers wheeled and cried sadly like the spirits of creatures too greatly outnumbered.

Edward was a dream; God's Little Mountain was an old tale—something forgotten, mist-begirt.

Twilight thickened, and birds began to shrill in the dew. Voices came up from the farm. They were back from church. Hazel felt crushed, bruised, robbed.

"Now, up you get, Hazel!" said Reddin, who wanted his supper badly, and no longer wanted Hazel. "Up you get and tidy yourself, and then home." He felt rather sorry for her.

She made no comment, no demur. Instinctively she

felt that she belonged to Reddin now, though spiritually she was still Edward's. She looked at Reddin, passive, doubtful; the past evening had become unreal to her.

So they regarded one another mistrustfully, like two creatures taken in a snare. They both felt as if they had been trapped by something vast and intangible. Reddin was dazed. For the first time in his life, he had felt passion instead of mere lust. The same ideas that had striven within him on his way here uplifted their voices again.

Staring dully at Hazen, he felt a smarting at the back of his eyes and a choking in his throat.

"What ails you, catching your breath?" she asked. He could not speak.

"You've got tears in your eyne."

Reddin put his hands up.

"Tell us what ails you?"

He shook his head.

"What for not, my—what for not?"

She never called Reddin "my soul."

But he could not or would not speak.

Hazel's eyes were red also, with tears of pain. Now she wept again in sympathy with a grief she could not understand.

So they sat beneath the black, slow-waving branches under the threat of the oncoming night, weeping like children. They cowered, it seemed, beneath a hand raised to strike. All that they did was wrong; all that they did was inevitable. Two larches bent by the gales kept up a groaning as bole wore on bole, wounding each other every time they swayed. In the indifferent hauteur of the dark steeps, the secret arcades, the avenues leading nowhere, crouched these two incarnations of the troubled earth, sentient for a moment, capable of sadness, cruelty, terror and revolt, and then lapsed again into the earth.

Forebodings of that lapse—forebodings that follow the hour of climax as rooks follow the plough—haunted them now, though they found no words for what they felt, but only knew a sense of the pressure of night. It appeared to stoop nearer, blind, impassive, but intensely aware of them under their dark canopy of leaves. Some Being, it seemed, was listening there, and not only listening, but imposing in an effortless but inevitable way its veiled purpose. Hazel and Reddin—he no less than she—appeared to be deprived of identity, like hypnotic mediums. His hardness and strength took on a pitiful dolt-like air before this prescient power.

When he at last stopped choking and licking the tears away surreptitiously as they rolled down his cheeks, he was very angry—with himself for crying, with Hazel for witnessing his disgrace. That she should cry was nothing, he thought. Women always cried at these times. Nor did he distinguish between her tears of pain and of sympathy.

"You needn't stare," he snapped. "If I've got a cold, there's no reason to gape."

"What for be you——"

"Shut up! I'm not."

Crying made him less masc

They climbed the crackling wood, ghastly with a sound as of feet passing tiptoe into silence—the multitudinous soft noises of a wood, cones falling, twigs snapping, the wind in old driven leaves, the subdued rustle of the trees. They passed the place where she had talked with Edward at the bark-stripping. The prostrate larches shone as whitely as her shoulder did through her torn gown. She remembered Edward's look, and wept again.

"What is it now?" he asked.

"I was i' this place afore the bluebells died, along with—Ed'ard."

"Why d'you say the man's name like that? It's no better than other names."

She had no reply for that, and they came in silence to the tormented may-tree where the horse was tied, his black mane and smooth back strown with faded, faintly coloured blossom.

Reddin lifted her on and swung into the saddle. She leant against him, silent and passive, as with one arm round her he guided the horse down the difficult path.

A star shone through the trees, but it was not a friendly star. It was more like a stare than a tear. When the rest of them sprang out like an army at the réveillé, they were aloof and cold, and they rode above in an ironic disdain too terrible to be resented.

Reddin put the horse to a gallop. He wanted fierce motion to still the compunction that Hazel's quiet crying brought.

A sense of immanent grief was on her, grey loneliness and fear of the future. He tried to comfort her.

"Dunna say ought!" she sobbed. "You canna run the words o'er your tongue comforble like Ed'ard can!"

"What do you want me to say?"

"I dunno. I want our Foxy."

"I'll fetch her in the morning."

"No, you munna. She'm safe at Ed'ard's. Let her bide. I want to be at Ed'ard's, too."

"Who comes wailing in the black o' night?" said the voice of Vessons as they neared the hall door. "I thought it was the lady as no gold comforts—her as hollas 'Lost! Alost!' in the Undern Coppy."

CHAPTER XXVI

UNDERN was in its June mood. Pinks frothed over the edges of the borders, and white bush-roses flung their arms high over the porch. All was heavily fragrant, close, muffling the senses. The trees brooded; the house brooded; the hill hung above, deeply recollected; the bats went with a lagging flight. It was like one of those spell-bound places built for an hour or an æon or a moment on the borders of elfdom, full of charms and old wizardry, ready to fall inwards at a word, but invincible to all but that word. The hot scent of the trees and the garden mingled with the smell of manure, pigsties, cooking pigwash, and Vesson's "Tom Moody" tobacco. It made Hazel feel faint—a strange sensation to her.

Vessons stood surveying them as he had done on the bleak night of Hazel's first coming.

"Where," he said at last, the countless fine lines that covered his upper lip from nostril to mouth deepening—"where's the reverent?" Receiving no reply but a scowl from his master, he led the horse away.

Reddin, with a kind of gauche gentleness, said: "I'll show you the house."

They went through the echoing rooms, and looked out of the low, spider-hung casements, where young ivy-leaves, soft and vivid, had edged their way [illegible] cracks. They stood under ceilings dark [illegible] oke of fires and lamps that had been lit un- [illegible] years ago for some old pathetic revelry. In cupboards left ajar by a hurried hand that had long been still hung gowns with flower-stains or wine-stains on their faded folds. The doors creaked and sighed after them, the floors groaned, and all about the house, though the summer air was so light and low, there was a moaning of wind. It was as if all the storms that had blown round it, the terror that had been felt in it, the tears that had fallen in it, had crept like forgotten spirits into its innermost recesses and now made complaint there for ever. A lonely listener on a stormy night might hear strange voices uplifted—the sobbing of children; songs of feasters; cries of labouring women; young men's voices shouting in triumph; the long intonations of prayer; the death-rattle.

And as Reddin and Hazel—surely the most strangely met of all couples that had owned and been owned by this house—went through the darkening rooms they were not, it seemed, alone. A sense of witnesses perturbed Hazel, a discomfort as from surveillance. A soft rumour, as of a mute but moving multitude, crept along the passages in their wake.

"Be there ghosses?" she whispered. "I'd liefer sleep under the blue roof-tree. I feel like corn under a millstone in this dark place."

"It's said to be haunted, but I don't believe it." He glanced over his shoulder.

"Who by?"

"People that failed. Weaklings. Men that lost their money or their women, and wives and daughters of the family that died young."

"What for did they fail?"

"Silly ideas. Not knowing what they wanted."

"Dear now! Foxy and me, we dunna allus know what we want."

"You want me."

"Maybe."

"If you don't, you must learn to. And if you don't know what you want, you'll come to smash."

"But when I do know, folk take it off me."

A long, mournful cry came down the passages.

Hazel screamed.

"Be that the lady as no gold comforts?" she whispered.

"No, you silly girl. It's a barn owl. But she's said to cry in the coppy on midsummer night."

"Things crying out as have been a long while hurted," murmured Hazel. "To-night's midsummer. Was she little, like me?"

"I don't know."

"Did summat strong catch a holt of her?"

"A man did." He laughed.

"Did she go young?"

"Yes; she died at nineteen."

"And so'll it be with me!" she cried suddenly. "So'll it be with me! Dark and strong in the full of life."

She flung herself on a faded blue settee and wept.

The impression of companionship—of whispers breaking out, hands stretched forth, the steady magnetism of countless unseen eyes—was so strong that Hazel could not bear it, and even Reddin was glad to follow her back to the inhabited part of the house.

"This is the bedroom," Reddin said, opening the door of a big room papered in faded grey, and full of the smell of bygone days. The great four-poster, draped with a chintz of roses on a black ground, awed her. Reddin opened a chest and took out the green dress. He watched her with an air of proud proprietorship as she put it on. She went down the shallow stairs like a leaf loosened from the tree.

Vessons, a beer-bottle in either hand, was so aghast at the pale apparition that he nearly dropped them.

"I thought it was a ghost," he said—"a comfortless ghost."

"So I be comfortless," Hazel said to Reddin when Vessons had retired. Her voice had a sound of tears in it, like a dark tide broken on rocks. "And when I was comfortless at the Mountain Ed'ard was used to read 'Comfort ye, my people,' as nice as nice."

"Are you fonder of Marston than of me?"

"I dunno."

She sat down sadly in the home that was not home. She remembered the half-finished collar she was knitting for Foxy. Also, a custom had grown up that she sang hymns in the evenings to Edward's accompaniment. She missed these things. She missed the irritations of that peaceful life—Mrs. Marston's way of clearing her throat softly and pertinaciously; Martha's habit of tidying all her little treasures into the kitchen grate; Edward's absurd determination that she should have clean nails; the ever-renewed argument, "Foxy's a bad dog!" "She inna. She's a good fox." "In my sight she's a bad dog."

Now she had floated free of all this. She was out of haven on the high seas. She felt very lonely—as the dead might feel, free of the shackles of life. It was certainly pleasant to wear the green dress. But she missed her little duties—clearing away the supper, Martha being gone; fetching the candles (Mrs. Marston always shook her head at the third, not from economy, but from vicarious philoprogenitiveness).

Edward's reading of the Book last thing had made her restless; she had thought it a bother. Now it seemed a privilege. To most girls, God's Little Mountain would have been purgatory. To her it was wonderful. It was the first time she had shared in the peculiar beauty of home, the daily sacrament of love. Edward never forgot to kiss them both when he came in; brought them flowers; was always carpentering at surprises for them. These last never turned out very well, his technical skill not keeping pace with his enthusiasm; but Hazel was not critical.

She, in common with the other little creatures, sat down in his shadow as in a city of refuge. Mrs. Marston shared this feeling. She always fell asleep at once when Edward was at home in the evening, ceasing to invent alarms about black men creeping through the kitchen window, Foxy getting into the larder, and a great tempest from the Lord blowing them all to perdition because Lord's Day was not kept as it used to be.

Into the parlour, at his own good time, Vessons brought the supper, and dumped it on the large round table, veneered like mahogany, heavily Victorian, and ornamented with brass feet. There were bread and cheese, bacon, and a good deal of beer.

Hazel saw nothing amiss with it, for though she had begun to grow accustomed to respectable middle-class meals, life at the Callow still seemed the homelier. Reddin looked up from cutting bacon to say with unwonted thoughtfulness, "Like some tea and toast?" He felt that toast was a triumph of imagination. He was rather dubious about asking Vessons to do it, so instead he repeated, "You'll have some tea and toast?"

Vessons went into the kitchen and shut the door. They waited for some time, and Hazel, who, whatever her fate, her faults and sorrows, was always as hungry as Foxy, looked longingly at Reddin's cheese and beer. Physical exhaustion brought tears of appetite to her eyes. At last Reddin went to the kitchen door.

"Where's that tea?" he asked.

"Tay?"

"Yes, you fool!"

"I know nothing about no tay."

"I said you were to make some."

"Not to me."

"And toast."

"I've douted the fire."

He had just done so.

"Look here, my man, there's a missus at Undern now. You please her or go. She tells me what she wants. I tell you. You do it."

"I'll 'ave no woman over me!" said Vessons sullenly. "Never will I! Never a missus did I take, not for all the pleasures of bed and board—no, ne'er a one I ever took. Maiden I am to my dying day."

The coupling of the ideas of Vessons and maidenhood was so funny that Reddin burst out laughing and forgot his anger.

"Now, make that tea, Vessons."

"She unna be here long?" asked Vessons craftily.

"Yes, for good."

Hazel heard him.

"For good." Did she want to be in this whispering house for good? Who did she want to be with for good? Not Reddin. Edward? But he had not the passion of the greenwood in him, the lust of the earth. He was not of the tremulously ecstatic company of wild, hunted creatures. If Reddin was definitely antagonistic, a hunter, Edward was neutral, a looker-on. They were not her comrades. They did not live her life. She had to live theirs. She wished she had never seen Reddin, never gone to Hunter's Spinney. Edward's house was at least peaceful.

"And what," she heard Vessons say, "will yer lordship's Sally Virtue say?"

She did not hear Reddin's reply: it was fierce and low. She wondered who Sally Virtue was, but she was too tired to think much about it. Afterwards Reddin had some whisky, and Vessons drank his health. Then Reddin picked out "It's a Fine Hunting Day" on the old piano, and sang it in a rough tenor. Vessons joined in from the kitchen in a voice quite free from any music, and the roaring chorus echoed through the house.

"Eh, stop! I canna abide it!" cried Hazel; but they did not hear.

Vessons came and stood in the doorway with the teapot in one hand and the expression of acute agony he always wore when singing.

> "All trouble and care
> Will be left far behind us at home!"

"Not for the little foxes!" cried Hazel, and she plucked the music from the piano and ran past Vessons, knocking the teapot out of his hand. She stuffed the music into the kitchen grate.

Vessons was petrified.

"Well," he said, "you've got the ways of wild cats and spinsters the world over." This was an unwilling compliment. "And I'll say this for you, whatever else I canna say, you've got sperit enough for the eleven thousand virgins!"

Reddin felt that the scene was hardly festive enough. He wondered that he himself did not feel more jubilant; reaction had set in. He wished that all should be gay as for a bridal, for he felt that this *was* a bridal in all but the name.

But the old house, like a being lethargic after long revelry, clad in torn and stained garments, seemed unready for mirth. Andrew was highly antagonistic. The hound had bristled, growling, at the intruder; and Hazel——?

He looked at Hazel under half-closed lids. Did she know what had happened? He thought not. Perhaps intuition whispered to her. Certainly she avoided his eyes. She sat drinking the tea, which Reddin, with much exertion of authority, at last caused to appear. She was wan, and her face looked very thin. Panic lingered about her eyes, at the corners of her lips.

He realized that she was afraid of him—his look, his touch. Immediately he wanted to exercise his power. He went across and took her chin in his hand, laying the other on her shoulder.

Her eyelids trembled.

"What'n you after, mauling me?" she said.

Then a passion of tears shook her.

"Oh, I want Ed'ard and the old lady! I want to go back to the Mountain, I do! Ed'ard'll be looking me up and down the country."

"Good Lord, so he will!" said Reddin, "and rousing the whole place. You must write a letter, Hazel, to say you're safe and happy, and he's not to worry."

"But I amna."

Reddin frowned at the spontaneity of this. But he made her write the note.

"Saddle the mare, Vessons, and take this to the Mountain."

"You dunna mind how much——" began Vessons. But Reddin cut him short.

"Get on," he said, and Vessons knew by the tone that he had better. "Push it under the parson's door, knock, and make yourself scarce, Vessons," Reddin ordered.

"You can go up to bed if you like, Hazel."

Left alone, he walked up and down the room, puzzled and uneasy.

According to his idea, he had done Hazel the greatest honour a man can pay to a woman. He could not see in what he had failed. He was irritated with his conscience for being troublesome. He had, as he put it, merely satisfied a need of his nature—a need simple and urgent as eating and drinking. He did not understand that in failing to find out whether it was also a need of Hazel's nature—and in nothing else at all—lay his unpardonable crime.

That he had offended against the views of his Church did not worry him. For, like many Churchmen, he had the happy gift of keeping profession and practise, dogma and deeds, in airtight compartments. How many of the most fervent Churchmen are not, or have not been at some period of their lives, exactly like Reddin?

"Of course, I've been a bit of a beast in the past," he thought. "But that's done with. Besides, she doesn't know."

He reflected again.

"I suppose I was a bit rough, but she ought to have forgotten that by now. I do wish she wouldn't keep on so about the parson."

He ran upstairs.

"Sorry I was rough, Hazel," he said shamefacedly. Hazel stood at the open window in a nightdress that she had found in one of the chests—a frail, yellowish thing with many frills of cobwebby lace made and worn by some dead woman on a forgotten bridal. It was symbolic of Hazel's whole life that she came in this way both to Undern and the Mountain—as bare of woman's regalia as a winter leaf is of substance.

Hazel was speaking when he entered. He stood still, astonished and suspicious.

"Who are you talking to?" he asked.

She turned. "Him above," she said. "I was saying the prayer Ed'ard learnt me. I said it three times, it being midsummer, and ghosses going to-and-agen and the jeath-pack about. He'll be bound to hearken to Ed'ard's prayer."

She looked small and pitiful standing in the flickering candlelight. She turned again to the window, and Reddin went downstairs, quite overwhelmed and abashed.

The house seemed eerier than ever, full of subdued complaints and whisperings. The faces of the roses round the window were woe-begone in the lamplight. The rustle of the leaves had an expostulatory sound. The wan poplars down the meadow looked accusing. It was almost as if the freemasonry of the green world was up in arms for Hazel. She had its blood in her veins, and shared with it the silent worship of freedom and beauty, and had now been plunged so deeply into  human life that she was lost to it. It was as if every incarnation of perfection that she had seen in leaf and flower (and she had seen much, though remaining without expression of it), every moment of deep comradeship with earthy, dewy things, every illumined memory of colours and lights that her vivid mind had gathered and cherished in its rage of love and rapture, had come now, pacing disdainfully through this old haunt of crude humanity; passing up the stairs; standing about the great four-poster where so many Reddins had died and been born; gazing upon this face that had known dreams (however childish) of their eternal magic; grieving as the tree for the leaf that has fallen. They grieved, but they did not forgive. For the spirits of beauty and magic are (as the bondsman of colour knows and the bondsman of poetry) inimical to the ordinary life and destiny of man. They break up homes. They lead a thousand wanderers into the unknown. They brook no half service.

It is only the rarest exception when a man loves a woman and yet excels in his art, and a woman must have an amazing genius if she is still a poet after childbirth.

But though sometimes these proud spirits will tolerate, will even be sworn companions of human love, it is only when it is a passion pure and burning that they know it for a sister spirit. In the sexual meeting of Hazel and Reddin there was nothing of this. Though it brought out the best in Reddin, the best was so very poor. And Hazel was merely passive.

So they stood and wept above her, and they foreswore her company for ever more. She might regard the primrose eye to eye, but she would receive no dewy look of comprehension. No lift of the heart would come with the lifting leaves, no pang of mysterious pain with bird-song, star-set, dewfall. Even her love of Foxy would become a groping thing, and not any longer would she know, when her blind bird made its tentative music, all it meant and all it dreamed. This very night she had forgotten to lean out and listen as of old to the soft voices of the trees. She had said her prayer, and then she had been so tired, and pains had shot through her, and her back had ached, and she had cried herself to sleep.

"What for did I go to the Hunter's Spinney?" she asked herself. But the answer was too deep for her, the traitorous impulse of her own being too mysterious. She could not answer her question.

Reddin, pacing the room downstairs, drinking whisky, and fuming at his own compunction, at last grew tired of his silent house.

"Damn it! why shouldn't I go up?" he said.

He opened Hazel's door.

"Look here," he said; "the house is mine, and so are you. I'm coming to bed." He was met by that most intimidating reply to all bluster—silence.

She was asleep; and all night long, while he snored, she tossed in her sleep and moaned.

CHAPTER XXVII

EARLY next morning Vessons was calling the cows in for milking. He leant over the lichen-green gate contemplatively.

All the colours were so bright that they were grotesque and startling. Above the violently green fields the sky shone like blue glass, and across the east were two long vermilion clouds. Behind the black hill the sun had shouldered up, molten, and the shadow of Vessons, standing monkey-like on the lowest bar of the gate, lay on the stretch of wet clover behind him—a purple, elfin creature, gifted with a prehensile dignity. The cows did not appear after his first call. He lifted his head and called again in a high, plaintive tone, as one reasons with a fretful child, "Come o-on, come o-on!" Then he sank into the landscape again. After an interval, a polished red and white cow appeared at a distance of five fields, coming serenely on at her own pace. A white one and a roan followed her at long distances. They advanced through the shadows, each going through the exact middle of the many gateways, always kept open like doors in a suite of rooms at a reception. Vessons waited patiently—more as a slave than a ruler—only uttering his plaintive "Come o-on!" once, when the last cow dallied overlong with a tuft of lush grass in the hedge. This was the daily ritual. Every morning he appeared, neutral-tinted, from the house, and cried upon an apparently empty landscape; every morning they meandered through the seven gates from the secret leafy purlieus where they spent the night.

Mysterious of eye, leisured, vividly red and white, they followed the old man as queens might follow an usher.

Hazel was coming down the path from the house. With morning, her abundant vitality had returned. The outer world was new and bright, and she wanted, shyly, to be up and dressed before Reddin awoke.

She was full of merriment at the subservience of Vessons to the cows.

"D'you say 'mum' to 'em?" she inquired.

Vessons looked her up and down. He was very angry, not only at her criticism, but at the difficulty of retort, since he supposed she was now "missus." His friendliness for her had entirely gone, not, as would have seemed natural, since her last night's instalment at Undern, but since her marriage with Edward. He felt that she had gone back on him. He had taken her as a comrade, and now she had gone over to the enemy. He was also injured at having been kept up so late last night.

He chumbled his straw for some time, until the last cow had disappeared. Then he said: "You'm up early for a married 'ooman, or whatever you be, missus."

Hazel laughed. She had lived so completely outside the influence of the canons of society that the taunt had no sting.

"Ha! you're jealous!" she said.

Then, with a mercilessly accurate imitation of his voice and face, she added:

"A missus at Undern! Never will I!"

He quailed under her mocking amber eyes, her impish laughter. Then, looking from side to side with suppressed fury, he said: "Them birds is after the cherries! I'll get a gun. I'll shoot 'em dead."

"If you shoot a blackbird, the milk'll turn bloody," said Hazel; but Vessons paid no heed.

All morning, at any spare moment, and after dinner (which he brought in in complete silence, and which was exceedingly unpalatable), he lurked behind trees and crept along hedges, shooting birds. Even Reddin felt awed, and could not gather courage to expostulate with him. In and out of the stealthy afternoon shadows, black and solemn, went the shambling old figure with his relentless face and outraged heart. He shot thrushes as they fluted after a meal of wild raspberries; he shot tiny silky willow-wrens, robins, and swallows—their sacredness did not awe him—a pigeon on its nest, blackbirds, a dipper, a goldfinch, and a great many sparrows. The garden and fields were struck into silence because of him; only a flutter of terrified wings showed his whereabouts. He piled his trophies—all the delicate, ruffled plumage of summer's prime—on the kitchen table, draggled and bloody.

Hazel and Reddin crept from window to window, silent, watching his movements. Undern grew ghostlier than ever, seeming, as the shots rang out startlingly loud in the quiet, like a moribund creature electrified by blows.

"He'd liefer it was me than the birds!" said Hazel. "Wheresoever I go, folk kill things. What for do they?"

"Things must be killed."

"It seems like the earth's all bloody," said Hazel. "And it's allus the little small uns. There! He's got a jenny-wren. Oh, deary me! it's like I've killed 'em; it's all along of me coming to Undern."

"Hush!" said Reddin sharply. "What I'm afraid of is that he'll shoot himself, he's so damned queer."

The last cow had sauntered to the gate before Vessons opened it and milked them that night. Afterwards he went in with the pails, set them on the parlour floor, and said with fury to Hazel: "Bloody, is it?"

She owned, faintly, that it was not.

"And now," said Vessons, turning on Reddin, "it's notice. Notice has been give—one month—by Andrew Vessons to John Reddin, Esquire, of Undern."

With tragic dignity he turned to go.

He saw neither Hazel nor Reddin, but only the swan, the yew-tree swan, his creation, now doomed to be for ever unfinished. The generations to come would look upon a beakless swan, and would think he had meant it so. Tears came into his eyes—smarting, difficult tears. The room was full of brooding misery. Reddin felt awkward and astounded.

"Why, Vessons?" he said in rather a sheepish tone.

Vessons did not turn. He fumbled with the door-handle. Reddin got up and went across to him.

"Why, Vessons?" he said again, with a hand on his shoulder. "You and I can't part, you know."

"We mun."

"But why, man? What's up with you, Andrew?"

The rare Christian name softened Vessons. He deigned to explain. "She is," he said, with a sidelong nod at Hazel. "She mocked me."

"Did you, Hazel?"

"Now then, missus!" Vessons glared at her.

"I only said——"

"Her said, 'Never will I!' " shouted Vessons. "Ah, that's what her said—'Never will I!' That's what *I* say," he added with the pride of a phrase-maker.

Reddin could make nothing of them, one so red and angry, the other in tears.

"I'll do no 'ooman's will!" said Vessons.

"Look here, Vessons! Be reasonable. Listen to me. I'm your master, aren't I?"

"Ah! Till a month."

"Well, you take orders from me; that's all that matters. I'm master here."

The tones of his ancestry were in his voice—an ancestry that ruled over and profited by men and women as good as themselves, or better.

"So we'll say no more about it," he finished, with the frank and winning smile that was one of his few charms.

Vessons stared at him for some time, and, as he stared, an idea occurred to him. It was, he felt, a good idea. It would enable him to keep his swan and his self-respect and to get rid of Hazel. As he pondered it, his face slowly creased into smiles. He touched his forelock—a thing only done on pay-days—and withdrew, murmuring, "Notice is took back."

They saw him go past the window with the steps and the shears, evidently to attend to the swan.

Reddin thought how easy it was to manage these underlings—a little authority, a little tact. He turned to Hazel, crying in the high armchair of black oak with its faded rose-coloured cushions. She was crying not only because Vessons had come off victorious, and because her position was now defined, and was not what she would have liked, but also because Reddin's manner to her jarred after last night.

Last night, in the comfortless darkness of Hunter's Spinney, he had seemed for a little while to be a fellow-fugitive of hers, one of the defenceless, fleeing from the vague, unknown power that she feared.

Then she had pitied him—self-forgetfully, fiercely—gathering his head to her breast as she so often gathered Foxy's. But now he seemed to have forgotten—seemed once more to be of the swift and strong ones that rode down small creatures.

She sobbed afresh.

"Look here, Hazel," said he, in a tone that he intended to be kind but firm—"look here: I'm not angry with you, only you must leave Vessons alone, you know."

"You want that old fellow more than you want me!"

"Don't be silly! He has his uses; you have yours."

He spoke with a quite unconscious brutality; he voiced the theory of his class and his political party, which tacitly or openly asserted that women, servants, and animals were in the world for their benefit.

"I'm not grass to be trod on," said Hazel, "and if you canna be civil-spoken, I'll go."

"You can't," he replied, "not now."

She knew it was true, and the knowledge that her own physical nature had proved traitorous to her freedom enraged her the more.

"You can't go," he went on, coming towards her chair to caress her. "Shall I tell you why?"

Hazel sat up and looked at him, her eyes gloomy, her forehead red with crying. He thought she was awaiting his answer; but Hazel seldom did or said what he expected. She let him kneel by her chair on one knee; then, frowning, asked: "Who cried in Hunter's Spinney?" He jumped up as if he had knelt on a pin. He had been trying to forget the incident, and hoped that she had. He was bitterly ashamed of that really fine moment of his life.

"Don't, Hazel!" he said.

He felt quite frightened when he remembered how

he had behaved. A strange doubt of himself, born that night, stirred again. Was he all he had thought? Was the world what he had thought? Misgivings seized him. Perhaps he ought not to have brought Hazel here or to the Spinney. An older code than those of Church and State began to flame before him, condemning him.

Suddenly he wanted reassurance. "You did want to come, didn't you? I didn't take advantage of you very much, did I?" he asked. "You want to stay?"

"No, I didna want to come till you made me. You got the better of me. But maybe you couldna help it. Maybe you were druv to it."

"Who by?" he asked, with an attempt at flippancy.

Hazel's eyes were dark and haunted.

"Summat strong and drodsome, as drives us all," she said.

She had a vision of all the world racing madly round and round, like the exhausted and terrified horse Reddin had that morning lunged. But what power it was that stood in the centre, breaking without an effort the spirit of the mad, fleeing, tethered creature, she could not tell.

Reddin sat brooding until Hazel, recovering first in her mercurial way, said:

"Now I've come, I mun bide. D'you think the old fellow'd let me cook summat for supper? It's been pig-food for us to-day."

But when they went to investigate, they found Vessons preparing a tremendous meal, hot and savoury as a victorious and penitent old man could make it. He showed in his manner that bygones were to be bygones, and night came down in peace on Undern. But it was a curious, torrid peace, like the hush before thunder.

CHAPTER XXVIII

IT was the Friday after Hazel's coming, and Reddin was away, much against his will, at a horse fair. He was quite surprised at the hurt it gave him to be away from Hazel. So far he had never been, in the smallest sense, any woman's lover. He had taken what he wanted of them in a kind of animal semi-consciousness that almost amounted to a stark innocence. Virility, he felt, was not of his seeking. There it was, and it must be satisfied. Now he was annoyed to find that he felt guilty when he remembered these women, and that he wanted Hazel, not, as with them, occasionally, but all the time. He had been accustomed to say at farmer's dinners, after indulging pretty freely:

"Oh, damn it! what d'you want with women between sun-up and sun-down?" His coarseness had been received with laughter and reproof. Now he felt that the reproof was juster than the laughter. It was curious, too, how dull things became when Hazel was not there. Hazel had something fresh to say about everything, and their quarrels were the most invigorating moments he had known. Hazel was primitive enough to be feminine, original enough to be boyish, and mysterious enough to be exciting. As Vessons remarked to the drake, "Oh, maister! you ne'er saw the like. It's 'Azel, 'Azel, 'Azel the day long, and a good man spoilt as was only part spoilt afore."

Vessons and Hazel were spending the afternoon quarrelling about the bees. When Reddin was away, Hazel put off her new dignity and was Vessons' equal, because it was so dull to be anything else. Vessons tolerated her presence for the sake of the subacid remarks it enabled him to make, but chiefly because of the sardonic pleasure it give him to remember how soon his resolve would be put in action.

They were in the walled garden, and the bees were coming and going so fast that they made, when Hazel half closed her eyes, long black threads swaying between the hive doors and the distant fields and the hilltop. They hung in cones on the low front walls, and lumped on the hive-shelves in that apparently purposeless unrest that precedes creation. But whether they intended, any of them, to create a new city that day, none might know. Vessons said not. Hazel, always for adventure, said they would, and said also that she could hear the queen in one hive "zeep-zeeping"—that strange music which, like the maddeningly soft skirl of the bagpipes or the fiddling of Ned Pugh, has power to lure living creatures away from comfort and full hives into the unknown—so darkly sweet.

"I canna hear it," said Vessons obstinately.

"Go on! You're deaf, Mr. Vessons."

"Deaf, am I? Maybe I hear as much as I want to, and more. Ah! that I do!"

"Well, then, why canna you hear 'em? Listen at 'em now. D'you know the noise I mean?"

"Do I know the noise?" Vessons' voice grew almost tearful with rage. "Do I know?' Me! As can make a thousand bees go through the neck of a pint bottle each after other, like cows to the milking! Me! Maybe you'd like to learn me the beekeeping?" he continued with salty humility. "Maybe you would! Never will I!"

He began to tear off the tops of the hives.

"Oh, Mr. Vessons, dunna be so cross!" Hazel was afraid there would be another scene like Monday's. "You take 'em off very neat," she added, with a pathetic attempt to be tactful—" as neat as my dad."

"I'd have you know," said Vessons, "as I take 'em off neater—ah! a deal neater. Bees and cows and yew-tree swans," he went on reflectively, "I can manage better than any married man. For what he puts into matrimony I put into my work. Now I asks you"—he fixed his eyes on her with the expression of a fanatic—"I ask you, was there ever a beekeeper or a general or a sea-captain as was anything to boast of, being married? Never! Marriage kills the mind! Why's bees clever? Why's the skip allus full of honey at summer's end? Because they're all old maids!"

"The queen inna. They all come from her."

Vessons glared for a moment; then, realizing defeat, turned on his heel and went to feed the calves. He had an ingenious way of getting the calves in. He had no dog; it was one of his dreams to have one. But he managed very well. First he opened the calfskit door; then he loosed the pigs; then he fetched a bucket and went to the field where the calves were, followed by a turbulent, squealing, ferocious crowd of pigs. He walked round the calves, and the calves fled homewards, far more afraid of the pigs than of a dog. This piece of farm economy pleased Vessons, and, peace being restored, they laid tea amicably.

When Reddin came home to a pleasant scent of toast and the sight of Hazel's shining braids of hair, new brushed and piled high on her head, he felt very well pleased with himself. He stretched in the red armchair and flung an arm round her. His hard blue eyes, his hard mouth, smiled; he felt that he could make a success of marriage, though the parson (as he called Edward) could not. Women, he reflected, were quite easy to manage. "Just show them who's master straight off, and all's well." Here was Hazel, radiant, soft, submissive, all the rough prickly husk gone since Sunday. Why had he behaved so strangely in the Spinney? Well, well, he must forget about that.

The hot tea ran very comfortably down his throat; the toast was pleasantly resistant to his strong teeth, He felt satisfied with life. Later on, no doubt, Hazel would have a child. That, too, would be a good thing. Two possessions are better than one, and he could well afford children. It never occurred to him to wonder whether Hazel would like it, or to be sorry for the pain in store for her. He felt very unselfish as he thought, "When she can't go about, I'll sit with her now and again." It really was a good deal for him to say. He had never taken the slightest notice of Sally Haggard at such times.

"Got something for you," he said, pulling at his pocket.

"Oh! It's an urchin!" cried Hazel delightedly.

Reddin began bruising and pulling at its spines with his gloved hands.

"Dunna!" cried Hazel.

Reddin pulled and wrenched until at last the hedgehog screamed—a thin, piercing wail, most ghastly and pitiful and old, ancient as the cry of the death's-head moth, that faint ghostly shriek as of a tortured witch. Centuries of pain were in it, the age-long terror of weakness bound and helpless beneath the knife, and that something vindictive and terrifying that looks up at the hunter from the eyes of trapped animals and sends the cuckoo fleeing in panic before the onset of little birds. Hazel knew the sound well. It was the watchword of the little children of despair, the password of the freemasonry to which she belonged.

Before the cry had ceased to horrify the quiet room, she had flung herself at Reddin, a pattern of womanly obedience no longer, but a desperate creature fighting in that most intoxicating of all crusades, the succouring of weakness.

On Reddin's head, a moment ago so smooth, on his face, a moment ago so bland, rained the blows of Hazel's hard little fists. Her blows were by no means so negligible as most women's, for her hands were muscular and strong from digging and climbing, and in her heart was the root of pity which nerves the most trembling hands to do mighty deeds.

"What the devil!" spluttered Reddin. "Here, stop it, you little vixen!"

He caught one of her hands, but the other was too quick for him.

"Give over tormenting of it, then!"

The hedgehog rolled on the floor, and the foxhound came and sniffed it. Reddin had her other hand now.

"What d'you mean by it?" he asked, very angry, and tingling about the ears.

"Leave it be! It's done you no harm. Lookee! The hound-dog!" she cried. "Drive him off!"

"I'm going to have some fun seeing the dog kill it."

Hazel went quite white.

"You shanna! Not till I'm jead," she said. "It's come to me to be took care of, and took care of it shall be." She reached a foot out and kicked the hound.

Reddin's mood changed. He burst out laughing.

"You're a sight more amusing than hedgehogs," he said; "the beast can go free, for all I care."

He pulled her on to his knee and kissed her.

"Send the hound-dog out, then."

When the hound had gone, resentfully, the hedgehog—a sphinx-like, protestant ball—enjoyed the peace, and Hazel became again (as Reddin thought) quite the right sort of girl to live with.

During the uproar they had not heard wheels in the drive, so they were startled by Vessons' intrigué insertion of himself into a small opening of the door, his firm shutting of it as if in face of a beleaguering host, and his stentorian whisper:

" 'Ere's Clombers now!" as if to say, "When you let a woman in you never know what'll come of it."

"Tell 'em I'm ill—dead!" said his master. "Tell 'em I'm in the bath—anything, only send them away!"

They heard Vessons' recitative.

"The master's very sorry, mum, but he's got the colic too bad to see you. It's heave, curse, heave, curse, till I pray for a good vomit!"

The Clombers, urgent upon his track, shouldered past and strode in.

"What the devil do they want?" muttered Reddin. He rose sulkily.

"I hear," said the eldest Miss Clomber, who had read Sordello and was very clever, "that young Lochinvar has taken to himself a bride."

This was quite up to her usual standard, for not only had it the true literary flavour, but it was ironic, for she knew who Hazel was.

"Er?" queried Reddin, shaking hands in his rather race-coursey manner.

"Introduce me, Mr. Reddin!" simpered Amelia Clomber. It was painful when she simpered; her mouth was made for sterner uses.

They surveyed Hazel, who shrank from their gaze. Something in their eyes made her feel as if they were her judges, and as if they knew all about Hunter's Spinney.

They looked at her with detestation. They thought it was detestation for a sinner. Really, it was for the woman who had, in a few weeks after meeting him, found favour in Reddin's eyes, and attained that defeat which, to women even so desiccated as the Clombers, is the one desired victory.

They had come, as they told each other before and after their visit, to snatch a brand from the burning. What was in the heart of each—the frantic desire to be mistress of Undern—they did not mention.

Miss Clomber had taken exception to Amelia's tight dress. For Amelia had a figure, and Miss Clomber had not. She always flushed at the text, "We have a little sister, and she hath no breasts."

Amelia was aware of her advantage as she engaged Reddin in conversation. He fell in with the arrangement, for he detested her sister, who always prefaced every remark with "Have you read——?"

As he never read anything, he thought she was making fun of him.

"And what," asked Miss Clomber of Hazel, lowering her lids like blinds, "was your maiden name?"

"Woodus."

"Where were you married?"

"The Mountain."

"Shawly there's no church there?"

"Ah. Ed'ard's church."

"Edward?"

"Ah! He's minister."

"You mean the chapel. So that's your persuasion. Now Mr. Reddin is such a sta'nch Charchman."

Reddin looked exceedingly discomfited.

"And when did this happy event take place?"

A cat with a mouse was nothing to Miss Clomber with a sinner.

At this point Reddin saw, as he put it, what she was driving at. He was very sleepy, having been out all day and eaten a large tea, and he never combated a physical desire. So he cut across a remark of Amelia's to the effect that marriage with the *right* woman so added to a man's comfort, and said:

"I'm not married, if that's what you mean."

"Then who——" said Miss Clomber, feeling that she had him now.

"My keep," said he baldly. He thought they would go at that. But they sat tight. They had, as Miss Clomber said afterwards, a soul to save. They both realized how pleasant might be the earthly lot of one engaged in this heavenly occupation.

"Hah! You call a spade a spade, Mr. Reddin," said Miss Clomber, with a frosty glance at Hazel; "you are not, as our dear Browning has it, mealy mouthed."

"In the breast of a true woman," said Amelia authoritatively, as a fishmonger might speak of fish, "is no room for blame."

"True woman be damned!"

Miss Clomber saw that for to-day the cause was lost.

At this point Miss Amelia uttered a piercing yell. The hedgehog, encouraged by being left to itself, and by the slight dusk that had begun to gather in the northerly rooms of Undern—where night came early—had begun to creep about. Surreptitiously guided by Hazel's foot, it had crept under Amelia's skirt and laid its cold inquiring head on her ankle, thinly clad for conquest. Hazel went off into peals of laughter, and Miss Amelia hated her more than before.

Vessons, in the kitchen, shook his head.

"I never heerd the like of the noise there's been since that gel come. Never did I!" he said.

"Leave him!" said Miss Clomber to Hazel on the doorstep. She was going to add "for my sake," but substituted "his." "You are causing him to sin," she added.

"Be I?" Hazel felt that she was always causing something wrong. Then she sighed. "I canna leave 'im."

"Why not?"

"He wunna let me."

With that phrase, all unconsciously, she took a most ample revenge on the Clombers; for it rang in their ears all night, and they knew it was true.

CHAPTER XXIX

ON Sunday Vessons put his resolve—to go to the Mountain and reveal Hazel's whereabouts—into practice. If he had waited, gossip would have done it for him. He set out in the afternoon, having "cleaned" himself and put on his pepper-and-salt suit, buff leggings, red waistcoat, and the jockey-like cap he affected. He arrived at the back door just as Martha was taking in supper.

"Well?" said Martha, who wanted to have her meal and go home.

"Well?" said Vessons.

"When I say 'well,' I mean what d'you want?"

"Allus say what you mean."

"Who d'you want? Me?"

"The master."

"The master's out."

"I'll wait, then."

He sat down by the fire, and looked so fixedly at Martha as she poured out her tea that she offered him some in self-defence. He drew up his chair. Now that he was receiving hospitality, he felt that he must be agreeable and complimentary.

"Single, I suppose?" he asked.

"Ah," said Martha coyly, "I'm single; but I've no objection to matrimony."

"Oh!" Vessons spoke sourly, "I'm sorry for you, then."

"Maybe you're a married man yourself?"

"Never."

"Better late than never!"

"If I've kep' out of it in the heat of youth, is it likely I'll go into it in the chilly times? Maiden I am to my dying day!"

"But if you was to meet a nice tidy woman as had a bit saved?" To Martha, a bridegroom of sixty-five seemed better than nothing.

"If I met a score nice tidy women, if I met a gross nice tidy women, it 'ud be no different."

"Not if she could make strong ale?"

"I can make ale myself. No woman shall come into my kitchen for uncounted gold."

Martha sighed as she changed the subject.

"What do you want the master for?"

"Never tell your tidings," said Vessons, "till you meet the king."

"Martha!"

Mrs. Marston stood at the kitchen door in the most splendid of her caps—a pagoda of white lace—and her voice was, as she afterwards said, "quite sharp," its mellifluousness being very slightly reduced.

Vessons rose, touching his hair.

"What is it, my good man?"

"A bit of news, mum."

"For my son?"

"Ah!"

"You may go, Martha," said Mrs. Marston, and Martha went without alacrity.

"Now," Mrs. Marston spoke encouragingly.

"It's for the master."

"He cannot see you."

The two old faces regarded each other with silent obstinacy, and Vessons recognized that, for all Mrs.

Marston's soft outlines, she was as obstinate as he was. He cleared his throat several times.

Mrs. Marston produced a lozenge, which he ate reluctantly, chumbling it with nervous haste. He was so afraid that she would give him another that he told her his news.

"Thank you," she said, keeping her dignity in a marvellous manner. "Mrs. Edward Marston, of course, wrote to the minister, but she forgot to give her address."

"Accidents will 'appen," Vessons remarked, as he went out.

It was some time before Edward came in. He had spent most of his time since last Sunday tramping the hillsides. It was not till he had finished his very cursory meal that his mother said calmly, looking over her spectacles:

"I know where Hazel is."

"You *know,* mother? Why didn't you tell me?"

"I am telling you, dear. There's nothing to be in a taking about. You've had no supper yet. A little preserve?"

Edward, in a sudden passion that startled her, threw the jam-dish across the room. It made a red splash on the wall. Mrs. Marston stopped chumbling her toast, and remained with the rotary motions of her mouth in abeyance. Then she said slowly:

"Your poor father always said, dear, that you'd break out some day. And you have. The best dish! Of course the jam I say little about; jam is but jam, after all; but the cut-glass dish——!"

"Can't you go on with the tale, mother?"

"Yes, my dear, yes. But you fluster me like the Silverton Cheap-jack does; I never *can* buy the dish he holds up, for I get in such a fluster for fear he'll break it, and then he does. And now you have."

Edward pushed back his chair in desperation.

"For pity's sake!" he said.

"I'm telling you. I never thought Hazel was steadfast, you know."

"Where *is* she? Why will you torment me?"

"An old man came. A very untrustworthy old man, I fear. A defiant manner, and that is never pleasant. There he was in the kitchen with Martha! Age is no barrier to wrong, and Martha was very flushed. There was a deal of laughter, too."

"Mother! If you keep on like this, I shall go mad."

"Why, Edward, you are all in a fever. There, there! It's more peaceful without her, and I wish Mr. Reddin well of her."

"Reddin? What Reddin?"

"Mr. Reddin of Undern. Who else?"

"Damn the fellow!"

"Edward! What words you take on your lips! And just think," she went on sorrowfully, "that he seemed such a nice man. He liked the gooseberry-wine so much, and gave me a ma'am, which is more than Martha does half her time. Where are you going?"

"To Undern?"

"What for?"

"Hazel."

Mrs. Marston sat bolt upright.

"But, of course, she'll never darken the door again!"

"I shall bring her back to-night, of course."

"But, my dear! You must divorce her, however unpleasant on account of the papers. Remember, she has been there a week."

"What of that?"

"But a week, dear!"

"Mother, I did not think to hear the talk of the filthy world from you."

Mrs. Marston quailed a little. There is nothing in the world so pure, so wonderful, so strong, as a young man's love can be—nothing so spiritual, nothing so brave.

Mrs. Marston, in her own words, "shed tears."

"Don't cry, mother, but help me," Edward said. "Be ready for her, love her. She is as pure as a dew drop. I know it. And I want her more than life."

"But if she doesn't want you, Edward, what more is to do?"

"To seek and to save," snapped Edward, and he banged the door and went hatless down the path between the heavy-browed tombstones. But he came back to suggest that there should be some tea ready.

As he went down the batch, owls were shrieking in the woods, and the sky was pied with grey and crimson, like bloodstained marble. The cries of the owls were hard as marble also, and of a polished ferocity. They would have their prey.

He walked fast through the lonely fields where Hazel had passed on her mushrooming morning. The roses that had then been in bud were falling.

At Alderslea people stared at him as he went by, flushed and hatless.

From Alderslea to Wolfbatch was some miles; from there to Undern the way lay over Bitterley Hill, where he missed the path. So it was quite dark when he came past Undern pool, lying black and ghastly in its ring of skeleton trees. The foxhound set up a loud baying within. Only one window was lit.

Edward hammered on the knocker, and the sound echoed in the hollow house.

There was a noise within of a door opening, and

Hazel's voice cried: "I wouldna go. It's a tramp, likely."

Then Reddin laughed, and Edward clenched his hands in rage at the easy self-confidence of him. The bolt was drawn back, and Reddin stood in the doorway, outlined by pale light.

"Who is it?" he asked in rather a jovial tone. He felt at peace with the world now Hazel was here.

"Beast!" Edward said tersely.

"Just come in a minute, my lad, and let's have a look at you. People don't call me names twice."

Hazel had heard Edward's voice.

She ran to the door, and the apple-green gown rustled about her.

"Ed'ard! Ed'ard! Dunna go for to miscall him! He'll hurt 'ee! He's stronger'n you. Do 'ee go back, Ed'ard!"

"Never! till you come, too."

"I like that," said Reddin. "Can't you see she's got my gown on her back? She's mine. She was never yours."

He looked meaningly and triumphantly at Edward.

"Oh, dunna, Jack! What for do you go to shame me?" said Hazel, twisting her hands.

Edward took no notice of her.

"I don't know what evil means you used, or how you brought the poor child here," he said, controlling himself with an effort. "But you have tried to rob me, and you have insulted her——"

"Oh, don't come here talking like an injured husband," Reddin said; "you know you aren't her husband."

"Keep your foul mouth shut before innocence! To try and rob a poor child of her freedom, of her soul——"

Hazel wondered at him. His eyes darkened so upon Reddin, his face was so powerful, irradiated with love and anger.

"So young!" he went on—"so young, and as wild as a little bird. How could anyone help letting her take her own way? She wanted to go free in the woods. I let her; and there you were like a sneaking wolf."

He threw a look at Hazel so full of wistful tenderness that she flung the green skirt over head and sobbed.

"Stow it, can't you?" said Reddin. "If you want a fight, say so; but don't preach all night."

His tone was injured. He felt that he had been particularly considerate to Edward in sending him the letter. Also, he was convinced that he had only taken what Edward did not want. That Edward could love Hazel was beyond his comprehension. If a man loved a woman, he possessed her, took his pleasure of her. Love that was abnegation was to his idea impossible. So that, now, when Edward spoke of his love, Reddin simply thought he was posing.

"Why didn't you let her be?"

"Women don't want to be let be," said Reddin with a very unpleasant laugh.

"Oh! stop talking about me as if I wunna here!" cried Hazel.

"If she loved you, I'd say nothing," Edward went on, staring at Reddin fixedly. "The fact that I'm her husband would not have counted with me, if you'd loved her and she you."

"A fine pastor!"

"But you don't. You only wanted—— Oh! you make me sick!"

"Indeed! Well, I'm man enough to take what I want; you're not."

"You trapped her; you would have betrayed her. But, thank God! a young girl's innocence is a wonderful and powerful thing."

Reddin was astounded. Could Marston really be such a fool as to believe in Hazel still?

"The innocent young girl——" he begun, but Hazel struck him on the mouth.

"All right, spitfire!" he said; "mum's the word." He was surprisingly good-humoured.

"Well, Hazel"—Edward spoke in a matter-of-fact tone—"shall we go home now?"

"Dunna ask me, Ed'ard! I mun bide."

"Why?"

Hazel was silent. She could not explain the strange instinct, stronger than her wildness, that Reddin had awakened in her, and that chained her here with invisible chains.

"Come home, little Hazel!" he pleaded.

"I canna," she whispered.

"Why? You can if you want to. Don't you want to?"

"Ah! I do that."

She was torn between her longing to go and her powerlessness to leave Reddin.

The light went out of Edward's face.

"Do you love this man?" he asked.

"No."

"Does it make you better to live with him?"

"No. It was living with you as did that."

Reddin was so enraged that he struck her, and her expression of submission as she cowered under the blow was worse to Edward than the blow itself. He forgot his views about violence, and struck Reddin back.

"Come outside," said Reddin in a tone of relief. The

situation had now taken a comprehensible turn for him.

"If it's fighting you're after, I'm with you; that's settling it like gentlemen. What are you grinning at?" He spoke huffily.

"Dunna snab at each other! What for do you?" said Hazel.

"Because your husband's jealous."

Edward was exasperated by the realization that his action in coming did look like that of the commonplace husband. But, after all, what did it matter? Nothing mattered but Hazel. He looked across at her crouched in the armchair, sobbing. He went to her and patted her shoulder.

"No one's angry with you, dear," he said. "Afterwards, when we're home, you shall explain it all to me."

"If you win!" put in Reddin.

Edward stooped and kissed Hazel's hand. The momentary doubt of her—cruel as hell—had gone. She was his lady, and he was going to fight for her. Hazel looked up at him, and in that instant she almost loved him.

They went out. It was a black moonless night. They stood near the lit window.

"Draw the blind up!" shouted Reddin.

Hazel drew it up. They faced each other in the square of light. They were both quite collected. It seemed difficult to begin. The humour of this struck Reddin, and he laughed.

Edward looked at him disgustedly. Reddin began to feel a fool.

"We must begin," he said.

Seeing that Edward was waiting for him to strike the first blow, and not being angry enough to do so, Reddin said coarsely:

"No good fighting, parson! She's mine—from head to foot."

He received as good a blow as Edward was capable of. They fought with hard-drawn breath, for they were neither of them in training. To Edward it seemed ridiculous to be fighting; to Reddin it seemed ridiculous to be fighting such an opponent.

They moved out of the light and back again in the tense silence of the night. A rat splashed in the pool, and silence fell again.

Edward could not do much more than defend himself, and Reddin's eyes shone triumphantly. Within, Hazel leaned against the glass faintly. It was as if evil and good, angels and devils, fought for her. And whichever won, she was equally forlorn. She did not want heaven; she wanted earth and the green ways of earth.

"Oh, he'll kill Ed'ard!" she moaned.

Edward staggered under a blow, and she hid her eyes. Suddenly she thought of Vessons. Where was he? She ran to the kitchen calling him. He was not there. She went to the stables. He was nowhere to be found. Drawn by an irresistible curiosity, she rushed back to the front of the house. Under the yew-tree she ran into Vessons.

"Sh!" he whispered. "Say nought! I'll tell you what's a mortal good thing for a dog-fight—pepper!" He held up the kitchen pepper-pot. In the other hand he had the poker.

"Now I'll part 'em, missus, you see!"

"Quick, then!"

But as she spoke Reddin got in a blow on Edward's jaw, and he fell.

Hazel rushed forward.

"You murderer!" she screamed, and she bit Reddin's hand as he stretched it out to catch her, and bent over Edward. The victor in the fight was fated to be the loser with Hazel, for she had a never-broken compact with all creatures defeated.

She ran to the pool for water.

"Catch a holt on him!" she cried to Vessons; "he's a murderer!"

Reddin stood by, confused and mystified at Hazel's unlooked-for behaviour. Vessons bent over Edward. He struck a match and held it to the end of his nose, chuckling as Edward winced.

"I'll tell you summat as is mortal tough!" he remarked. "A minister of the Lord! Will the gen'leman stay supper?" he inquired of Reddin.

"No!" said Hazel; "Mr. Reddin'll take supper alone, for all us, to his dying day. Put the horse in, please, Mr. Vessons."

"Right you are, missus."

Reddin was so taken aback by the turn of events, and his head ached so much, that he had nothing to say. He watched Vessons bring the horse round, blinked at Hazel as she tore off the silk dress and borrowed Edward's coat instead, and glowered dumbly at Edward as he was helped into the trap. Hazel sat between the two men.

"Pluck up!" said Vessons to the cob unemotionally, and the trap jogged through the gate and out on to the open hill.

"And if it cosses me my place, I'll tell ye one thing!" Vessons said to himself: "There's as good to be had, and better."

"Well, I'm damned!" said Reddin as they disappeared in the darkness. He went in and finished the whisky in a state of mystification that ended in sleep.

CHAPTER XXX

AS the horse trotted along the hard road, rabbits scuttled across in the momentary lamplight. Hazel tied her handkerchief round Edward's head.

All the windows were dark in Alderslea, except one faint dormer where an old woman was dying. They began to climb the lane that led up to the Mountain. Cattle looked over hedges, breathing hard with curiosity. In an upland field a flock of horned sheep were racing to and fro through a gap in the hedge, coughing and stamping at intervals, and looking, as the moon rose, like fantastic devils working sorcery with their own shadows.

The lamps dimmed in the moonlight and the world seemed to widen infinitely, like life at the coming of love. The country lay below like a vast white mere, and the hill sloped vaguely to a silver sky. Vessons walked up the Batch to ease the cob, and Edward looked down at Hazel and murmured:

"My little child!"

"Dunna talk," said Hazel quickly; "it's bad for 'ee!" She was afraid to break the magical silence, afraid that the new peace that came with Marston's presence would vanish like the moon in driven cloud, and that she would feel the dragging chain that pulled her back to Reddin.

Edward was silent, puzzling over the question, Why

had not Hazel asked for his help? Reddin must have seen her at least several times, must have persecuted her. He grew very uneasy. He must ask Hazel.

They drew up before the white-sentried graveyard. Vessons went up the path and knocked at the silent house. Then he threw handfuls of white spar off a grave at the windows. The minorca cockerel crew reedily.

"That's unlucky," said Hazel.

Mrs. Marston put her head out, very sleepy, and asked who it was.

"The conquering 'ero!" said Vessons, as Edward and Hazel came up the path, deeply shadowed. He got into the trap and drove off.

"Well, Undern'll be summat like itself again now," he thought.

"It was a deal more peaceable without her, naughty girl!" thought Mrs. Marston as she sadly and lethargically put on her clothes.

"Well, Edward!" she exclaimed when she came down in her crimson shawl with the ball fringe, "here's a to-do! A minister of grace with a pocket-handkerchief round his head coming to his house in the dead of night with a wild old man. What's happened? Oh, my dear, is it your arteries? We wondered where you were, Hazel Marston!"

"I'm very shivery, mother," Edward said.

"Something hot and sweet!" She bustled off. They were alone for the first time.

"Hazel, why didn't you tell me about this man? It was not kind or right of you."

"There was nought to tell." She fidgeted.

"But he must have seen you several times."

"I was near telling you, but I thought you'd be angered."

"Angry! With you! Oh, to think of you in such danger!"

"What danger?"

"Of things that, thank God, you never dream of. He forged that letter, I suppose? Or did he frighten you into writing it?"

"Ah."

"But why did you ever go?"

"He pulled me up on the horse and took me."

"The man's a savage."

Hazel checked a hasty denial that was on her lips.

"What a pity you happened to meet him!" Edward said.

"Ah!"

"But why didn't you want to come at once when I came to fetch you? Were you so afraid of him as that?"

"Ah."

"Well, it's over now. He won't show his face here again; we've done with him."

Hazel sighed. But whether it was her spiritual self sighing with relief at being with Edward, or her physical self longing for Reddin, she could not have said.

"Only you could come through such an experience unchanged, my sweet," Edward said.

"I mun go to Foxy!" she cried desperately. "Foxy wants me."

"Foxy wants a good beating," said Mrs. Marston benignly, looking mercifully over her spectacles. Her wrath was generally like the one drop of acid in a cell of honey, smothered in loving-kindness and *embonpoint.*

When Hazel had gone, she said:

"You will send her away from here, of course?"

Edward went out into the graveyard without a word. He sat on one of the coffin-shaped stones.

"God send me some quiet!" he said.

Mrs. Marston came and draped her shawl round him. He got up, despairing of peace, and said he would go to bed.

"There's a good boy! So will I. You'll be as bright as ever in the morning. Then she whispered: "You won't keep her here?"

"Keep her! Who? Hazel? Of course Hazel will stay here."

"It's hardly right."

"Pleasant, you mean, mother. You never liked her. You want to be rid of her. But how you can so misjudge a beautiful soul I cannot think. I tell you she's as pure as a daisy. Why, she could not even bear, in her maidenly reserve, the idea of marriage. It is sheer blasphemy to say such things."

"Blasphemy, my dear, is not a thing you can do against people. It is disagreeing with the Lord that is blasphemy."

"I must ask you, anyway, never to mention Hazel's name to me until you can think of her differently."

When, after saying good-night to Hazel and Foxy, Edward had gone to bed, Mrs. Marston shook her head.

"Edward," she said, "is not what he was." She waited till Hazel came in.

"You're no wife for my son," she said; "you've sinned with another man."

"I hanna done nought nor said nought; it's all other folk's doing and saying, so I dunna see as I've sinned.

And I never could abear 'ee," Hazel cried; "I'd as lief you was dead as quick!"

She rushed up to her room and flung herself on her bed sobbing. She felt dazed, like a child taken into a big toy-shop and told to choose quickly. Life had been too hasty with her. There were things, she knew, that she would have liked; but she had so far not had time to find out what they were.

She wished she could tell Edward all about it. But how could she explain that strange inner power that had driven her to Hunter's Spinney? How could she make him understand that she did not want to go, and was yet obliged to go? She could not tell him that, although she was furious with Reddin on his behalf, although she hated Reddin for the coarseness and cruelty in him, yet parting with him had hurt her.

How could this be? She did not know. She only knew that as she lay in her little bed she wanted Reddin, his bodily presence, his kisses or his blows. He had betrayed her utterly, bringing to his aid forces he could not gauge or understand. His crime was that he had made of a woman who could not be his spiritual bride (since her spirit was unawakened, and his was to seek) his body's bride. All the divine paradoxes of sex—the mastery of the lover and his deep humility, his idealization of his bride and her absolute surrender—these he had dragged in the mud. So instead of the mysterious, transcendant illumination that passion brings to a woman, she had only confusion, darkness, and a sense of something dragging at the roots of her being in the darkness.

Her eyes needed his eyes to stare them down. The bruises on her arms ached for his hard hands. Her very tears desired his roughness to set them flowing.

"Oh, Jack Reddin! Jack Reddin! You've put a spell on me!" she moaned. "I want to be along of Ed'ard, and you've bound me to be along of you. I dunna like you, but I canna think of ought else!"

She fought a hard battle that night. The compulsion to get up and go straight to Undern was so strong that it could only be compared to the pull of matter on matter. She tried to call up Edward's voice—quiet, tender, almost religious in its tone to her. But she could only hear Reddin's voice, forceful and dictatorial, saying, "I'm master here!" And every nerve assented, in defiance of her wistful spirit, that he *was* master.

That, when morning came, she was still at the Mountain showed an extraordinary power of resistance, and was simply owing to the fact that Reddin had, in what he called "giving the parson a good hiding," opened her eyes very completely to his innate callousness, and to his temperamental and traditional hostility to her creed of love and pity. Soon, in the mysterious woods, the owls turned home—mysterious as the woods—strong creatures driven on to the perpetual destruction of the defenceless, destroyed in their turn and blown down the wind—a few torn feathers.

CHAPTER XXXI

EDWARD did not notice the strained relationship between Mrs. Marston and Hazel. He supposed that his mother's suspicions had faded before Hazel's frank presence.

Outwardly there was little change in the bearing of the two women; it was only in feminine pinpricks and things implied that Mrs. Marston showed her anger and Hazel her dislike, and it was when he was out that Martha spoke so repeatedly and emphatically of being respectable. His coming into the house brought an armoured peace, but no sooner was he outside the door than the guns were unmasked again.

Hazel wished more and more that she had stayed at Undern.

She found a man's roughness preferable to women's velvet slaps, his most masterful demands less wearing than their silent criticism. At Undern she could not call her physical self her own. Here, her heart and mind were attacked. She could not explain to Mrs. Marston that something had made her go. Mrs. Marston would simply have said "Fiddlesticks!" She could not explain that Reddin's touch drugged her. If Mrs. Marston had ever been made to feel that madness of passivity—which seemed impossible, so that Edward's existence was a paradox—she had long since forgotten it. Besides, Hazel had no words in which to express these things; she was not even clear about them herself.

She never tried to explain anything to Edward. She dreaded his anger, and she felt that only by complete silence could she keep the look of loving reverence in his eyes. She understood how very differently Reddin looked at her. It did not matter with him, but Edward—it was everything to her in Edward.

Only once there had been a keen look of criticism in Edward's eyes, and her heart had fluttered. Edward said:

"Why, when you were dragged to Undern against your will, did you wear the man's gown? It wasn't dignified. And why did you cry out on him not to shame you? He could not shame you. You had done nothing wrong."

"He said such awful things, Ed'ard, and the dress—the dress was so pretty."

"You poor child! you dear little one! So it was a pretty colour, was it?"

"Ah!"

"You shall have one like it."

He went off whistling.

It was when she had been back nearly six weeks, and the August days were scorching the Mountain, that the strain became unbearable. She was not feeling well.

Reddin had made no sign. This had at first calmed her, then piqued her; now it hurt her. Mysteriously she felt that she must be with him.

"He'm that proud, he'd ne'er ask me to go back. And if I went, there'd be no peace. Oh, Jack Reddin, Jack Reddin! You've put a spell on me! There inna much peace days, nor much rest nights, in your dark house. And yet——"

Yet, whenever she went for a walk, she felt her feet taking her towards Undern.

Then, quite suddenly, one morning Reddin rode past the house. Mrs. Marston saw him.

"Edward must know of this," she said, very much flustered. "You ought to go away somewhere, Hazel."

"Away? Why ever?"

"Out of temptation. Why not to your aunt's?"

"Aunt Prowde wouldna have me. And Ed'ard wouldna like me to go."

"Edward, I am sure, thinks as I do."

"Gospel?"

"Do not be irreverent."

"I dunna think you know what Ed'ard thinks as well as me."

"Don't say dunna, Hazel. Of course, I know what Edward thinks a great deal better than you. I've known him all his life."

Afterwards, when Mrs. Marston was not in the room, Martha said in her contemptuous tones:

"I s'pose you know, Mrs. Ed'ard, how he's going on?"

"Who?"

"Why, that Mr. Reddin."

"What's he done?"

"Oh, I know! But I wouldn't soil me mouth, only I'm thinking you'd ought to know."

She looked triumphant.

"He's after that there Sally something as lives near by. They do say as all her brats be his."

"Mr. Reddin's? Is he—like—married to her, Martha?"

"About as much as he was to you, I reckon!"

"And does she—live there now?"

"I dunno."

"Is she pretty?"

"It inna allus the prettiest as get lovers."

"But is she prettier than me?"

"I've heard she's bigger and finer."

"But she hanna got abron hair?"

"How should I know?"

This was desolate news to Hazel; for Reddin, now that she was going to bear his child, had become necessary to her. She was unconscious of the reason of this need—not a spiritual one, but purely physiological. She did not hate him for this news. Such hatred is abnormal. Nor did she love him. That would have been still more abnormal. But she must be in his house; she must sew for him, share his daily doings, sleep in the big four-poster, and not in the small virginal bed at the Mountain. It would be grievous to leave Edward. He was the shelter between her flickering spirit and the storms of life. She had hesitated, putting off the inevitable, feeling that Undern was always there, like an empty room, for her re-entry, so she had not hurried. Now the room was occupied, her place taken. Immediately she felt that she must go. Feverishly she decided to go this very night and peer in (no one but herself had ever drawn the blinds at Undern of late years) and see for herself. Mrs. Marston and Martha both seemed to be pushing her over the brink.

When, after tea, she crept from the house, she was crying—crying at leaving Edward, the master and the comrade of her unknown self. It was as if she gave up immortality. Yet she was relieved to be going—that is, if she could stay at Undern. Both her tears and her relief were natural. The pity was that body and soul had been put in opposition by belonging to different men.

She left a little blotted note for Edward.

"Dunna think too bad of me, Ed'ard. I be bound to go to Undern and live; I ud liefer bide along of you."

She went through the shadow-sweet meadows where birds hopped out across green stretches in the cool, the high corn that had once been her comrade, the honeysuckle hedges that used to bring so childish a glee. They wore an air of things estranged and critical. All was so sad, like a dear friend with an altered countenance. She was an exile even in the seeing and hearing. It was strange to her as a town under the tides. There it was, clear and belfried as of old, but fathoms deep, and the bells had so faint a chime that Reddin's voice drowned them. She was turned out of the Eden of the past that she had known in wood and meadow. She was denied the Eden of the future that she might have had in Edward's love. She had the present—Reddin—unless the other woman had robbed her of him also.

She sat down in the heavy shadow of the trees at the far side of Undern Pool. The water looked cold and ghastly even on this golden day. She watched the wagtails strut magisterially, the moorhens with the worried air of overworked charwomen, all the mysterious evening life of a summer pool, but she had no smile for them to-day. The swallows slid and circled across the water; their silence was no longer intimate, but alien. She looked across at Undern. There were roses everywhere, but the house had so strong a faculty for imposing its personality that it gave to the red roses and the masses of traveller's joy that frothed a deep sadness, as if they had blown and dropped long since and were but memoried flowers. The shadows of swallows came and went on the white western wall, and smoke stood up blue and straight from Vessons' kitchen fire. She watched the cows go down the green lane, and the shadows go over the meadows in triumphal state. When all was shadow, and the sky was as suddenly vacant of swallows as at dawn it had been full of them, she went stealthily towards the house.

A light appeared in the parlour. She came close up and looked in.

Reddin was in the easy-chair, reading the paper, a pipe in the corner of his mouth. No one else was there.

"Jack Reddin!" she said.

"Hullo!" He turned. "So you've come? I thought you'd have come long ago."

That was all he said. But she assured herself that he was glad she had come, because he shouted to Vessons for tea. She was certain he was glad to see her. Yet there was something vaguely insolent in his manner. He was a man who must never be sure of a woman. The moment she committed herself for him and was at a disadvantage he despised her.

"Come over here!" he said. "There! I suppose you've forgotten what it's like to be kissed, eh? And to live with a man? You can never go away again now."

"Why?"

"Well, you are a simpleton! D'you think he'd have you back after this? The first time was my fault, he thinks; but the second! It won't wash." He laughed.

"This time's your fault as much as the other. You made me come both times. There's Vessons! Let me get up."

"No. Why should I?"

Vessons entered.

"This 'ere game of tether-ball," he said, "fair makes me giddy."

"Jack," said Hazel when he had gone, "Martha said there was a woman here."

"Martha's a liar."

"Hanna there bin?"

"No. Never anyone but you."

"Hanna you bin fond of anyone?"

"Only you."

"She said there was a woman as had a lot of little children, as was yours."

"Damn her!"

"And I thought she'd ought to live along of you, and to be married-like, and wear the green dress."

"No one shall wear that but you, nor have my children but you."

She was, as he had calculated, entirely overwhelmed, and so startled that she forgot to question him any more.

"Oh no," she said; "that'll never be."

He raised his eyebrows at her extraordinary denseness, but he judged it best to say no more.

He must get rid of Sally. He supposed she would make him pay heavily. He was sick of the sight of her and the children. They were not nice children. He looked at Hazel contemplatively. If his conjecture was right, he would have to try and legalize things during the next few months. He badly wanted a son—born in wedlock. He would have to go and beg the parson to divorce her. It would be detestable, but it would have to be done. He would wait and see.

Meanwhile, Vessons also made plans, his obstinate mouth and pear-shaped face more dour than ever.

Hazel had a letter from Edward in the morning; it was very short. She could not tell what he thought of her.

He only said that if she ever wanted help she was to come to him. She cried over it, and hid it away. She knew well how Edward would have looked as he wrote it. She knew he would be grieved. She had not the slightest idea that he would be utterly overwhelmed and wrecked. She had not the least notion how he felt for her.

She was very glad to be away from Mrs. Marston and Martha. She found this household of two men a great rest after the two women, although Vessons did not relax his disapproval. If it had not been for her passionate, spiritual longing for Edward, she would have been happy, for the deep law of her being was now fulfilled in thus returning to Reddin. He, for his part, liked to see her about. Roses appeared in the rooms; it was strange to him, who had never had a woman in his house, to find his bedroom scented with flowers. He liked to watch her doing her hair.

He always pretended to be asleep in the morning, so that she should get up first—shyly anxious to be dressed before he awoke. So morning after morning he would watch her through his eyelashes. He never felt that, as she obviously wished for privacy, he was mean or indelicate.

"I've got a right to. She's mine," was his idea.

It was not till a week after Hazel's coming that Reddin pulled himself together, and went to interview Sally Haggard. Vessons, observing the fact, repaired to Sally's cottage on his master's return, and found her in tears. To this see heavy-browed, big-boned woman crying so startled him that he contemplated her in silence.

"Well, fool, can't you speak?" she said.

"I dare say now as he wants you to move on?" queried Vessons.

"Ah."

"Because of this other young 'ooman he's brought?"

"Ah, what's the good o' mouthing it? I bin faithful to 'im; I hanna gone with others. All the chillun's his'n. And never come near me, he didna, when my time come. And now it's 'go!' " She broke out crying again.

"What I come for was to show you a way to make *her* go. If I tell you, you mun swear never to come and live at Undern."

"Struth I will!"

"Well, then, just you come and see 'er some time when the master's away. And bring the chillun."

"Thank you kindly."

"Not till I say the word, though! I wunna risk it till he's off for the day. If he found me out, it'd be notice. Eh, missus, he's like a lad with his first white mouse! And the parson! Laws, they'm two thrussels wi' one worm, and no mistake."

"And yet she's only a bit of a thing, you tell me?"

"Ah! But she'm all on wires, to and agen like a canbottle."

"Why canna she bide with the minister?"

"Lord only knows! It's for 'er good, and for the maister's and yours, not to speak of mine. It's werrit, werrit, all the while, missus, and the fingers in the tea-caddy the day long! It's Andrew this and Andrew that, and a terrible strong smell of flowers—enough for a burying."

Vessons waited eagerly for his opportunity; but Reddin was afraid to leave Hazel alone, in case she might see Sally; so September came and drew out its shining span of days, and still Vessons and Sally were waiting.

CHAPTER XXXII

MORNING by morning Hazel watched the fuchsia-bushes, set with small red flowers, purple-cupped, with crimson stamens, sway in beautiful abandon. The great black bees pulled at them like a calf at its mother. Their weight dragged the slender drooping branches almost to the earth. So the rich pageantry of beauty, the honied silent lives went on, and would go on, it seemed, for ever. And then one morning all was over; one of Undern's hard early frosts took them all—the waxen red-pointed buds, the waxen purple cups, the red-veined leaves. The bees were away, and Hazel, seeking them, found a few half alive in sheltered crevices, and many frozen stiff. She put those that were still alive in a little box near the parlour fire. Soon a low delighted humming began as they one by one recovered and set off to explore the ceiling. Into this contented buzzing came Reddin, who had just been again to Sally's, and was much put out by her refusal to go away before November.

"What the h—— is all this humming?" he asked.

"It's bees. I've fetched 'em in to see good times a bit afore they die."

"What a child's trick!" he said, fending off an inquiring bee. "Why, they'll stay here all winter! We shall get stung." Then he saw the hospital full of bees by the fire.

"More?" he said. "Good Lord!" He threw the box into the fire.

Hazel was silent with horror. At last she gasped: "I was mothering 'em!"

"You're very keen on mothering! Wouldn't you like a kid to mother?"

"No. I'd liefer mother the bees and foxes as none takes thought on. I dunna like babies much—all bald and wrinkly. Martha said as having 'em made folk pray to die, but as it was worth anything to get one. But I dunna think so. I think they'm ugly. I seed one in a pram outside that cottage in the Hollow" (Reddin jumped), "and it was uglier than a pig. I think you're a cruel beast, Jack Reddin, to burn my bees, and they so comforble, knowing I was taking care on 'em."

She would not speak to him for the rest of the day. He was so bored in the evening that he went out and demanded a boxful of bees from Vessons.

"The missus wants 'em," he said sheepishly.

Vessons was prepared to be pleasant in small matters. He fetched some from the hive.

"'Ere you are," he said patronizingly; "but you munna be always coming to me after 'em."

He was oblivious of the fact that they were Reddin's bees.

Reddin presented them.

"There," he said gruffly; "now you can be civil again."

"But these be hive-bees!" said Hazel, "and they was comforble to begin with! I dunna want that sort. I wanted miserable uns!"

"Hang it! how could I know?" asked Reddin irritably.

"No. I suppose you couldna," said Hazel; "you'm terrible stupid, Jack Reddin!"

So life went on at Undern, and Hazel adapted herself to it as well as she could. It was strange that the longer she lived there the more she thought of Edward. She always saw his face lined with grief and very pale, not tanned and ruddy with fresh air as she had known it. It was as if his mentality reached across the valley to hers and laid its melancholy upon her. Sometimes she was very homesick for Foxy, but she would not have her at Undern. She did not trust the place. She never went out anywhere, for people stared, and when Reddin, with some difficulty, persuaded her to amble round the fields with him on a pony he picked up cheap for her, she always wanted to keep in his own fields.

It was not until nearly the end of October that Vessons got his chance. Reddin had to go to a very important fair. He wanted Hazel to go with him, but she said she was tired, and, guessing the reason, he immediately gave in.

In spite of Vessons' earnest desire to get him off, he started late. He galloped most of the way, determined to get in early. He liked coming home to tea and seeing Hazel awaiting him in the firelight.

As soon as he had gone, Vessons set out for Sally's, anxious that she should be quick. But Sally would not hurry. It was washing-day, and she also insisted on making all the children very smart, unaware that their extreme ugliness was her strength. It was not till three o'clock that she arrived at the front door, baby in arms, the four children, heavily expectant, at her heels, and Vessons stage-managing in the background.

Hazel had been looking at two of the only books at Undern—"The Horse" and "The Dog," illustrated. Vessons had views about books. He considered them useful in their place.

"There's nought like a book," he would say, "one of these 'ere big fat novels or a book of sermons, to get a nice red gledy fire. A book at the front and a bit of slack behind, and there you are!"

There the books were, too.

So Hazel looked at the "Book of the Horse" until she knew all the pictures by heart. She had fallen asleep over it, and she jumped up in panic when Sally spoke.

"Who be you?" she asked in a frightened voice as they eyed her.

"I'm Sally Haggard, and these be my children." She surveyed them proudly. "D'you notice that they favour anyone?"

Hazel looked at them timidly.

"They favour you," she said.

"Not Mr. Reddin?"

"Mr. Reddin?"

"Ah. They'd ought to. They'm his'n."

"His'n?"

"Yes, parrot."

"Be you the 'ooman as Martha said Jack lived along of?"

"He did live along of me."

"Why, then, you'd ought to be Mrs. Reddin, and wear this gownd, and live at Undern," said Hazel.

"Eh?" Sally was astonished.

"And he said there wunna any other but me."

Sally laughed.

"You believed that lie? You little softie!"

Hazel looked at the children.

"Be they *all* his'n?" she said.

"Every man-jack of 'em, and not so much as a thank you for me!"

The children were ranged near their mother—on high chairs. They gaped at Hazel, sullen and critical. An irrepressible question broke from Hazel.

"What for did you have 'em?"

Sally stared.

"What for?" she repeated. "Surely to goodness, girl, you're not as innicent-like as that?"

"I ain't ever going to have any," Hazel went on with great firmness, as she eyed the children.

"God above!" muttered Sally. "He's fooled her worse'n me!"

"Come and look at the baby, my dear," she said in a voice astonishingly soft. She looked at Hazel keenly. "Dunna you know?" she asked.

"What?"

"As you're going to have a baby?"

Hazel sprang up, all denial. But Sally, having told the children to play, spoke for a long time in a low tone, and finally convinced a white, sick, trembling Hazel of the fact. Not being sensitive herself, she did not realize the ghastly terror caused by her lurid details of the coming event.

Hazel looked so ill that Sally tried to administer consolation. "Maybe it'll be a boy, and you'll be fine and pleased to see 'un growing a fine tall man like Reddin."

Hazel burst into tears, so that the children stopped their play to watch and laugh.

"But I dunna want it to grow up like Jack," she said. "I want it to grow up like Ed'ard, and none else!"

"Well! You *are* a queer girl. If you like him as you call Ed'ard, what for did you take up with Jack?"

"I dunno."

"Well, the best you can do," said Sally, "is to go back to your Edward, lithermonsload and all. And if he wunna take you——"

"Eh, but he will!" A wonderful tender smile broke on Hazel's face. "He'll come to the front door and pull me in and say, 'Come in, little Hazel, and get a cup of tea.' And it'll be all the same as it was used to be."

"Well, he must be a fool! But so much the better for you. If I was you, I'd go right back to-neet. Now what'd you say to a cup o' tea? I'm thinking it's high time I took a bite and sup in this parlour!"

They got tea; and Vessons, hovering in the yard, was in despair. He could not appear, for Hazel must not know his part in the affair. "Laws! If they've begun on tea, it's all up with Andrew," he remarked to the swan in passing.

Dusk came on and still no Sally appeared. The two chimneys smoked hospitably, and he wanted his tea. He was a very miserable old man. He repaired to the farthest corner of the domain and began to cut a hedge, watching the field track. Soon Reddin appeared, and Vessons was unable to repress a chuckle.

"Rather 'im than me!" he said.

Reddin, having fruitlessly shouted for Vessons, took the cob round to the yard himself. Then he went in. As he entered the parlour, aware of a comfortable scent of tea and toast, he met the solemn gaze of seven pairs of eyes, and for a moment he was, for all his tough skin, really staggered.

Then he advanced upon Sally with his stock firmly grasped in his hand.

"Get out of this!" he said.

The baby set up a yell. Sally rose and stood with her arm raised to fend off the blow.

"Jack," said Hazel, "she'm got the best right to be at Undern. Leave her stay! She'm a right nice 'ooman."

Reddin gasped. Why would Hazel always do and say exactly the opposite to what he expected?

"But you're the last person——" he began.

"You're thinking she'd ought to be jealous of me, Jack Reddin," said Sally. "But we'm neither of us jealous! I tell you straight! She's too good for you. You've lied to me; I'm used to it. Now you'm lied to her—poor innicent little thing!"

"What for did you tell me lies, Jack?" asked Hazel.

What with the unfaltering gaze of the two women, and the unceasing howls of the baby, Reddin was completely routed.

"Oh, damn you all!" he said, and went hot-foot in a towering passion to look for Vessons. A man to rage at would be a very great luxury. Having at last found Vessons, harmlessly hedge-brushing, he was rather at a loss.

"How dare you let Sally in?" he began.

"Sally?"

"Yes. Why the h—— did you come away here and leave the house?"

"The 'edge wanted doing."

His tone was so innocent that Reddin was suspicious.

"You didn't bring her yourself, did you?"

"Now, *is* it me," said Vessons, reasonable but hurt, "as generally brings these packs of unruly women to Undern?"

"I believe you're lying, Vessons."

Vessons opened his mouth to say, "Notice is giv' "; but seeing that in his master's present mood it might be accepted, he closed it again.

When Reddin went in, Sally was gone, and Hazel, much as usual, ministered to his comfort. The only signs of the recent tumult were the constrained silence and the array of cups and plates.

"You'd better understand once and for all," he said at last, "that I'll never have that woman here."

"Not if I went?"

"Never! I'd kill her first."

"What for did you tell me lies?"

"Because you were so pretty and I wanted you."

The flattery fell on deaf ears.

"Them chil'en's terribly ugly," said Hazel wearily.

Reddin came over to her.

"But yours'll be pretty!" he said.

"Dunna come nigh me!" cried Hazel fiercely. "She says I'm going to have a little un! It was a sneak's trick, that; and you're a cruel beast, Jack Reddin, to burn my bees and kill the rabbits and make me have a little un unbeknown."

"But it's what all women expect!"

"You'd ought to have told me. She says it's mortal pain to have a baby, and I'm feared—I'm feared!"

"Hazel," he said humbly, "I may as well tell you now that I mean to marry you. The parson must divorce you. Then we'll be married. And I'll turn over a new leaf."

"I'll ne'er marry you!" said Hazel, "not till Doom breaks. I dunna like you. I like Ed'ard. And if I mun have a baby, I'd lief it was like Ed'ard, and not like you."

With that she went out of the room, and he noticed that she was wearing the dress she had come in, and not the silk.

He sat by the fire, brooding; but at last managed to cheer himself by the thought that she would get over it in time. She was naturally upset by Sally just now.

"And, of course, the parson'll never take her back, nor her father," he reflected. "Yes, it'll all come right."

He was upheld in this by the fact that Hazel's manner next day was much as usual, only rather quiet.

CHAPTER XXXIII

IT was the night of the great storm. Undern rattled and groaned; its fireless chimneys roared, and doors in unused passages banged so often that the house took on an air of being inhabited. It seemed as if all the people that had ever lived here had come back, ignoring in their mournful dignity of eternal death these momentary wraiths of life. Hazel had always been afraid of the place, and had sat up until Reddin wanted to go to bed, so that she need not traverse the long passages alone. But to-night she was afraid of Reddin also—not just a little afraid, as she had always been, but full of unreasoning terror.

All things were confused in her mind, like the sounds that were in the wind: Reddin's face, distorted with rage, as he advanced on Sally with his arm raised; the howling of the baby; the sound of her bees burning—going off like apple-pips. A scene came back to her from the week before—it seemed years ago. They had gone into the harvest-field after a hot, yellow day haunted by the sound of cutting. Only a small square of orange wheat was left; the rest of the field lay in the pale disorder of destruction. The two great horses stood at one corner, darkly shining in the level light. The men who had been tying sheaves stood about, some women and children were coming over the stubble, and several dogs lay in the shadow. They all seemed to be waiting. They were, in fact, waiting for Reddin, who was always present at the dramatic finish of a field. Hazel knew what drama was to be enacted; knew what the knobbed sticks were for; knew who crouched in the tall, kindly wheat, palpitant, unaware that escape was impossible.

"Plenty o' conies, sir!" called one of the men, whose face was a good deal more brutal than that of his mongrel dog.

Hazel knew that the small square must be packed with rabbits, stark-eyed and still as death, who had, with a fated foolishness, drawn in from the outer portions of the field all day as the reaper went round.

"Jack," she said, "I hanna asked for a present ever."

"No. You didn't want the bracelets, you silly girl."

"I want one now."

"You do, do you?"

"Ah! If you'll give it me, Jack, I'll do aught you want. What'd you like best in the 'orld?"

He considered. He was feeling very fit and almost too much alive.

"Hunter's Spinney over again—up to when we got so gloomy."

Hazel never wanted to think of that night again, nor see the Spinney again. There had been many times since, in the grey-tinted room, that had been nearly as bad. But for evoking a shuddering, startled horror in her mind, nothing came up to that Sunday night.

The reaper was moving again. Soon the rabbits would begin to bolt.

"I'll do ought and go anywhere if you'll do this as I want, Jack."

"Well?"

"Call 'em off! Leave the last bit till morning.

Let 'em creep away in the dark and keep living a bit longer!"

"What nonsense!"

"Call 'em off, Jack! You can. You'm maister!"

"No."

She sobbed. "I be going, then."

"No. You're to stay. You'll have to be cured of this damned silliness, and learn to be sensible."

While she struggled to wrench herself free, two rabbits bolted, and hell broke loose. One would not have thought that the great calm evening under its stooping sky, the peaceful, omniscient trees, the grave, contented colours, could have tolerated such hideousness. The women and children shrieked with the best, and Hazel stood alone—the single representative, in a callous world, of God. Or was the world His representative, and she something alien, a dissentient voice to be silenced?

Such scenes, infinitely multiplied, bring that question to one's mind.

A rabbit had dashed across the field close to them, and Reddin, relaxing his grip of her, had slashed at it with his stick. The look of its eye, white and staring, as it fled past her with insensate speed, came back to her now, and its convulsive roll over and recovery under the blow; and then the next blow—— She had fled from the place.

She thought again of what Sally had said, and a deep, smouldering rage was in her at this that he had done to her—this torture to which, according to Sally, he had quite consciously condemned her.

Now that she knew him better, his daily acts of callousness tormented her. She would go. She was not wanted here. Sally had said so. There had been letters from her aunt, from Reddin's vicar, from the eldest Miss Clomber. In them all she was spoken of as the culprit for being at Undern. Well, she did not want to be at Undern. She would go.

"Well, Hazel, child, what's the matter?" asked Reddin, looking up from doing his quarterly accounts. "Haven't you got a stocking to mend, or a hair-ribbon to make?"

"A many and a many things be the matter."

"Come here, and I'll see if I can put 'em right."

"Harkee!" she said suddenly. "It's like as if the jeath-pack was i' full cry down the wind."

"Anyone would think you were off your head, Hazel. But come and tell me about the things that are the matter."

"It's you as makes 'em the matter."

"Oh, well, sulk as long as you like."

He returned angrily to his accounts. In the kitchen Vessons, very spondaic, was singing "The Three Jolly Huntsmen."

In a few minutes Hazel rose and lit a candle. She looked, as she walked to the door in her limp muslin dress, like the spectre of some unhappy creature of the past.

"Where are you going?" asked Reddin.

"I thought to go to bed."

"I'm not ready."

"I'll go by my lonesome."

"All right, sulk! It doesn't hurt me."

But it did hurt him. He wanted her to be fond of him, to cling to him. When at last he went up through the screaming house, he thought she was asleep. She lay still in the big bed and made no sign.

Reddin was soon snoring, for accounts implied a

strenuous intellectual effort. He would have left them to Vessons, but Vessons always had to notch sticks when he did them, and the manual labour ensuing on any accounts running into pounds would have seriously interfered with his other work. The cheese fair accounts usually took a long time. He could be heard saying in a stupendous voice, "One and one and one——" until the chant ended in, "Drat it! what *do* 'em maken?"

So Reddin did the accounts, and slept the sleep of the intellectual worker afterwards.

Hazel looked out from the tent of the bed canopy into the dark, creaking room and the darker, roaring night. She grew more afraid of Reddin and Undern as the hours dragged on.

Reddin's presence tore to pieces the things she loved—delicate leafy things—as if they were tissue-paper and he had walked through it. Her pleasure seemed to mean nothing when he was with her, and before his loud laughter her wonderful faery-haunted days shrivelled. All she knew was that, now she lived at Undern, she never went out in the green dawn or came home wreathed in pansy and wild snapdragon.

Reddin had imposed a deeper change on her than the change from maid to wife. He had robbed her of a thing frailer and rarer than maidenhood—the sacramental love of Nature. It is only the fairest, the highest and fullest matings that do not rob the soul of this, even when it is an old, tried joy. He had wronged her as deeply as one human being can wrong another. His theft was cruel as that of one who destroys a man's God. And the strange part of it was that never, as long as he lived, would he know that he had done so, or even guess that there had been any treasury to rifle. He would probably, as an old man, long past desire, repent of the physical part of the affair. Yet this was so much the lesser of the two. Indeed, if he had been able to win her love, it would have been, not wrong-doing, but righteousness. That a woman should, in the evolution of life, cease to be a virgin and become a mother is a thing so natural and so purely physical as hardly to need comment; but that the immortal part of her should be robbed, that she should cease to be an entity in a world where personality is the only rare and precious thing—this is tragic.

Reddin could not help his over-virility, nor could he help having the insensitive nature that could enjoy the physical side of sex without the spiritual; probably he could not help being the kind of man that supplies the most rabid imperialists, reactionaries, materialists. (He always spoke of heathen Chinee, lower orders, beastly foreigners, mad fanatics, and silly sentimentalists, these last being those who showed any kind of mercy.) It seemed that he could not help seeing nothing outside his own narrow views.

But it did seem a pity that he never tried to alter in the least. It did seem a pity that, after so many centuries, so many matings and births, all his emblazoned and crested ancestors should have produced merely—Reddin, a person exactly like themselves.

Rain rustled on the window and the wind roared in the elms. The trees round Undern Pool stooped and swung in the attitude of mowers. Hazel knew that the Mountain would be even wilder to-night. Yet the Mountain shone in paradisal colours—her little garden; her knitting; the quiet Sundays; the nightly prayers;

above all, Edward's presence, in the aura of which no harm could come—for all these things she passionately longed.

They were not home as the wild was, but they were a haven. They were not ecstasy, but they were peace.

In her revulsion from Reddin and her terror of Undern, she forgot everything except the sense of protection that Edward gave her. She forgot Mrs. Marston's silent, crushing criticism and Martha's rude righteousness. She forgot that she had sinned against the Mountain so deeply that the old life could never return.

She remembered it as on the night of her wedding—the primroses, red and white and lilac; the soothing smell of the clean sheets, that made her feel religious; the reassuring tick of the wall-clock; Mrs. Marston's sliding tread; Foxy and the rabbit, the blackbird, and the one-eyed cat.

She struck a match softly and crept across the room to the old mahogany tallboy. From beneath a drawerful of clothes she took out Edward's letter. She read it slowly, for she was, as Abel said, no scholar. Edward wanted her, that was quite clear. Comfort flowed from the half-dozen lines.

The ethics of the thing held no place in her mind. She was not made for the comforts or the duties of social life, and it was not in her—nor would it have been, however she had been educated—to consider what effect her actions might have on the race. Humanity did not interest her.

The ever-circling wheels of birth, mating, death, so all-absorbing to most women, were nothing to her. Freedom, green ways, childlike pleasures of ferny, mossy discoveries, the absence of hunger or pain, and the presence of Foxy and other salvage of her pity—these were the great realities. She had a deeper fear than most people of death and any kind of violence or pain for herself or her following. Her idea of God had always been shadowy, but it now took shape as a kind of omnipotent Edward.

When she had read the letter, she went to the window. A tortured dawn crept up the sky. Vast black clouds, shaped like anvils for some terrific smithy-work, were ranged round the horizon, and, later, the east glowed like a forge. The gale had not abated, but was rising in a series of gusts, each one a blizzard. Hazel was not afraid of it, or of the shrieking woods. The wind had always been her playmate. The wide plain that lay before the Undern windows was shrouded in rain—not falling, but driving. Willows, comely in the evening with the pale gold of autumn, had been stripped in a moment like prisoners of a savage conqueror for sacrifice. The air was full of leaves, whirling, boiling, as in a cauldron. From every field and covert, from the lone hill-tracts behind the house, from garden and orchard, came the wail of the vanquished.

Even as she watched, one of the elms by the pool fell with a grinding crash. Reddin stirred in his sleep and muttered restlessly. She waited, frozen with suspense, until he was quiet again.

She could hear the hound baying, terrified at the noise of the tree. She dressed hurriedly, crept downstairs, and went out by the back way, leaving the house, with its watchful windows, its ancient quiet which was not peace, and the grey, flapping curtains of the rain closed in behind her.

She found a little shelter in the deep lanes, but

when she came to the woods leading up to the Mountain the wind was reaping them like corn. Larches lay like spellicans one on another. Some leant against those that were yet standing, and in the tops of these last there was a roaring like an incoming tide on rocks. Crackings and groanings, sudden crashes, loud reports like gun-fire, were all about her as she climbed—a tiny figure in chaos.

When she came to the graveyard, havoc was there also. Several crosses had fallen, and were smashed; the laburnum-tree, rich with grey seed-vessels, lay prone, and in its fall it had carried half the tomb away with it, so that it yawned darkly, but not as a grave from which one has risen from the dead. A headstone lay in the path, and the text, "In sure and certain hope of the resurrection," was half obliterated.

Hazel crept into the porch of the chapel to shelter, utterly exhausted. She went to sleep, and was awakened by the breakfast-bell. She went to the front door and knocked.

CHAPTER XXXIV

EDWARD, coming downstairs, felt such a rush of joy and youth at sight of her that he was obliged to stand still and remember that joy and youth were not for him, that his love had gone of her own will to another man, and must be to him now only a poor waif sheltered for pity. He was very much altered. His face frightened Hazel.

"Have you come to stay, Hazel, or only for a visit?" he asked.

"Oh, dunna look at me the like o' that, and dunna talk so stern, Ed'ard!"

"I wasn't aware that I was stern."

Edward's face was white. He looked down at her with an expression she could not gauge. For there had come upon him, seeing her there again, so sweet in her dishevelment, so enchanting in her suppliance, the same temptation that tormented him on his wedding-day. Only now he resisted it for a different reason.

Hazel, his Hazel, was no fit mate for him. The words flamed in his brain; then, fiercely, he denied them. He would not believe it. Circumstance, Hazel, his mother, even God might shout the lie at him. Still, he would not believe.

But he must have it out with her. He must know.

"Hazel," he said, "after breakfast I want you to come with me up the Mountain."

"Yes, Ed'ard," she said obediently.

She adored his sternness. She adored his look of weariness. She longed hopefully and passionately for his touch.

For now, when it was too late, she loved him—not with any love of earth; that was spoilt for her—but with a grave amorousness kin to that of the Saints, the passion that the Magdalen might have felt for Christ. The earthly love should have been Edward's, too, and would have run in the footsteps of the other love, like a young creature after its mother. But Reddin had intervened.

"First," Edward said, "you must have some food and a cup of tea."

He never wavered in tenderness to her. But she noticed that he did not say "dear," nor did he, bringing her in, take her hand.

Breakfast was an agony to Edward, for his mother, who had from the first treated Hazel with silent contempt as a sinner, now stood, on entering with the toast, and said:

"I will not eat with that woman."

"Mother!"

"If you bring that woman here, I will be no mother to you."

"Mother! For my sake!"

"She is a wicked woman," went on Mrs. Marston, in a calm but terrible voice; "she is an adulteress."

Edward sprang up.

"How dare you?" he said.

"Are you going to turn her out, Edward?"

"No."

"Eddie! my little lad!"

Her voice shook.

"No."

"My boy that I lay in pain for two days and a night, to bring you into the world!"

Edward covered his face with his hands.

"You will put me before—her?"

"No, mother."

"You were breast-fed, Eddie, though I was very weak."

There was a little silence. Edward buried his face in his arms.

"Right is on my side, Edward, and what I wish is God's will. You will put duty first?"

"No. Love."

"I am getting old, dear. I have not many more years. She has all a lifetime. You will put me first?"

He lifted his head. He looked aged and worn.

"No! And again no!" he said. "Stop torturing me, mother!"

Mrs. Marston turned without a word to go out. Hazel sprang up, breaking into a passion of tears.

"Oh, let me go!" she cried. "I'll go away and away! What for did you fetch me from the Calla? None wants me. I wunna miserable at the Calla. Let me go!"

She stared at Mrs. Marston with terrified eyes. "She's as awful as death," she said, "the old lady. As awful as Mr. Reddin when he's loving. I'm feared, Ed'ard! I'd liefer go."

But Edward's arm was round her. His hand was on her trembling one.

"You shall not frighten my little one!" he said to his mother; and she fled to the kitchen, where, frozen with grief, she remained all morning in a kind of torpor. Martha was afraid she would have a stroke. But she dared not speak to Edward, for, hovering in the passage, she had seen his face as he shut the door.

He made Hazel eat and drink. Then they went out on the hill.

"Now, Hazel," he said, "we must have truth between us. Did you go with that man of your own will?" good question

She was silent.

"You must have done, or why go a second time? Did you?" His eyes compelled her. She shivered.

"Yes, Ed'ard. But I didna want to. I didna!"

"How can both be true?"

"They be."

"How did he compel you to go, then?"

Hazel sought for an illustration.

"Like a jacksnipe fetches his mate out o' the grass," she said.

"What did he say?"

"Nought."

"Then how——?"

"There's things harder than words; words be nought."

"Go on."

"It was like as if there was a secret atween us, and I'd got to find it out. Dunna look so fierce, Ed'ard!"

"Did you find out?"

A tide of painful red surged over Hazel; she turned away. But Edward, rendered pitiless by pain, forcibly pulled her back, and made her look at him.

"Did you find out?" he repeated.

"There inna no more," she whispered.

"Then it is true what he said, that you were his from head to foot?"

"Oh, Ed'ard, let me be! I canna bear it!"

"I wish I could have killed him!" Edward said. "Then you were his—soul and body?"

"Not soul!"

"You told a good many lies."

"Oh, Ed'ard, speak kind!"

"What a fool I was! You must have detested me for interrupting the honeymoon. Of course you went back! What a fool I was! And I thought you were pure as an angel."

"I couldna help it, Ed'ard; the signs said go, and then he threw me in the bracken."

Something broke in Edward's mind. The control of a life-time went from him.

"Why didn't I?" he cried. "Why didn't I? Good God! To think I suffered and renounced for this!" He laughed. "And all so simple! Just throw you in the bracken!"

She shuddered at the knife-edge in his voice, and also at the new realization that broke on her that Edward had it in him to be like Reddin.

"What for do you fritten me?" she whispered.

"But it's not too late," Edward went on, and his face, that had been grey, flushed scarlet. "No, it's not too late. I'm not particular. You're not new; but you'll do."

He crushed her to him and kissed her.

"I'm your husband," he said, "and from this day on I'll have my due. You've lied to me, been unfaithful to me, made me suffer because of your purity—and you had no purity. To-night you sleep in my room; you've slept in his."

"Oh, let me go, Ed'ard! let me go!" She was lost indeed now. For Edward, the righteous and the loving, was no more. Where should she flee? She did not know this man who held her in a desperate embrace. He was more terrible to her than all the rest—more terrible, far, than Reddin—for Reddin had never been a god to her.

"I knelt by your bedside and fought my instincts, and they were good instincts. I had a right to them. I gave up more than you can ever guess."

"I'm much obleeged, Ed'ard," she said tremblingly.

"I've disgraced my calling, and I've this morning hurt my mother beyond healing."

"I'd best be going, Ed'ard. The sun'll soon be undering."

The day blazed towards noon, but she felt the chill of darkness.

"And now," Edward finished, "that I have no mother, no self-respect, and no respect for you, I will at least have my pleasure and—my children."

The words softened him a little.

"Hazel," he said, "I will forgive you for murdering my soul, when you give me a son; I will almost believe in you again, next year—Hazel——"

He knelt by her with his arms round her. She was astonished at the mastery of passion in him. She had never thought of him but as passionless.

"To-night," he said, and tenderness crept back into his voice, "is my bridal. There is no saving for me now in denial, only in fulfilment. I can forgive much, Hazel, for I love much. But I can't renounce any more."

Hazel had heard nothing of what he said since the words, "when you give me a son."

They rang in her brain. She felt dazed. At last she looked up affrightedly.

"But," she said, "when I have the baby, it unna be yours, but his'n."

"What?"

"It—it'll be his'n."

"What?"

He questioned foolishly, like a child. He could not understand.

"It's gone four month since midsummer," she said, "and Sally said I was wi' child of—of——"

"You need not go on, Hazel."

Edward's face looked pinched. The passion had gone, and a deathly look replaced it. He was robbed, utterly and cruelly. He could no longer believe in a God, or how could such things be? Manhood was denied him. The last torture was not denied him—namely, that he saw the full satire of his position, saw that it was his own love that had destroyed them both. Out of his complete ruin he arose joyless, hopeless, but great in a tenderness so vast and selfless that it almost took the place of what he had lost.

Hazel was again his inspiration, not as an ideal, but as a waif. In his passion of pity for her he forgot everything. He had something to live for again.

"Poor child!" he said. "Come home. I will take care of you."

"But—the old lady?"

"You are first."

She caught his hands; she flung herself upon his shoulder in a rush of tears. If this was his tragic moment, it was also hers.

"Oh, Ed'ard, Ed'ard!" she cried, "it's you as I'd lief have for my lover! It's you as I'm for, body and soul, if I'm for mortal man! It's your baby as I want, Ed'ard, and I wouldna be feared o' the pain as Sally told of if it was yours. What for didna you tell me in the spring o' the year, Ed'ard? It be winter now, and late and cold."

"There, there! you don't know what you're saying. Come home!"

Edward had not listened to her, she knew. And, indeed, his brain was weary, and could take in no more. He only knew he must care for Hazel as Christ cared for the lambs of His fold. And darkly on his dark mind loomed his new and bitter creed, "There is no Christ."

CHAPTER XXXV

MARTHA met them on the doorstep, crying, hiccoughing, and enraged.

"Why, Martha!" Edward looked at her in astonishment. It is usually the supers, and not the principals, that raise lamentation in the midst of tragedy—"why, Martha, have you lost someone dear to you?"

He knew all about that loss.

"I've lost nought, sir; thank God my good name's my own, and not gone like some folk's; but I'm bound to give notice, sir, not having fault to find, being as good a master as ever stepped. But seeing the missus is going——"

"The missus?"

"Ah. The mother as God give you, sir, the very next time the trailer goes by, and the letter wrote and all. And when she goes, I go. For I've kep' myself respectable, and I'll serve no light woman, nor yet live in a house give over to sin."

Edward saw Martha in a new light, as he now saw all things.

"What a filthy mind you have, Martha!" he said in a strange weary voice. "The minds of all respectable people are obscene. You are a bad woman!"

But Martha, setting up a shriek, had fled from the house. She told her brother that the master was mad, bewitched. She never entered the house again.

Edward found his mother in the kitchen.

"Mother, you are not really going?"

"Yes, Edward, unless"—a flicker of hope lit her eyes—"unless you have sent her away."

"Let me explain, mother. It is not as it seems in the world's eyes."

"She is an adulteress. And you—oh, Edward, I thought you were a good man, like your father! Not even the common decency to wait till the other man's child is born. Why, the merest ploughman would do that!"

If any face could have expressed despair, torture, and horror, Edward's face did now. He looked at her for a long while, until she said:

"Don't fix your eyes so, Edward! What are you looking at?"

"The world. So that is what you think of me?"

"What else can I think? Why do you say 'The world' so strangely?"

"The world!" he said again. "A place of black mud and spawning creatures. No soul, no God, no grace. Nothing but lust and foul breath and evil thoughts."

"I will not hear such talk. I will keep my room till I go." Mrs. Marston rose and went upstairs. She would not have his arm. And though for the next two days he waited on her with his old tenderness, she barely spoke, and there was between them an estrangement wider than death. She prayed for him night and day, but not as one that had much hope.

Meanwhile, Hazel managed the house. She put all her worship of Edward into it, all her passion of tenderness. And she, who had hitherto spoilt all the food she touched, now cooked almost with genius. She found an apron of Martha's and washed it; she read Mrs. Marston's receipts till her head ached; she walked over God's Little Mountain each day to buy dainties. When she asked Edward for money, he gave her the keys of his desk. Four times a day appetizing meals went up to Mrs. Marston, and were brought down again barely touched. Hazel ate them, for the urgent necessity of coming maternity was on her, and she would not waste Edward's money. Four times a day Edward's favourite dishes were set in the parlour by a bright hearth. Edward, as soon as Hazel had returned to the kitchen, threw them into the fire.

It was Hazel who packed Mrs. Marston's boxes while the old lady slept, and made up the fire in her room in the middle of the night.

Then, closing her own door, she would fling herself on her bed in passionate weeping as she thought what might have been if, when Edward had said, "To-night is my bridal," she had had a different reply to make.

She knew that nothing except what she had said would have made any impression on Edward; she knew he would not have listened to her. She was glad to know this. The momentary fear of him was gone. All was right that he said and did. The whole love of her being was his now. He had filled the place of nature and joy and childish pleasures. She was not meant for human love. But through her grief she loved better than those that were meant for it.

All the sweet instincts of love and wifehood; the beauty of passion; the pride of surrender; the forgetfulness of self that creates self; the crying of the spirit from its delicate marble minaret to the flesh in its grassy covert, and the wistful, ascending answer of flesh to spirit—all these were hers. And as she lay and wept, and remembered how many a time Edward had stood on her threshold and hastily, though gently, shut her door upon her, she realized what Edward meant to her, and what he was. Then she would rise and stand at her window, fingered and shaken by the autumn winds, and look up at the hard-eyed stars.

"If there's anybody there," she would say, "please let the time go quick till the baby comes, and let Ed'ard have his bridal like he said, and see his little uns running up and down the batch."

And, looking round the room at all the signs of his love, she would suddenly find unbearable the innocent stare of the buttercups and daisies on the walls, and would bury her face, flushed red with fluttering possibilities of unearthly rapture. Then she would sleep and dream that once more Edward stood upon the threshold and kissed her and turned to his cold room; but she—she had made a noble fire in her little grate; and the room was full of primroses, red and white and lilac; and the wall-clock chimed instead of striking—an intoxicating fairy chime; and there were clean sheets as of old. She forgot her shyness; she forgot to be afraid of his criticism; she caught his hands. He turned. And at the marvel of his face she woke, trembling and happy.

Mrs. Marston went without any farewell to Hazel. Edward carried her box down the quarry and helped her into the trailer. He stood and watched it bump away round the corner, Mrs. Marston sitting, as she had done on that bright May morning, majestic in her grape-trimmed hat and the mantle with the bugles. Her face and attitude expressed the deep, though unformulated, conviction that God was "not what He was."

Then he turned and went home, numb, without vitality or hope.

A new Hazel met him on the threshold, no longer timorous, deprecating, awkward, but bravely and sweetly maternal. She led him in. Tea was laid with the meticulous reverence of a sacrament.

"Now draw your stocking foot along the floor!" Hazel commanded.

At this remembrance of his mother and Hazel's careful love, he broke down and wept, his face in her lap.

"Now see!" she whispered. "She'll come back, Ed'ard, when the anger's overpast."

"The anger of good people is never overpast, Hazel."

"See, I'll write her a letter, Ed'ard, and I'll say I'm a wicked girl, and she's to teach me better ways. She'll come like Foxy for bones, Ed'ard."

Comfort stole into Edward's heart.

"And see, my dear, I'll send his baby to him, and maybe, after——" She stumbled into silence.

"What, Hazel?"

"Maybe, Ed'ard, after—a long and long while after——" She began to cry, covering her face. "Oh, what for canna you see, my soul," she whispered, "as I love you true?"

Edward looked into her eyes, and he did see. Strangely, as an old forgotten tale, there came to him the frail hope of the possibility of joy. And with it came faith, storm-tossed and faint, but still living, in Hazel's ultimate beauty and truth. He did not know how this could be. He only knew it was so. He did not know how it was that she, whom all reviled, was pure and shining to him again, while the world grovelled in slime. But so it was.

"Harkee, Edward!" she said, "I'm agoing to mother you till she comes back. And some day, when you've bin so kind as to forgive me, maybe I unna be mother to you, but—anything you want me to be. And, maybe, there'll be a—a—bridal for you yet, my soul, and your little uns running down the batch."

"Yes, maybe. But don't let's talk of such things yet, not for many years. They are so vile."

She was cut to the heart, but she only said softly:

"Not for a many years, my soul! I'm mothering of you now!"

"That's what I want," he said, and fell asleep while she stroked his tired head.

Peace settled again on the chapel and parsonage, and a muted happiness. Summer weather had returned for a fleeting interval. The wild bees were busy again revelling in the late flowers, but taking their pleasure sadly; for the flowers were pale and rain-washed, and the scent and the honey were fled.

"Eh! I wish I could bring 'em all in afore the frosses, and keep 'em the winter long," Hazel said. "But they've seen good times. It inna so bad for folks to die as have seen good times. Afore I'm old and like to die, I want to see good times, Ed'ard—good times along with you."

"What sort of good times?"

"Oh, going out of a May morning, you and me—and maybe Foxy on a string—and looking nests, and us with cobwebs on our boots, and setting primmy-roses, red and white and laylac, in my garden as you made, and then me cooking the breakfast, and you making the toast and burning it along of reading some hard book, and maybe us laughing over a bit o' fun. And then off to read to somebody ill, and me waiting outside, pleased as a queen, and hearkening to your voice coming quiet through the window. And picking laylac, evenings, and going after musherooms at the turn of the year. Them days be coming, Ed'ard, inna they? I dunna mind ought if I know they're coming."

"Yes, perhaps they are," he said, smiling a little at her simple hopes, and even beginning himself to see the possibility of a future for them.

Two days went by in this calm way, for no one came near them, and while they were alone there was peace. They did not go beyond the garden, except when Hazel went to the shop. Edward did not go with her; he felt sensitive about meeting anyone.

In the evenings, by the parlour fire, Edward read aloud to her. He did not, however, read prayers, and she wondered in silence at the change.

She felt a great peace in these evenings, with Foxy on the hearthrug at her feet. They neither of them looked either backward or forward, but lived in the moated present, that turreted heaven whose defences so soon fall.

On the third morning Reddin came. Hazel had gone to the shop, and, coming back, she had lingered a little to watch with a sense of old comradeship the swallows wheeling in hundreds about the quarry cliffs. Their breasts were dazzling in the clear hot air. They had no thought for her, being so filled with a rage of joy, dashing up and down the smooth white sides of the quarry, multiplied by their blue shadows. They would nestle in crevices, like bits of thistledown caught in a grass-tuft, and would there sun themselves and chirrup. So many hundreds were there, and their shadows so multiplied them, that they seemed less like birds than like some dream of a bird heaven—essential birdhood. They were so quick with life, so warm, with their red-splashed breasts and blue flashing bodies; they wove such a tireless, mazy pattern, like bobbins weaving invisible lace, that they put winter far off. They comforted Hazel inexpressibly. Yet to-morrow they would, in all likelihood, be gone, not even a shadow left. Hazel wished she could catch them as they swept by, their shining breasts brushing the grasses. She knew they were sacred birds, "birds with forkit tails and fire on 'em." If sacredness is in proportion to vitality and joy, Hazel and the swallow tribe should be red-letter saints.

It was while she was away that Reddin knocked at the house door, and Edward answered the knock. Something in his look made Reddin speak fast. He had triumphed at their last encounter through muscle. Edward triumphed in this through despair.

"I felt I ought to come, Marston. As things are, the straight thing is for me to marry her—if you'll divorce her."

He looked at Edward questioningly, but Edward stared beyond him with a strange expression of utter nausea, hopeless loss, and loathing of all created things. Reddin went on:

"Her place is with me. It's my duty to look after her now, as it's my child she's going to have."

He could not resist this jibe of the virile to the non-virile. Besides, if he could make Marston angry, perhaps he would fight again, and fighting was so much better than this uncomfortable silence.

"I should naturally pay all expenses and maintenance wherever she was; I never mind paying for my pleasures."

Edward's eyes smouldered, but he said nothing.

"Of course, she can't *expect* either of us to see to her in her position" (Edward clenched his hands), "but I intend to do the decent thing. I'm never hard on a woman in that state; some fellows would be; but I've got a memory, hang it, and I'm grateful for favours received."

Why he should be at his very worst for Edward's benefit was not apparent, except that complete silence acts on the nerves, and nervousness brings out the real man.

"Well, think it over," he concluded. "You seem to be planning a sermon to-day. I shall be round here on Saturday—the meet's in the woods. I'll call then, and you can decide meanwhile. I don't mind whether she comes or not—at present. Later on, if I can't get on without her, I can no doubt persuade her to come again. But if you say divorce, I'll fetch her at once, and marry her as soon as you've got your decree. Damn you, Marston! Can't you speak? Could I say fairer than that, man to man?"

Edward looked at him, and it was such a look that his face and ears reddened.

"You are not a man," Edward said, with complete detachment; "you are nothing but sex organs."

He went in and shut the door.

Edward said nothing to Hazel of Reddin's visit. He forgot it himself when she came home; it slipped into the dreary welter of life as he saw it now—all life, that is, other than Hazel's. Brutality, lust, cruelty—these summed up the world of good people and bad people. He rather preferred the bad ones; their eyes were less awful, and had less of the serpent's glitter and more of the monkey's leer.

He did not shrink from Reddin as he shrank from his mother.

Hazel came running to him through the graves. She had a little parcel specially tied up, and she wrote on it in the parlour with laborious love. It was tobacco. She had decided that he ought to smoke, because it would soothe him.

They sat hand in hand by the fire that evening, and she told him of her Aunt Prowde, and how she first came to know Reddin, and how he threatened to tell Edward of her first coming to Undern. She was astonished at the way his face lit up.

"Why didn't you tell me that before, dear? It alters everything. You did not go of your own choice at first, then. He had you in a snare."

"Seems as if the world's nought but a snare, Ed'ard."

"Yes. But I'm going to spend my life keeping you safe, little Hazel. I hope it won't make you unhappy to leave the Mountain?"

"Leave the Mountain?"

"Yes. I must give up the ministry."

"Why ever?"

"Because I know now that Jesus Christ was not God, but only a brave, loving heart hunted to death."

"Be that why you dunna say prayers now?"

"Yes. I can't take money for telling lies."

"What'll you do if you inna a minister, Ed'ard?"

"Break stones—anything."

Hazel clapped her hands.

"Can I get a little 'ammer and break, too?"

"Some day. It will only be poor fare and a poor cottage, Hazel."

"It'll be like heaven!"

"We shall be together, little one."

"What for be your eyes wet, Ed'ard?"

"At the sweetness of knowing you didn't go of your own accord."

"What for did you shiver?"

"At the dark power of our fellow-creatures set against us."

"I inna feared of 'em now, Ed'ard. Maybe it'll come right, and you'll get all as you'd lief have."

"I only want you."

"And me you."

They both had happy dreams that night.

Outside, the stars were fierce with frost. The world hardened. In the bitter still air and the greenish moonlight the chapel and parsonage took on an unreal look, as if they were built of wavering, vanishing material, and stood somewhere outside space on a pale, crumbling shore.

Without, the dead slept, each alone, dreamless. Within, the lovers slept, each alone, but dreaming of a day when night should bring them home each to the other.

As the moon set the shadows of the gravestones lengthened grotesquely, creeping and creeping as if they would dominate the world.

In the middle of the night Foxy awoke, and barked and whimpered in some dark terror, and would not be comforted.

CHAPTER XXXVI

HAZEL looked out next morning into a cold, hostile world. The wind had gone into its winter quarter, storming down from the top of the Mountain onto the parsonage and raging into the woods. That was why Edward and Hazel never heard the sounds—some of the most horrible of the English countryside—that rose, as the morning went on, from various parts of the lower woods, whiningly, greedily, ferociously, as the hounds cast about for scent. Once there was momentary uproar, but it sank again, and the Master was disappointed. They had not found. The Master was a big fleshy man with white eyelashes and little pig's eyes that might conceal a soul—or might not. Miss Amelia Clomber admired him, and had just ridden up to say, "A good field. Everybody's here." Then she saw Reddin in the distance, and waited for him to come up. She was flushed and breathless and quite silent—an extraordinary thing for her. He certainly was looking his best, with the new zest and youth that Hazel had given him heightening the blue of his eyes and giving an added hauteur of masculinity to his bearing. She would, as she watched him coming, cheerfully have become his mistress at a nod for the sake of those eyes and that hauteur.

He was entirely unconscious of it. He never was a vain man, and women were to him what a watch is to a child—something to be smashed, not studied. Also, his mind was busy about his coming interview with Edward. He was ludicrously at a loss what to say or do. Blows were the only answer he could think of to such a thing as Edward had said. But blows had lost him Hazel before, and he wanted her still. He was rather surprised at this, passion being satisfied. Still, as he reflected, passion was only in abeyance. Next May——

If Miss Clomber had seen his eyes then, she would probably have proposed to him. But he was looking away towards the heights where Edward's house was. There was in his mind a hint of better things.

Hazel had been sweet in the conquering; so many women were not. And she was a little, wild, frail thing. He was sorry for her. He reflected that if he sold the cob he could pay a first-rate doctor to attend her, and two nurses. "I'll sell the cob," he decided. "I can easily walk more. It'll do me good."

"Good-morning, Mr. Reddin!" cried Miss Clomber as sweetly as she could.

"May your shadow never grow less!" he replied jocosely, as he cantered by with a great laugh.

"If she'd only die when she has the child!" thought Miss Clomber fiercely.

Up on the Mountain Edward and Hazel were studying a map to decide in which part of the country they would live. Round the fire sat Foxy, the one-eyed cat, and the rabbit in a basket. From a hook hung the bird in its cage, making little chirrupings of content. On the window-sill a bowl of crocuses had pushed out white points.

But upon their love—Edward's dawn of content and Hazel's laughter—broke a loud imperious knocking. Edward went to the door. Outside stood Mr. James, the old man with the elf-locks who shared the honey prizes with Abel, two farmers from the other side of the Mountain, Martha's brother, and the man with the red braces who had won the race when Reddin turned.

They coughed.

"Will you come in?" asked Edward.

They straggled in, very much embarrassed.

Hazel wished them good-morning.

"This young woman," Mr. James said, "might, I think, absent herself."

"Would you rather go or stay, Hazel?"

"Stay along of you, Ed'ard."

Hazel had divined that something threatened Edward.

They sat down, very dour. Foxy had retired under the table. The shaggy old man surveyed the bird.

"A nice pet, a bird," he said. "Minds me of a throstle I kep'——"

"Now, now, Thomas! Business!" said Mr. James.

"Yes. Get to the point," said Edward.

James began.

"We've come, minister, six God-fearing men, and me spokesman, being deacon; and we 'ope as good will come of this meeting, and that the Lord'll bless our endeavour. And now, I think, maybe a little prayer?"

"I think not."

"As you will, minister. There are times when folk avoid prayer as the sick avoid medicine."

James had a resonant voice, and it was always pitched on the intoning note. Also, he accented almost every other syllable.

"We bring you the Lord's message, minister. I speak for 'Im."

"You are sure?"

"Has not He answered us each and severally with a loud voice in the night-watches?"

"Ah! He 'as! True! Yes, yes!" the crowd murmured.

"And what we are to say," James went on, "is that the adulteress must go. You must put her away at once and publicly; and if she will make open confession of the sin, it will be counted to you for righteousness."

Edward came and stood in front of Hazel.

"Had you," James continued in trumpet tones—"had you, when she played the sinner with Mr. Reddin, Esquire, leading a respectable gentleman into open sin, chastened and corrected her—ay, given her the bread of affliction and the water of affliction and taken counsel with us——"

"Ah! there's wisdom in counsel!" said one of the farmers, a man with crafty eyes.

"Then," James went on, "all would 'a been well. But now to spare would be death."

"Ah! everlasting death!" came the echoes.

"And now" (James' face seemed to Hazel to wear the same expression as when he pocketed the money) —"now there is but one cure. She must go to a reformatory. There she'll be disciplined. She'll be made to repent."

He looked as if he would like to be present.

They all leant forward. The younger men were sorry for Edward. None of them were sorry for Hazel. There was a curious likeness, as they leant forward, between them and the questing hounds below.

"And then?" Edward prompted, his face set, tremors running along the nerves under the skin.

"Then we would expect you to make a statement in

a sermon, or in any way you chose, that you'd cast your sins from you, that you would never speak or write to this woman again, and that you were at peace with the Lord."

"And then?"

"Then, sir"—Mr. James rose—"we should onst again be proud to take our minister by the 'and, knowing it was but the deceitfulness of youth that got the better of you, and the wickedness of an 'ooman."

Feeling that this was hardly enough to tempt Edward, the man with the crafty eyes said:

"And if in the Lord's wisdom He sees fit to take her, then, sir, you can choose a wife from among us." (He was thinking of his daughter.) He said no more.

Edward was speaking. His voice was low, but not a man ever forgot a word he said.

"Filthy little beasts!" he said, but without acrimony, simply in weariness. "I should like to shoot you; but you rule the world—little pot-bellied gods. There is no other God. Your last suggestion" (he looked at them with a smile of so peculiar a quality and such strange eyes that, as the old beeman afterwards said, "It took you in the stomach") "was worthy of you. It's not enough that unselfish love can't save. It's not enough" (his face quivered horribly) "that love is allowed to torture the loved one; but you must come with your foul minds and eyes to 'view the corpse.' And you know nothing—nothing."

"We know the facts," said James.

"Facts! What are facts? I could flog you naked through the fields, James, for your stupidity alone."

There was a general smile, James being a corpulent man. He shrank. Then his feelings found relief in spite.

"If you don't dismiss the female, I'll appeal to the Presbytery," he said, painfully pulling himself together.

"What for?"

"Notice for you."

"No need. We're going. What d'you suppose I should do here? There's no Lord's day and no Lord's house, for there's no Lord. For goodness' sake turn the chapel into a cowhouse!"

They blinked. Their minds did not take in his meaning, which was like the upper wind that blows coldly from mountain to mountain and does not touch the plain. They busied themselves with what they could grasp.

"If you take that woman with you, you'll be accurst," said James. "I suppose," he went on, and his tone was, as he afterwards said to his wife with complacency, "very nasty"—"I suppose you dunno what they're all saying, and what I've come to believe, in this shocking meeting, to be God's truth."

"I don't know or care."

"They're saying you've made a tidy bit."

"What d'you mean?"

James hesitated. Filthy thoughts were all very well, but it was awkward to get them into righteous words.

"Well, dear me! they're saying as there was an arrangement betwixt you and 'im—on the gel's account"—(the old beeman tried to hush him)—"and as cheques signed 'John Reddin' went to your bank. Dear me!"

Slowly the meaning of this dawned on Edward. He sat down and put his hands up before his face. He was broken, not so much by the insult to himself as by the fixed idea that he had exposed Hazel to all this. He traced all her troubles and mistakes back to himself, blaming his own love for them. While he had been fighting for her happiness, he had given her a mortal wound, and none had warned him. That was why he was sure there was no God.

They sat round and looked at their work with some compunction. The old beeman cleared his throat several times.

"O' course," he said, "we know it inna true, minister. Mr. James shouldna ha' taken it on his lips." He looked defiantly at James out of his mild brown eyes.

Edward did not hear what he said. Hazel was puzzling over James' meaning. Why had he made Edward like this? Love gave her a quickness that she did not naturally possess, and at last she understood. It was one of the few insults that could touch her, because it was levelled at her primitive womanhood. Her one instinct was for flight. But there was Edward. She turned her back on the semicircle of eyes, and put a trembling hand on Edward's shoulder. He grasped it.

"Forgive me, dear!" he whispered. "And go, now, go into the woods; they're not as cold as these. When I've done with them we'll go away, far away from hell."

"I dunna mind 'em," said Hazel. "What for should I, my soul?"

Then she saw how dank and livid Edward's face had become, and the anguished rage of the lover against that which hurts her darling flamed up in her.

"Curse you!" she said, letting her eyes, dark-rimmed and large with tears, dwell on each man in turn. "Curse you for tormenting my Ed'ard, as is the best man in all the country—and you'm nought, nought at all!"

The everlasting puzzle, why the paltry and the low should have power to torment greatness, was brooding over her mind.

"The best!" said James, avoiding her eyes, as they all did. "A hinfidel!"

"I have become an unbeliever," Edward said, "not because I am unworthy of your God, but because He is unworthy of me. Hazel, wait for me at the edge of the wood."

Hazel crept out of the room. As she went, she heard him say:

"The beauty of the world isn't for the beautiful people. It's for beef-witted squires and blear-eyed people like yourselves—brutish, callous. Your God stinks like carrion, James. *Nunc Dimittis.*"

Hazel passed the tombstone where she had sat on her wedding-day. She went through the wicket where she and her mother had both passed as brides, and down the green slope that led near the quarry to the woods. The swallows had gone. She came to Reddin's black yew-tree at the fringe of the wood, and sat down there, where she could watch the front door. In spite of her bird-like quickness of ear, she was too much overwhelmed by the scene she had just left to notice an increasing, threatening, ghastly tumult that came, at first fitfully, then steadily, up through the woods. At first it was only a rumour, as if some evil thing, imprisoned for the safety of the world, whined and struggled against love in a close underground cavern. But when it came nearer—and it seemed to be emerging from its prison with sinister determination—the wind had no longer any power to disguise its ferocity, although it was still in a minor key, still vacillating and scattered. Nor had it as yet any objective; it was only vaguely clamorous for blood, not for the very marrow of the soul. Yet, as Hazel suddenly became aware of it, a cold shudder ran down her spine.

"Hound-dogs!" she said. She peered through the trees, but nothing was to be seen, for the woods were steep. With a dart of terror, she remembered that she had left Foxy loose in the parlour. Would they have let her out?

She ran home.

"Be Foxy here?" she asked.

Edward looked up from the chapel accounts. James was trying to browbeat him over them.

"No. I expect she went out with you."

Hazel fled to the back of the house, but Foxy was not there. She whistled, but no smooth, white-bibbed personality came trotting round the corner. Hazel ran back to the woods. The sound of the horn came up intermittently with tuneful devilry.

She whistled again.

Reddin, coming up the wood at some distance from the pack, caught the whistle, and seeing her dress flutter far up the wood, realized what had happened.

"Bother it!" he said. He did not care about Foxy, and he thought Hazel's affection for her very foolish; but he understood very well that if anything happened to Foxy, he would be to blame in Hazel's eyes. Between him and Hazel was a series of precipitous places. He would have to go round to reach her. He spurred his horse, risking a fall from the rabbit-holes and the great ropes of honeysuckle that swung from tree to tree.

Hazel ran to and fro, frantically calling to Foxy.

Suddenly the sound, that had been querulous, interrogative, and various, changed like an organ when a new stop is pulled out.

The pack had found.

But the scent, it seemed, was not very hot. Hope revived in Hazel.

"It'll be the old scent from yesterday," she thought. "Maybe Foxy'll come yet!"

Seeing Reddin going in so devil-me-care a manner, a little clergyman (a "guinea-pig" on Sundays and the last hard-riding parson in the neighbourhood on weekdays) thought that Reddin must have seen the fox, and gave a great view-halloo. He rode a tall raw-boned animal, and looked like a monkey.

Hazel did not see either him or Reddin. With fainting heart she had become aware that the hounds were no longer on an old scent. They were not only intent on one life now, but they were close to it. And whoever it was that owned the life was playing with it, coming straight on in the teeth of the wind instead of doubling with it.

With an awful constriction of the heart, Hazel knew who it was. She knew also that it was her momentary forgetfulness that had brought about this horror. Terror seized her at the dogs' approach, but she would not desert Foxy.

Then, with the fearful inconsequence of a dream, Foxy trotted out of the wood and came up to her. Trouble was in her eyes. She was disturbed. She looked to Hazel to remove the unpleasantness, much as Mrs. Marston used to look to Edward.

And as Hazel, dry-throated, whispered "Foxy!" and caught her up, the hounds came over the ridge like water. Riding after them, breaking from the wood on every side, came the hunt. Scarlet gashed the impenetrable shadows. Coming, as they did, from the deep gloom, fiery-faced and fiery-coated, with eyes frenzied by excitement, and open, cavernous mouths, they were like devils emerging from hell on a foraging expedition. Miss Clomber, her hair loose and several of her pin-curls torn off by the branches, was one of the first, determined to be in at the death.

The uproar was so terrific that Edward and the six righteous men came out to see what the matter was. Religion and society were marshalled with due solemnity on God's Little Mountain.

Hazel saw nothing, heard nothing. She was running with every nerve at full stretch, her whole soul in her feet. But she had lost her old fleetness, for Reddin's child had even now robbed her of some of her vitality. Foxy, in gathering panic, struggled and impeded her. She was only halfway to the quarry, and the house was twice as far.

"I canna!" she gasped on a long terrible breath. She felt as if her heart was bursting.

One picture burnt itself on her brain in blood and agony. One sound was in her ears—the shrieking of the damned. What she saw was Foxy, her smooth little friend, so dignified, so secure of kindness, held in the hand of the purple-faced huntsman above the pack that raved for her convulsive body. She knew how Foxy's eyes would look, and she nearly fainted at the knowledge. She saw the knife descend—saw Foxy, who had been lovely and pleasant to her in life, cut in two and flung (a living creature, fine of nerve) to the pack, and torn to fragments. She heard her scream.

Yes; Foxy would cry to her, as she had cried to the Mighty One dwelling in darkness. And she? What would she do? She knew that she could not go on living with that cry in her ears. She clutched the warm body closer.

Though her thoughts had taken only an instant, the hounds were coming close.

Outside the chapel James said:

"Dear me! A splendid sight! We'll wait to verify the 'aypenny columns till they've killed."

They all elbowed in front of Edward. But he had seen. He snatched up his spade from the porch, and knocked James out of the way with the flat of it.

"I'm coming, dear!" he shouted.

But she did not hear. Neither did she hear Reddin, who was still at a distance, and was spurring till the blood ran, as in the tale of the death-pack, yelling: "I'm coming! Give her to me!" Nor the little cleric, in his high-pitched nasal voice, calling: "Drop it! They'll pull you down!" while the large gold cross bumped up and down on his stomach. The death that Foxy must die, unless she could save her, drowned all other sights and sounds.

She gave one backward glance. The awful resistless flood of liver and white and black was very near. Behind it rode shouting devils.

It was the death-pack.

There was no hope. She could never reach Edward's house. The green turf rose before her like the ascent to Calvary.

The members of the hunt, the Master and the huntsmen, were slow to understand. Also, they were at a disadvantage, the run being such an abnormal one—against the wind and up a steep hill. They could not beat off the hounds in time. Edward was the only one near enough to help. If she had seen him and made for him, he might have done something.

But she only saw the death-pack; and as Reddin shouted again near at hand, intending to drag her on to the horse, she turned sharply. She knew it was the Black Huntsman. With a scream so awful that Reddin's hands grew nerveless on the rein, she doubled for the quarry.

A few woodlarks played there, but they fled at the oncoming tumult.

For one instant the hunt and the righteous men, Reddin the destroyer, and Edward the saviour, saw her sway, small and dark, before the staring sky. Then, as the pack, with a ferocity of triumph, was flinging itself upon her, she was gone.

She was gone with Foxy into everlasting silence. She would suck no more honey from the rosy flowers, nor dance like a leaf in the wind. Abel would sit, these next nights, making a small coffin that would leave him plenty of beehive wood.

There was silence on God's Little Mountain for a space.

Afterwards a voice, awful and piercing, deep with unutterable horror—the voice of a soul driven mad by torture—clutched the heart of every man and woman. Even the hounds, raging on the quarry edge, cowered and bristled.

It echoed in the freezing arches of the sky, and rolled back unanswered to the freezing earth. The little cleric, who had pulled a Prayer-Book from his pocket, dropped it.

Once again it rang out, and at its awful reiteration the righteous men and the hunt ceased to be people of any class or time or creed, and became creatures swayed by one primeval passion—fear. They crouched and shuddered like beaten dogs as the terrible cry once more roused the shivering echoes:

"Gone to earth! Gone to earth!"

CPSIA information can be obtained
at www.ICGtesting.com
Printed in the USA
BVOW09s1758171017
497893BV00031B/1193/P